Helping Clumsy Children

This book is to b[...]
the last date stamped below.

In school, the main difficulty
is in writing, although the
teachers are very helpful when
they know it is a a ~~problem~~
disability. I also have difficulty
with drawing etc. although I am
taking and enjoying Art ~~lessons~~.
I am ~~not~~ bad at P. E ~~although~~
I do enjoy this lessons.
Wood- and metal-work
are not compulsory this year
and I do not take them but
in previous years I have been
very unproductive in these
subjects.
　　　Outside school, the
difficulty is not as ~~so~~ ~~distress~~
~~distressing~~
but writing is again sometimes
a problem. The biggest
problem is being generally
clumsy and unhandy.

Helping Clumsy Children

Edited by

Neil Gordon
MD, FRCP (Ed. & Lond.), FCST (Hon.)
Consultant Paediatric Neurologist to the Children's
Hospitals, Manchester

and

Ian McKinlay
BSc (Hons.) MB ChB, DCH, MRCP
Consultant Paediatric Neurologist to the Children's
Hospitals, Manchester

Foreword by
Marcel Kinsbourne
DM (Oxon.), MRCP (Lond.)
Professor of Paediatrics, University of Toronto, Faculty
of Medicine;
Professor of Psychology, University of Toronto, Faculty
of Arts and Sciences;
Professor of Psychology, University of Waterloo

CHURCHILL LIVINGSTONE
EDINBURGH LONDON AND NEW YORK 1980

129916

CHURCHILL LIVINGSTONE
Medical Division of the Longman Group Limited

Distributed in the United States of America by Churchill
Livingstone Inc., 19 West 44th Street, New York, N.Y.
10036, and by associated companies, branches and
representatives throughout the world.

First published 1980

ISBN 0 443 01868 5

British Library Cataloguing in Publication Data

Helping clumsy children.
    1. Movement disorders in children
    I. Gordon, Neil   II. McKinlay, Ian
    618.9'27'406   RJ496.M/   79–41208

Printed in Singapore by Singapore Offset Printing Pte Ltd

Foreword

A quiet revolution has occurred in medicine in recent years. Broadening out from its traditional narrow forms of healing those whose problems derive from diagnosable disease, medical practice now increasingly takes note of those human differences which, though not due to disease states, hamper their victims' efforts to participate fully in our society and gain that minimum of acceptance and approbation usually a prerequisite to a sound outlook on oneself and one's life. It is now recognised that human well-being is not guaranteed by the mere absence of disease. It is furthered by exercising one's abilities; and if these are lacking or deficient for any reason, they should be fostered by whatever effective training methods ingenuity can devise.

The increasing concern of medicine with health as a road to successful living is only partly due to grudging step-by-step retreat of diseases in the face of advancing medical knowledge, hygiene and social change. It is also symptomatic of the democratic mentality, which is as jealously concerned with the rights of the few as the liberties of the many. The rights of minorities, when threatened, are safeguarded. More subtly, those minorities which are ill-equipped to assert themselves socially or vocationally on account of flaws in physique or mentality, are no longer left to fend for themselves as best they can or sequestered in sheltered isolation. Rather, they are helped as far as possible to function effectively and competitively in the mainstream of society. Genetic diversity is responsible for much of the enriching variety of human intellect, temperament and emotional style that so well serves the diverse requirements of our intricate and complex social structure. But in its extreme this source of 'normal' variation creates harrowing problems in the sense of deviation from the norm, deviations so great that the individual becomes a social misfit.

Those who are slow to acquire language, reading skills or numerical abilities (the 'learning disabled') and those whose ability to maintain concentration is deficient (the 'hyperactive') are now well recognised and are the subject of a sprawling and contentious literature. The critical need for interdisciplinary cooperation and concern in support of these children is now accepted as a matter of course (even if its implementation presents recalcitrant difficulties). In contrast, those whose motor development is delayed or imperfect, who are simply clumsy, have been neglected. Yet helping clumsy children improve their dexterity, and the effectiveness of their motor performance, is just as vital to their prospects of social and vocational success as is the correction of poor study habits or the remedial education of the child who is difficult to teach. If there is no disease there is no prospect of a dramatic remedy. Instead, hard facts must be recognised and faced. The remedial programme designed for the individual will inevitably call for more than the usual amount of strenuous and maintained effort from the child, as well as considerable patience and ingenuity from the professional concerned.

While clumsiness in the guise of various more pretentious labels does receive consideration in the literature, it has up to now been dealt with in rather fragmentary, or dogmatic fashion, depending on the profession and temperament of the author. The nature of the problem is such as to call for a more integrated approach. The physician who concerns himself with developmental differences such as clumsiness cannot affort to neglect the help of psychologists, speech pathologists, teachers of physical education, physical and occupational therapists, and the mental health personnel who provide emotional support while the actual efforts to help the child perform better are under way.

The present volume is, to my knowledge, the first that effectively prescribes and integrates these diverse viewpoints in the service of the child as a total person.

Toronto, 1980   Marcel Kinsbourne

Preface

In the past few years there has been increasing concern regarding the problems of children who are clumsy due to disorders of perception and motor organisation. Early diagnosis of this disability makes it possible not only to provide help when this is necessary but, by sympathetic management of the child's difficulties, to prevent the otherwise inevitable emotional and behavioural complications.

There is still much to be learnt about the causes of this disability, its assessment and the predictive value of any tests used. In particular, there is controversy over the ways these children can be helped. It has been suggested that it may be harmful to label a child as clumsy and to single out the child as different from his peers; but early diagnosis need not indicate life-long disability that cannot improve. On the contrary, the prognosis for children with perceptual motor disabilities is, in general, good, and helping these children is one of the most rewarding aspects of paediatrics. As with all developmental disabilities the degree of severity ranges from those so mildly affected that they can still be included in the 'normal range' to those so severely handicapped that they may best be classified among the milder types of cerebral palsy. However, even if extreme cases can be so diagnosed on medical grounds, it may still be best for practical purposes to include them among the clumsy children. Names affect attitudes and the term cerebral palsy tends to evoke the clinical picture of a life-long disability which does not improve, while the inference is that a developmental disorder will undoubtedly change for the better as the child grows older.

For the majority, who are mildly affected, the very recognition of the disability is all important. If it is realised that the child has real difficulties in acquiring motor skills it is essential that due credit is given for the extra effort he makes. If, as sometimes happens, the child is continually blamed for not trying, it is no wonder if he opts out of the situation and presents as a behaviour problem. Early screening (sensibly discussed with parents and teachers) does not mean the child has to be 'labelled', but the teacher can be alerted to the possibility of problems arising. If they do, the teacher will recognise the need for classroom remediation or referral for more detailed assessment.

To spend time and effort in recognising a disability and then to do nothing about it is worse than useless. It will increase the frustration of the child and the anxiety of the parents. Efforts must therefore be made to help the child in the home and in the school. This is the main justification for this book. It is right that there should be controversy as the efficacy of much that is now done to try and help these children is unproven; but this is no excuse for doing nothing. It is logical to encourage the child to practise those tasks which are difficult and to demonstrate ways of circumventing them if this is possible. Apart from treating the child's disability it is essential to identify his abilities and to ensure success in some field or other. Only then will the self-confidence be established which is so essential to successful learning. It is hoped that this book will be of use to those who ask the question 'how can we help' and will, as a result, improve the lot of these children which can so easily be an unhappy one.

Manchester, 1980   N.G.
                                                        I.M.

Acknowledgements

The editors wish to acknowledge their gratitude to Miss Jean Perry and her colleagues in the Medical Illustration Department of North Manchester General Hospital and Booth Hall Children's Hospital for illustrating this book. Professor John Dobbing made many detailed and helpful suggestions in the preparation of Chapter 2 and gave permission for the use of the illustration of dendrites. Permission for publishing the extract from *Helping Language Development — A Developmental Programme for Children with Early Language Handicaps* by J. Cooper, M. Moodley and J. Reynell was given by Edward Arnold Ltd. Willing contributions by clumsy children and their parents were particularly appreciated. Without the patient and tireless typing and secretarial support of Mrs Margaret Richardson preparation of this book would have been impossible.

To Ronnie MacKeith
whose inspiration has done so much to help
the handicapped child.

Contributors

Lynette Bradley Remedial Teacher and Research Fellow, Department of Experimental Psychology, Oxford University.

Marion Bryant Superintendent Occupational Therapist, Child Development Centre, Alder Hey Children's Hospital, Liverpool.

Lesley Cooke Lecturer in Physical Education, Newcastle University.

Maureen Garvey Area Speech Therapist, Salford AHA(T), Royal Manchester Children's Hospital, Salford.

Neil Gordon Consultant Paediatric Neurologist, Booth Hall Children's Hospital, Manchester.

Ann Grimley Superintendent Physiotherapist, Royal Manchester Children's Hospital and Swinton Hospital, Salford.

Ian McKinlay Consultant Paediatric Neurologist, Booth Hall Children's Hospital, Manchester.

Sheila McKinlay Specialist in Community Medicine (Child Health), Bolton Area Health Authority.

Valerie Mellor Principal Clinical Psychologist, Manchester AHA(T), Booth Hall Children's Hospital, Manchester.

David Thursfield Consultant Child Psychiatrist, Manchester AHA(T), Booth Hall Children's Hospital, Manchester.

Klaus Wedell Professor of Educational Psychology, University of London Institute of Education.

Contents

Definition

Clumsy children show difficulties in motor coordination out of proportion to their general abilities. They commonly, but not invariably, have co-existing learning difficulties. Their disabilities may lead to secondary emotional problems including frustration or social isolation. Thus, a child of whatever chronological age whose general abilities are those of an eight-year-old but whose coordination skills are typical of a five- or six-year-old will be regarded as 'clumsy'.

The motor difficulties may affect large movements involving balance or fine coordination or eye-hand coordination, and sometimes all these skills. While recognising the term is vague and that the word 'clumsy' carries other pejorative connotations as far as social behaviour is concerned, it is useful to describe a child's condition at a particular time. It does not imply a single cause although aetiology and management will affect prognosis. It will also be affected by the style of management and it is to promote good management that this book has been written.

Who are clumsy children?

Clumsiness in childhood may be due to many causes ranging from progressive conditions such as cerebral degenerative diseases and polyneuropathies, to static ones like head injuries and defective vision. Obviously many of these aetiologies are recognisable from the history and the findings on examination, and numerous as they may be they constitute the minority of clumsy children. In most instances the clumsiness appears to be a developmental disorder. This was recognised by Orton in 1937 and discussed in his book *Reading, Writing and Speech Problems in Children*. His fifth group of such disorders is developmental apraxia. He reports that Galen spoke of some children as being 'ambilevous', that is, doubly left-handed as if they were equipped with a lack of skill on both sides comparable to that of the left hand in a strongly right-handed person. He includes this disorder in the control of skilled movements among those of developmental language delays mainly because it extends to the motor patterns of both speech and writing. His description of such a child is a good one: 'such children are often somewhat delayed in learning even the simpler movements such as walking and running, and have great difficulty in learning to use their hands and to copy motions shown to them. They are slow in learning to dress themselves and are clumsy in their attempts to button their clothes, tie their shoes, handle a spoon and in other simple tasks'.

His remarks on treatment are particularly relevant. Having determined very simple patterns of movement over which the child has mastery these are combined into more complex patterns. Those children in whom gross body movements are affected can often become proficient in activities such as swimming and horse-riding where the body is supported without a particular need for equilibration. This may ensure success in at least one competitive field. When parents raise the question of attitudes to excessive awkwardness in the home it is helpful to stress that it is a constitutional disability and not just undue carelessness. Obviously in such cases punishment can be positively harmful, and Orton (1937) suggests that the best attitude for the parents to adopt is that of tolerant amusement towards each episode, but with careful observation of the faulty movements with a view to sympathetic instruction for their correction. Orton also stresses that in competition clumsy children are bound to develop feelings of inferiority as their limitations are exposed. The remedy is punctilious training in some sport or manual craft so that this can compensate for more general awkwardness.

In spite of this wise advice given such a long time ago, very little has so far been done to treat these children. Interest was renewed in the United Kingdom in the early 1960s by the publications of Walton *et al.* (1962) and Gubbay *et al.* (1963). The concept of the clumsy child was redefined, but the presumption that children only had to try harder to acquire motor skills was still well entrenched. They studied 21 children in detail and divided them into two groups: those with isolated apraxia and agnosia; and those with apraxia and agnosia with minimal neurological signs. They were confident that the syndrome was much commoner than was generally realised and recognised that the clumsy children with no overt neurological signs were less easily recognised than those with pyramidal, extrapyramidal or cerebellar dysfunction. Therefore these children usually receive less sympathy and understanding, and because of a reluctance to attempt motor tasks there is a tendency to accuse them of laziness or misbehaviour; or they may be suspected of being mentally dull. This leads to frustration with further disorders of behaviour which aggravates the problems of learning and performance.

The term minimal cerebral dysfunction was in favour during the 1960s (Bax and MacKeith, 1963), but this is a heterogenous group of behaviour syndromes, learning disorders, and motor disabilities. This term has served a useful purpose by drawing attention to a large number of children who are often in urgent need of help, but what is required is a detailed analysis of the child's difficulties. These may be delay in language development, defects in perception or of motor organisation, unacceptable overactivity or emotional immaturity, often in a variety of combinations. If it is accepted that 'minimal cerebral dysfunction' signifies that a child has minor degrees of such disabilities, they should be classified accordingly. This does seem to have been increasingly the case but some disabilities are less easily recognised than others. A number of children with impairment of perceptual motor function are still labelled as having minimal cerebral dysfunction, as their difficulties are of a fairly subtle kind, only manifesting themselves in certain situations.

There is no typically clumsy child. The clinical picture will vary greatly, depending on such factors as the reasons for the incoordination, sensory or motor, the age of the child and a variety of genetic and environmental influences. The child will more often be male than female, and possible explanations for this will be discussed later. Although population studies have suggested a male:female ratio of 2:1, the ratio in children referred to the neurology clinics of the children's hospitals in Manchester has been 4:1, perhaps because the behaviour of boys who are frustrated gives rise to greater management difficulty.

Early motor development may be delayed, the child sitting, standing and walking at a later age than usual and the infant may be unusually floppy. After the toddling age the grace of the average child is something to be admired but among those with perceptual motor disorders the parents may soon realise that movements are more awkward than they should be. Large movements may be affected because of defective balance. Falls will be frequent and the child always seems to be tripping over his feet. The gait can be awkward with abnormal postures of the feet, particularly when running. This often results in referral to the orthopaedic clinic. If the acquisition of balance is delayed this is bound to result in poor performance when it comes to sport and physical education. As a result no-one wants a child of this kind on their team or as a companion on holiday.

Impairment of fine movements more often causes trouble when it comes to developing motor skills. It means that the child's self-help with dressing is delayed, for example doing up buttons and tying shoe laces, and in the hustle of getting children ready for school it is often easier for the mother to do it herself than to allow the child the practice that is essential for success. Lack of manual dexterity will inevitably affect writing which will not only be untidy but will often start at the top left hand corner and drift towards the lower right hand one. If there are marked perceptual difficulties letters and numbers are likely to be incorrectly written or reversed to an excessive degree. This also applies to words such as 'saw' for 'was', and the sequence of letters in words may be confused.

The P.E. class is often dreaded, partly for the poor performance that is likely, and the possible ridicule of teacher and peers, but also because of the difficulties of dressing and undressing. Practical classes such as woodwork and sewing are also a problem among older children. Defects in eye-hand coordination will be particularly apparent in tasks such as catching balls, and will affect hobbies like modelling and drawing. It may also result in messy eating to the annoyance of the average parent. The list of tasks likely to result in failure could be extended to include almost any task a child is likely to attempt but there will be infinite variations between one child and another, and it sometimes is surprising how specific the difficulties can be. The child may not be able to write neatly for example but may be able to sew and do jigsaw puzzles without difficulty.

There will often be an association with difficulties of other types, which is not surprising if it is accepted that perceptual motor disabilities are more often than not acquired before, during, or shortly after birth. For example anoxia which causes foetal distress during prolonged labour can result in brain damage leading to epilepsy on the one hand and learning disorders on the other. It is therefore to be expected that children are often multiply affected. There may also be a more direct association between handicaps as will be discussed in greater detail in later chapters. A child who is clumsy because of a perceptual motor disability may also suffer from a delay in language development resulting from a common aetiology causing damage to different parts of the brain, but such a child will be particularly liable to speech disorder as articulation is dependent on coordination of a complex degree. It will depend on sensory information on the exact position of the lips, tongue and other organs of articulation, and on the working of the various muscles involved, including those of respiration. It is therefore not surprising that 'clumsy children' quite often exhibit various types of speech disorder, including so-called congenital (or developmental) articulatory dyspraxia.

The same arguments apply to various other learning difficulties. If a child has a severe perceptual disability and has no idea of the concept of shapes and sizes or has defects of orientation and sequencing, he is bound to experience troubles of some kind or another when he starts to try to read. Reading retardation is more often part of a disorder of language development but often those children most severely affected, particularly in the early years at school, show evidence of both audio-phonic and visual perceptual disabilities (Boder, 1973).

When considering learning difficulties of all kinds it is therefore essential not to take too narrow a view of the problem (Farnham-Diggory, 1978). For instance dyslexia as a term for delay in acquiring the skill of reading seems to have a fascination of its own. It is certainly an emotive term and if care is not taken the child so affected may receive intensive help with reading to the exclusion of many other needs. In addition to the difficulties with reading the child may fail in manual skills such as constructing models or in team games which tend to be of such importance as a status symbol. Particularly when of average or above average intelligence this may result in more frustration and unhappiness than the inability to read, as the level of intelligence is not reflected in performance. Categories of disabilities may be needed for administrative purposes and to concentrate the attention of those responsible for providing help for a certain type of disability when they are failing to do so. However, children seldom suffer from a single handicap and their progress must be assessed in its entirety. This is often accepted in principle as few people would suggest assessment units being set up to deal with a single disorder such as defective hearing, and support the idea of the team approach with experts in various disciplines working closely together; but this does not always happen in practice. It is therefore necessary constantly to stress the dictum that if one disability is found look for others. Also it must be emphasised that it is necessary not only to look for learning difficulties among children, but also to find out about their skills and ensure their success in some of the tasks they attempt.

It can be justifiably asked, 'when is a child clumsy,' or rather 'when do difficulties of coordination become significant?' There is no generally agreed cut-off point and generalisations can be dangerous. It could be said that if the clumsiness is causing anxiety to the parents or frsutration to the child, something should be done about it. However, this attitude of waiting for trouble and then dealing with it is not very satisfactory. Arguably by identifying the possibility of learning difficulties without attaching firm labels, much can be done to prevent them, and more especially the complication of emotional disorders.

Often the clumsy child is referred to the hospital clinic with symptoms of anxiety such as headache, abdominal pain and nocturnal enuresis. If there have been unrecognised learning difficulties for some time the child will frequently be depressed which of itself is bound to affect performance and can lead to an erroneous impression of low intelligence. If abnormal behaviour has resulted from the frustrations of failure or wrongful accusations of laziness they can be more difficult to treat than the primary disability.

There is another factor of importance which is related to the aspirations and sometimes the social class of the parents. In a recent, unpublished survey at the children's hospitals in Manchester, over half of the referrals of children, who proved to have significant perceptual-motor disabilities, to the out-patient clinics were from social classes 1 and 2. Obviously if learning has a high priority in a family, help for a child in difficulties will be sought at any early stage, but for many from other backgrounds this is not the case. If the incidence of significant perceptual motor disabilities is around 6 to 7 per cent (Bremner et al., 1967) at the age of seven or eight years it means that there will be one or two such children in most primary school classes for the younger children. The majority of these children cope, however. Perhaps a quarter run into sufficient difficulty to require further attention. This figure is likely to be higher in special schools of various types such as those for the maladjusted or for children with epilepsy because of common aetiologies. Environmental factors also play a part in the opportunities to acquire skills so that the number of clumsy children is likely to be higher among the children of manual workers than among those of the professional classes.

A more positive attitude to clumsiness therefore seems to be justified with early identification by appropriate tests and this is reviewed in Chapter 4.

The significance of handedness is often discussed in relation to clumsiness. Admittedly we live in a right-handed world and to be left-handed is bound to make such tasks as cutting out with scissors more difficult. However, in studying the effects of left-handedness certain distinctions have to be made. If a child is strongly left-handed and this has been recognised from an early age, and perhaps if there is a high incidence of left-handers in the family, the handedness is likely to be genetically determined, and there is no particular reason why the integration of cerebral function should be significantly affected or the child be handicapped except by awkwardness in certain tasks. There are other children who present as left-handers but their condition is different. It may have taken them a long time to show hand preference and even in adult life they may do some tasks such as writing with the left hand but perform others such as using a knife and fork or throwing a ball as right-handers. Also they may choose to kick a ball with the right foot rather than the left, or when using one eye prefer the right: so-called crossed laterality. Evidence from the past history, for example complications at birth, strongly suggests the possibility of 'forced left-handedness'. That is to say the child's endowment was that of a right-handed person, but due to brain damage at an early stage of development the left cerebral hemisphere suffered a disproportionately greater degree of damage so that a reorganisation of cerebral function had to take place. The right cerebral hemisphere takes over at least some of the roles which are normally those of the left. As a result the left-handedness and the crossed laterality in these individuals (though *not* in general) can be regarded as a symptom of this reorganisation; so also can the learning disorders which are such a frequent association.

It must of course be stressed that the majority of left-handers or 'crossed laterals' show neither clumsiness nor learning disorders. Reports sometimes refer to children as 'crossed lateral' as if this were abnormal in itself. The question of laterality is also more complex than it at first appears and the function tested must be taken into account. Some children kick with the right foot because they balance better on the left; others because the right foot is more skillful.

Disorganisation is particularly characteristic of the children with perceptual motor disabilities. This often affects many aspects of life and not just movements. They seem to live in a perpetual muddle and perhaps this is another aspect of the faulty cerebral integration that follows minor and scattered lesions in the brain. It is worth emphasising again how easily these children become emotionally upset and develop disorders of behaviour, due in part to learning disorders. Because of their difficulties they are particularly liable to demonstrate attention-seeking behaviour. These symptoms may also result from the same failure of cerebral integration. This may cause a lowered level of frustration so that upsets cannot be so easily tolerated. Also behaviour cannot be controlled as expected for the child's age, and a well-developed sense of failure is common.

Overactivity unacceptable for a child's age can be due to a variety of causes such as language disorders, perceptual disorders, manipulative difficulty, anxiety, inappropriate teaching in the classroom leading to boredom, and the use of sedative drugs, particularly barbiturates. Some children will be found to be overactive, with a short attention span and poor concentration for no particular reason. They may be said to suffer from 'the hyperkinetic syndrome' although this is rare. There appears to be a failure to develop an expected pattern of behaviour and in this sense the syndrome can be regarded as a conduct plus learning disorder. As with others it will occur among children with perceptual motor difficulties, although in those attending hospital clinics with such disabilities, which have not been recognised for long periods anyhow, depression and relative inactivity seems commoner.

In the hyperkinetic syndrome large motor movements may not be more frequent than among controls (Pope, 1970) but in situations which require attention differences are soon apparent. For example, for a child with language comprehension difficulty words may demand no more attention than background noises. Under-arousal seems an unlikely cause but a lack of inhibition and an impairment of selective attention is more probable. This will result in over-stimulation with the child responding in a series of seemingly endless disassociated actions, as normally much of the sensory input to the brain never reaches a conscious level (Conners, 1976). The ability to work, when someone is talking or playing music in the room, must be one of the most complex functions we ask of our brains. The system which underlies this ability is not well defined but must surely involve brain-stem activating pathways and their transmitter substances. The fact that barbiturates usually aggravate the condition may be due to an added impairment of a system already working inefficiently, while, rarely, stimulant drugs such as methylphenidate may have the opposite effect with significant benefit to a child who has a brief attention-span in all circumstances.

The terms agnosia and dyspraxia have not so far been mentioned as they are terms which have mostly been used in the field of acquired cerebral lesions in adults. As in the case of disorders of language the transfer of terms used to denote a loss of a well established function to the interference with its development can cause confusion. If this fundamental difference is borne in mind there is no particular objection to the use of these terms, especially if they are prefixed by the word developmental. Agnosia is defined as an inability to interpret sensory input when the peripheral pathways are intact. The perception of an object is achieved by the association of sensations from one sensory channel with those obtained from other channels and with memories of sensations derived from previous experience which includes actions in regard to it (Brain, 1955). If this secondary process fails to develop normally, perception will be faulty. Apraxia is an inability to carry out purposive movements in the absence of severe weakness, sensory loss and consistent incoordination. In other words, there is no memory of patterns of movements so that, although physical ability is adequate for their performance, the organisation is lacking. These terms indicate the two main categories of disability affecting the clumsy child, defects of perception and of motor organisation, and the child may show a predominance of one or other disorder. In those most severely affected there will be a marked involvement of both functions, and often of large and fine movements.

REFERENCES

Bax M, MacKeith R 1963 Minimal cerebral dysfunction. Little Club Clinics in Developmental Medicine No. 10. Heinemann, London
Boder E 1973 Developmental dyslexia: a diagnostic approach based on three atypical reading-spelling patterns. Developmental Medicine and Child Neurology 15: 663–687
Brain R 1955 Diseases in the nervous system. Oxford University Press, London
Brenner M W, Gillman S, Zangwill O L 1967 Visuo-motor disability in school children. British Medical Journal iv: 259–262
Conners C K 1976 Learning disabilities and stimulant drugs in children: theoretical implications. In: Knights R M, Bakker D J (ed) The neuropsychology of learning disorders. University Park Press, London.
Farnham-Diggory S 1978 Learning disabilities. Fontana/Open Books, London
Gubbay S S 1975 The clumsy child. Saunders, London

Gubbay S S, Ellis E, Walton J N, Cant S D M 1965 Clumsy children: a study of apraxic and agnostic defects in 21 children. Brain 88: 295–312
Orton S T 1937 Reading, writing and speech problems in children. Norton, New York
Pope L 1970 Motor activity in brain-injured children. American Journal of Orthopsychiatry 40: 783–794
Walton J N, Ellis E, Cant S D M 1962 Clumsy children: a study of developmental aprazia and agnosia. Brain 85: 603–612

SUGGESTIONS FOR FURTHER READING

Ashworth F 1978 Reading writing and talking too, Home and School Council Publications, 17 Jackson's Lane, Billericay, Essex.
Birch H G 1964 Brain damage in children: the biological and social aspects. Williams & Wilkins, Baltimore.
Geschwind N 1976 Selected papers on language and the brain. Reidel, Boston
Haber R N, Hershenson M 1973 The psychology of visual perception. Holt, New York
Hinshelwood J 1917 Congenital word blindness. Lewis, London
Kinsbourne M 1971 Cognitive deficit: experimental analysis. In: McGuage J L (ed) Psychobiology. Academic Press, New York
Lindsay P, Norman D 1977 Human information processing. Academic Press, New York
Luria A R 1966 Human brain and psychological processes. Harper & Row, New York
Miles T R 1974 The dyslexic child. Priory Press, Hove, (GB)
Owen F W, Adams P A, Forrest T, Stoltz L M, Fisher S 1971 Learning disorders in children: sibling studies. Monographs of the Society for Research in Child Development, Palo Alto
Strauss A 1947 Psychopathology and education of the brain-injured child. Grune & Stratton, New York.
Werner H 1961 Comparative psychology of mental development. Science Editions, New York.

Why are they clumsy?

Different factors, it has been speculated, may lead to problems with physical coordination (Taylor and McKinlay, 1979). These include processes affecting brain growth and development, including maturational rate and genetic factors, opportunity for learning (Essen, Fogelman and Head, 1978), experience and motivation. It is also possible that the child may seem to perform poorly when tested on an 'off day'. The older a child is when he is tested (say, after seven years) the greater is the influence of the development of skills as opposed to developmental variation. Family size (Belmont, *et al.*, 1976) and general intelligence also affect performance.

Brain growth and development
The development of the brain occurs in a complex but predictable sequential pattern. The effect of an insult depends on its timing in relation to the events of brain growth. In the first three to four weeks after conception a flat plate of cells becomes the neural tube. If this is disrupted the fetus may well suffer from gross abnormalities such as spina bifida or anencephaly and is much more likely than not to be spontaneously aborted (Nishimura, 1970).

From about the 10th to 18th weeks of gestation those cells which will become nerve cells multiply. Towards the end of this period they become differentiated, and after this their number is fixed since mature neurons cannot divide. Thus, by half way through pregnancy the majority of the brain's nerve cells are already present although they still have a great deal of growing to do, as well as some migration to their eventual locations. Problems during this early period lead to the most severe forms of mental retardation with microcephaly (disproportionately small brains) (*Lancet*, 1979), and spastic cerebral palsy (Hagberg, 1975).

The next phase of brain development is called the 'brain growth spurt' because it is a time when many things develop very rapidly. Three main aspects have been especially studied: the formation of interconnections (dendrites) between nerve cells and synapses, increase in the numbers of glial cells and myelination. The first two occupy the last half of pregnancy and the first two years or so of infancy. Myelination — the formation of lipid insulating sheaths round nerve fibres to speed conduction of electrical discharges — begins in the later weeks of pregnancy and is largely complete by four or five years after birth.

Study of the development of dendrites is already proving an exciting means of understanding functional abnormalities of the nervous system (Purpura, 1975). Though techniques for this have been available for over 100 years using silver stains, these are time consuming and unreliable and have not been very successful. The great majority of interconnections between nerve cells occur at synaptic junctions along the edges of the 'twigs' or 'spines' of the dendritic 'tree', a small minority connecting with the nerve cell bodies themselves (Fig. 2.1).

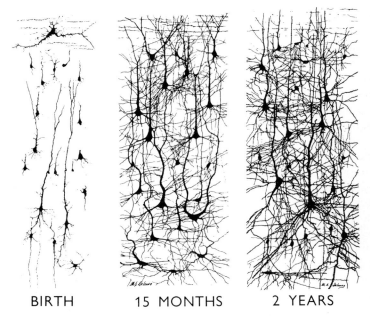

BIRTH   15 MONTHS   2 YEARS

Fig. 2.1 Normal brain development showing dendrite formation (from Dobbing (1976) with permission).

The number of interconnections received by each individual cell may be in the order of 800 for a Purkinje cell, 12 500 for a neurone in the visual cortex and up to 24 000 for a pre-frontal neurone. When it is realised that a rat's brain probably contains about 150 million neurones, and the human brain is 700 times as big as a rat's, the problem of counting synapses can be seen to be formidable, and the potential for disruption of such a sophisticated system need not be emphasised. Very advanced counting techniques have had to be devised (Thomas et al., 1979).

Glial cells accompany nerve cells in large numbers in the developed brain and come to outnumber nerve cells by about eight to one. Their functions are largely unknown, but they are involved in some way in nerve cell metabolism and one common variety is responsible for the formation of myelin. New counting techniques in serial sections of brain tissue and assay of deoxyribonucleic acid (DNA) have made it possible to quantify brain cell numbers (glial cells and neurones) in ways not open to conventional brain pathology. This has been applied both to animal experiments and to analysis of human brains (Dobbing and Sands, 1973). Biochemical assay (e.g. of cholesterol; Dobbing and Sands, 1973) has improved understanding of the rate of myelination, most of which occurs in pre-school years. It may be speculated that the main value of myelination is to allow rapid conduction of electrical impulses in a growing organism.

Against this general account of brain growth the particular features of the development of the cerebellum are of special interest. The growth spurt of the cerebellum begins a little later than that of the rest of the brain and ends earlier, being virtually complete by 9 to 10 months of post-natal life. By this time the cerebellum contains adult numbers of cells at a time when the forebrain and brainstem are about 60 per cent towards that target. The cerebellum has been shown to be disproportionately susceptible to processes affecting brain growth in late pregnancy and early infancy (Dobbing and Smart, 1973).

In rats transient undernutrition or irradiation during the brain growth spurt has been shown to lead to disproportionate underdevelopment of the cerebellum (Dobbing, 1970; Dobbing et al., 1970, 1971) with observed clumsiness subsequently in the mature animals. In low birth weight babies who are small for dates (i.e. with poor late intrauterine growth) impaired performance scores but normal verbal quotients have been reported (Davies, 1976). This was not true of premature babies of the same weight but appropriate for gestational age. Their performance and verbal scores were normal. However a quarter of the premature babies and a third of the small for dates babies under 1250 g showed learning difficulties though with IQs greater than 70. This may have implications for the special care of very small newborn babies (Harvey and Wallis, 1979).

Microcephaly and mental retardation in children irradiated as fetuses by the Hiroshima and Nagasaki bombs was largely confined to those irradiated prior to 18 weeks gestation (Miller and Blot, 1972).

Children exposed to cranial irradiation and chemotherapy for leukaemia before the age of four years (Fig. 2.2) have been shown to have impaired performance scores (but not verbal scores) in a way not observed when older children are so treated (Eiser and Lansdown, 1977). Thyroxine is generally believed to be an important hormone for the development of dendrites before and after birth (Grave, 1977). If the fetus suffers from thyroxine deficiency it cannot be compensated for by the mother's thyroid function as thyroxine does not cross the placenta. It is of great interest therefore that the long term follow-up of hypothyroid infants, subsequently treated, has shown them to have performance difficulty and clumsiness in later years (McFaul, *et al.*, 1978). The incidence is 1:4000 deliveries.

Fig. 2.2 Boy aged eight years, four months. Treated for leukaemia at age three. Now has some phonic basis for spelling but weak grasp of spelling rules and no concept of syllables. The isolated words are 'elephant', 'hippopotamus', 'gate' and 'new'.

In a study of 32 newborn babies showing symptoms after perinatal asphyxia, long-term follow-up showed 14 to be clumsy children (Brown, 1976) an incidence of 1.5 per 1000 deliveries.

The detailed observation of children with epilepsy has shown the importance of the time and nature of insult, the site of injury and the sex of the affected brain in determining the subsequent biography of the child. The greatest risk of becoming schizophrenic in people with temporal lobe epilepsy for example occurs in left-handed females with small tumours in the left temporal lobe giving rise to epilepsy after the development of organised speech (Taylor, 1975). The greatest risk of intellectual impairment occurs with ischaemic damage to the left brain (Stores, 1978).

The incidence of clumsiness in children with epilepsy is not known but deserves study. Two out of five children in a residential school for people with epilepsy were reported to have sufficient clumsiness to interfere with their work (Dunlop, unpublished data). One in three children with epilepsy in the Isle of Wight study showed significant educational retardation. Amongst the small number tested by a modified Oseretsky scale about half were thought to be moderately or severely clumsy (Rutter, et al., 1970).

The co-ordination skills of 15 children suffering from absences with generalised seizure discharge were recently tested in our department using Gubbay's test and the Lincoln-Oseretsky test. They performed significantly less well in both tests than a control, seizure-free group matched for sex and intelligence (Phillips and McKinlay 1979 unpublished data).

Observations of impaired motor performance in children with spina bifida (Minns et al., 1977), hydrocephalus (Anderson and Plewis, 1977) and cerebral palsy (O'Malley and Griffith, 1977) are also relevant. (Perceptuomotor disorder has been found in children with hemiplegia irrespective of the side clinically affected.) There is no doubt about the presence of an organic brain disorder in these conditions.

Further insight into the possible neuropathology of clumsiness and learning disorders in some children has come from the description of adults with acquired disorders. In some, the effect of a stroke, surgery or tumour has been to disconnect areas of the brain from each other. The individual areas may continue to function independently or in conjunction with other parts of the brain. The subject has been fully reviewed by Geschwind (1970) and Dimond (1976). For a review of auditory-visual integration in brain-damaged and normal children see Birch and Belmont (1965). Disordered auditory organisation is discussed by Bradley and Bryant (1978).

In 1892 Déjèrine described a patient who suddenly lost the ability to recognise words, letters or numbers after a stroke affecting the left occipital cortex and corpus callosum. He could, however, write correctly either spontaneously or to dictation though he could not read what he had written. The speech area seemed to have become disconnected from the visual cortex. (See also British Medical Journal, 1979).

After division of the corpus callosum for severe epilepsy some patients have lost the ability to write with the left hand, though they have continued to be able to copy shapes with that hand. The converse was true of the right hand (Bogen and Bogen, 1969). All patients operated on in this way are not so affected and many of those affected have recovered. Presumably other connections are formed or activated. However, one patient (von Wagenen and Herren, 1940) after such an operation was found simultaneously opening a door with one hand and shutting it with the other, putting a dress on with the right and taking it off with the left. The effect was temporary.

Other observed phenomena, after strokes usually, giving rise to puzzling inconsistency include retaining the capacity to repeat proverbs, swear and sing songs correctly in spite of severe loss of propositional speech (Geschwind et al., 1968). There is also the phenomenon of loss of recognition of body parts which may not be paralysed.

It is suggested that some children show features of non-connection or under-connection which contribute to coordination difficulty and learning difficulties. Whereas it is widely held that the immature brain has an enhanced capacity for compensation for insults this may apply more to focal lesions than to diffuse processes. Disturbance of brain development during the growth spurt may lead to limitation in the numbers of dendrites or glial cells. Alternatively maturational processes may be delayed leading to immature performance and behaviour with subsequent catch-up.

A variety of physical insults may lead to a variety of coordination and learning difficulties as opposed to a single process leading to a discrete 'clumsy child syndrome' or 'dyslexia syndrome'. The precise

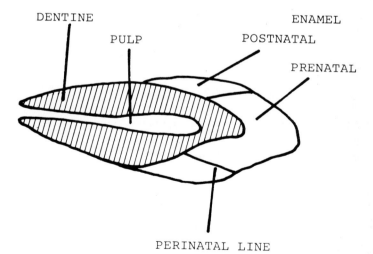

DENTINE   ENAMEL

PULP   POSTNATAL

PRENATAL

PERINATAL LINE

Fig. 2.3a Diagrammatic representation of an incremental growth line in a deciduous incisor. Such lines may be single or multiple, present or absent, slight or pronounced, and are usually seen in the enamel. In a current study in Cheshire 80 per cent of all children appear to have a definite perinatal line, 5 per cent have a prenatal line, and 30 per cent have a postnatal line. These are being correlated with physical coordination and educational attainments.

Fig. 2.3b Incremental growth lines (arrowed) in the enamel of a deciduous tooth. A dense horizontal line separates the enamel (above) from the dentine. Because of the high magnification, the crystalline matrix of enamel and dentine can be seen. The root of the tooth is to the left of this section. The lower of the two lines was formed in the perinatal period; the upper one developed about three weeks later. (From Levine *et al.*, 1979)

insult for a particular child is often unknown at present. However the possibility that a proportion of clumsy children have an organically based problem offers the possibility of prevention in future. It also implies that a physical-remedial style of management may be more appropriate than a universal attempt to apply a purely psycho-social analysis or remedy.

Techniques being applied in current research may elucidate the organic hypothesis further. Microscopic and microradiographic examination of longitudinal sections of the shed deciduous teeth of children can show incremental growth lines, particularly in the enamel, highly indicative of an insult or insults to growth in earlier development (Bergman *et al*. (1965), Levine *et al*.(1979) (Fig. 2.3).

Minimal brain damage; minimal cerebral dysfunction
The terms MBD/MCD have been loosely and variously applied to children whose problems have been thought to have a constitutional basis. However, evidence of brain damage has generally been lacking except in highly selected groups (e.g. Bergstrom and Bille, 1978). Behavioural traits ascribed to MBD (e.g. hyperactivity or sleep disturbance) have been too loosely applied to be useful (Rutter, Graham and Yule, 1970; Sandberg, Rutter and Taylor, 1978). There is extensive overlap with a 'normal' population. The term 'brain damage' has induced distress in parents and despondency amongst teachers. The difficulties experienced by some children are far from minimal. Thus, although the implications of a biological disorder may be well-founded, the terminology of MBD/MCD is not helpful.

Genetic factors
Just as there are families with a predisposition to be athletes or musicians there are bound to be families with relatively poor coordination skills. If retrospective developmental histories of children are notoriously inaccurate (Hart *et al*., 1978) so are developmental histories of parents or other relatives. Thus a family history needs to be interpreted with caution. Where no positive family history is elicited the child's problems are more likely to be organically based or attributable to inadequate learning experience. The genetic and acquired factors may overlap. A process affecting brain development may not lead to detectable effects in a child with a generous genetic endowment (or good learning experience). However, in a child with a lesser genetic spare capacity for balance, manipulation or language skills, the effect of an acquired developmental insult may be harder to conceal.

Learning opportunity and rehearsal
A child who has had restricted opportunities for play because of housing conditions, repeated illness, parental attitudes, lack of toys or nursery class facilities will not perform well on school entry screening tests. After a short period at school, performance may improve rapidly. Some of the young children who improve quickly with

intervention (e.g. by therapists) are likely to be in this category. The child may not have been encouraged to dress independently, explore imaginatively, take some risks or to play with other children. Such explanations are often proposed for clumsy children (e.g. 'overprotective mother') but it must be considered that the parent has been responding to the child's relative incompetence. They would seem to become less likely as the child moves through school with its wide opportunities for rehearsal of skills.

Effect of growth

The physical awkwardness of the adolescent is commonly observed. The effect of growth on body image perception and control of body movements has not been fully evaluated. It is possible that some children adapt better than others to the constant change in body size and weight.

Poor motivation at the time of testing

A child may perform poorly at the time of testing for many reasons though the tasks required are within his capability. He may be unwell, have poor rapport with the tester, may be anxious, depressed or preoccupied, may have had an unhappy experience of previous testing, may have low self-esteem and not try for fear of failure. He may have a hearing impairment or language difficulty and not understand the instructions. Such children are not truly clumsy children. Prolonged observation by the teacher together with discussion with the parents will clarify the issue. There is a congruence between behaviour problems and performance difficulties which requires skilled and patient elucidation. Just as false positives on screening may have an emotional basis so it is possible to overlook constitutional factors in a child with behaviour and learning problems. This is, at least potentially, one of the areas of expertise within the school health service, though additional specialist help may be required.

Conclusion

Children may be observed to be clumsy for a variety of reasons. These include organic factors affecting brain development, genetic factors, emotional state, learning experience, nature and timing of testing and the child's attitude to being tested. This may help to explain why 'clumsy children' are such a heterogeneous group.

REFERENCES

Anderson E M, Plewis I 1977 Impairment of a motor skill in children with spina bifida cystica and hydrocephalus: An exploratory study. Br. J. Psychol 68: 61.70

Bergman G, Bille B, Lyttkens G 1965 Tooth ring analysis in minimal brain dysfunction. Lancet i: 963

Bergstrom K, Bille B 1978 Computed tomography of the brain in children with minimal brain damage: a preliminary study of 46 children. Neuropadiatrie 9: 378–384

Birch H G, Belmont L 1965 Auditory visual integration in brain damaged and normal children. Develop Med Child Neurol 7: 135–144

Bogen J E, Bogen G 1969 Bull Los Ang Neurol Soc 34: 191–219

Bradley L, Bryant P E 1978 Difficulties in auditory organisation as a possible cause of reading backwardness. Nature 271:746–7

British Medical Journal leading article 1979 Acquired Cerebral Disorders of Reading 2: 350–351

Brown J K 1976 Infants damaged during birth; perinatal asphyxia In: Hull D (ed) Recent advances in paediatrics – 5, Churchill Livingstone, Edinburgh, Ch 3, p 73

Davies P A 1976 Outlook for the low birthweight baby — then and now. Arch Dis Child 51: 817–9

Dimond S J 1976 The disconnection syndromes. In: Williams D (ed) Modern trends in neurology. Butterworth, London, Ch 3

Dobbing J 1970 Undernutrition and the developing brain In: Heinrich W A (ed) Developmental neurobiology. Thomas, Springfield, Illinois, p 241

Dobbing J 1976 Vulnerable periods in brain growth and somatic growth. In: Roberts D F, Thomson A M (eds) The biology of human fetal growth. Taylor & Francis, London.

Dobbing J, Sands J 1973 Quantitative growth and development of human brain. Arch Dis Child 48: 757–767

Dobbing J, Smart J L 1973 Early undernutrition, brain development and behaviour. In: Barnett S A (ed) Ethology and development. Clinics in developmental medicine no 47. SIMP Heinemann, London

Dobbing J, Hopewell J W, Lynch A, Sands J 1970 Vulnerability of developing brain: I. Some lasting effects of x-irradiation. Exp Neurol 28: 442–449

Dobbing J, Hopewell J W, Lynch A 1971 Vulnerability of developing brain: VII Permanent deficit of neurons in cerebral and cerebellar cortex following early mild undernutrition. Exp Neurol 32: 439–447

Dunlop B 1964 Neurological survey of Lingfield Hospital School. (Quoted in: People with Epilepsy 1969 HMSO, London, p 38)

Eiser C, Lansdown R 1977 Retrospective study of intellectual development in children treated for acute lymphoblastic leukaemia. Arch Dis Child 52: 525–529.

Essen J, Fogelman K, Head J 1978 Childhood housing experiences and school attainment. Child Care Health and Development 4: 41–58

Geschwind N, Quadfasel F A, Segarra J M 1968 Neuropsychologia 6: 327–340

Geschwind N 1970 In: Williams D (ed) Modern trends in neurology, Butterworths, London

Gilman D 1977 Thyroid hormones and brain development. Raven Press, New York

Hagberg B 1975 Pre-, Peri and Postnatal prevention of major neuropaediatric handicaps. Neuropadiatrie 6: 331–338

Hart H, Bax M, Jenkins S 1978 The value of a developmental history. Develop Med Child Neurol 20: 442–452

Harvey D R, Wallis S M 1979 Neurological examination of children who were small for dates babies. Arch Dis Child 54: 725–726.

Lancet leader 1979 Unclassified mental retardation. (Lancet) 1: 250–251.

Levine R S, Turner E P, Dobbing J 1979 Deciduous teeth contain histories of developmental disturbances. Early Human Development 3: 211–220

McFaul R, Dorner S, Brett E M, Grant D B 1978 Neurological abnormalities in patients treated for hypothyroidism from early life. Arch Dis Child 53: 611–619

Miller R W, Blot W J 1972 Small head size after in utero exposure to atomic radiation. Lancet 2: 784

Minns R A, Sobkowiak C A, Skardoutsou A, Diuck K, Elton R A, Brown J K, Forfar J O 1977 Upper limb function in spina bifida. Z. Kinderchir 22: 4 493–506

Nichimura H 1970 Proceedings of the 3rd international conference on congenital malformations: The Hague 1969. (eds) Fraser F C, McKusick V A Excerpta Medica Amsterdam, p 275

O'Malley P J, Griffith J F 1977 Perceptuomotor dysfunction in the child with hemiplegia. Develop Med Child Neurol 19: 172–178

Purpura D P 1975 Dendritic differentiation in human cerebral cortex: normal and aberrant patterns. In: Kreutzberg G W (ed) Advances in neurology vol 12, physiology and pathology of dendrites. Raven Press, New York, p 91–116

Rutter M, Graham P, Yule W 1970 A neuropsychiatric study in childhood. Clinics in Developmental Medicine 35/36: SIMP, Heinemann, London

Sandberg S T, Rutter M, Raylor E 1978 Hyperkinetic disorder in psychiatric clinic attenders. Develop Med Child Neurol 20: 279–299

Stores G 1978 School children with epilepsy at rish for learning and behaviour problems. Develop Med Child Neurol 20: 502–508

Taylor D C 1975 Factors influencing the occurrance of schizophrenia-like psychosis in patients with TLE. Psychological Medicine 5: 249–254

Taylor D C, McKinlay I A 1979 What kind of thing is 'being clumsy'. Child Care Health and Development 5. 167–175

Thomas Y M, Bedi K S, Davies C A, Dobbing J 1979 A stereological analysis of the neuronal and synaptic content of the frontal and cerebellar cortex of weanling rats undernourished from birth. Early Human Development 3: 109–126

von Wagenen W P, Herren R Y 1940 Surgical division of commisural pathways in the corpus callosum – relation to spread of an epileptic attack Arch Neurol Psychiat (Chicago) 44: 740–759

Who says they are clumsy?

The problems of the clumsy child come to light in a variety of ways. It may be obvious to the parents, who then consult their family doctor. It may be the school situation which first highlights the child's shortcomings and then the teacher and clinical medical officer visiting the school will be involved. The latter may also identify clumsiness in the preschool child health clinic. The psychologist and the various therapists in the course of their assessment and treatment will often recognise that a child is having particular difficulties in the organisation of motor skills and will recommend special remedial measures. Also, very occasionally, a child will be particularly aware of his own clumsiness and be prepared to complain about it.

Parents start to assess their children from birth, though their interest will obviously vary. In coming to the conclusion that a child is abnormally clumsy they may evoke comparison with older siblings, or with other children of the same age in their neighbourhood. On the other hand, the conclusion may be forced on the parents by the comments of relatives or friends. If the child starts to complain of symptoms found to be the result of the stresses of trying to cope with a learning disorder, the parents may well take the symptoms at their face value without realising there is a significant underlying cause. However, if the child's behaviour is causing trouble at school or progress is said to be abnormally slow, this is likely to create increasing anxiety and cause at least the more vocal parent to demand that something be done to help the child.

Parents may well discuss these problems with the teachers at the child's school, but particularly in the case of the preschool child they will probably go to the family doctor in the first place. If a child presents with symptoms for which there seems to be no obvious cause, it is worthwhile enquiring into the school situation. For the same reasons these children may be referred to the paediatrician, either for help in their assessment, or because of unexplained symptoms. In the latter case it may be the paediatrician who is the first person to say that the child is clumsy, and to ensure that the necessary help is given in terms of an adequate analysis of the difficulties, treatment such as physiotherapy, and remedial education, if this is needed.

The clinical medical officer working in the child health clinic and in the schools is in a particularly good position to recognise the clumsy child. There are many children with a significant degree of clumsiness which is not recognised. These children may come to the clinic in the same way as they do to the family doctor; but equally it may be a matter of recognising a significant delay in motor development and a degree of incoordination unacceptable for the patient's age in the course of carrying out routine developmental checks. In the school these children are often seen because of slow progress and suspected mental retardation or because of behaviour problems. In these circumstances it can take considerable perspicacity to identify a specific learning disorder so that the necessary assessments can be carried out. This is particularly true if there are severe emotional disturbances, which can easily dominate the clinical picture.

The teacher can be the first to diagnose perceptual motor disabilities. It may well be that in the past there was a tendency almost automatically to blame the child if progress was not satisfactory, but that is no longer the case. There is no doubt that all of us could do better if we tried but for clumsy children their efforts must be directed in the most profitable manner and must be suitably rewarded. If the teacher recognises a child is in difficulty and asks the question 'why', this will ensure the possibility that a specific learning disability is considered. If this is severe, the child's movements, the way he holds his pencil, his drawings and writing may all give the clue to the type of disorder, which can then be investigated in greater detail so that a programme of remedial teaching can be formulated. If the child has been referred to the psychologist because of suspected mental retardation a marked discrepancy in abilities may be found. Likewise, the occupational therapist, physiotherapist and speech therapist may identify clumsiness as a specific disability in the course of their assessment and treatment.

Some children are referred by the family doctor to the orthopaedic surgeon because of repeated falls and an awkward gait and it is not at once apparent that this is part of a generalised disorder of balance and motor coordination. When this becomes evident onward referral to a paediatrician or paediatric neurologist may be made.

If the diagnosis is missed, the child may well present at a later age at the Child Guidance Clinic because of behaviour disorders, having been labelled as lazy or naughty because it has not been recognised that he is trying hard and doing his best and has learning problems for which he needs help.

If movements are not severely affected the diagnosis may result from a question of suspicion, or on the routine examination of young children to identify possible handicaps by the clinical medical officer. Large numbers of children are likely to be involved in the first instance, only a certain number of whom will need detailed and time-consuming assessment. Various screening tests can be devised, often using items from a number of different developmental and intelligence scales.

In the case of disorders of language development there is little doubt that the earlier the age at which this is identified the better, so that appropriate advice and treatment can be given. In the case of perceptual motor disorders the situation is not the same, except perhaps for those children severely affected. If before the age of five the parents have recognised that their child is abnormally clumsy and have started to worry about this, a full examination must be carried out and treatment given if this is needed. Others less severely affected may be identified under certain circumstances depending on such factors as their social class, concern of parents, and attendance at a nursery school. They are not likely to need any special treatment or education at this stage.

Pre-school developmental screening

The routine developmental screening tests carried out by the health visitors and doctors on pre-school children may not detect the clumsy child in the early years if the disability is slight or very specific. Suspicions will be aroused in the case of the toddler who often falls and has great difficulty in learning to feed himself with cup and spoon and, later on, in learning to fasten buttons and zip fasteners. It must always be remembered that some children fail to develop these skills because of lack of practice — their mothers have continued to feed them rather than put up with the mess they would make, and continued to dress them 'because it is quicker'. At school entrant age it is common to find children who cannot dress and undress themselves. An average child who has had the opportunity to practice can dress and undress himself, with the exception of difficult buttons, by the age of four years (Sheridan 1973).

The value of pre-screening questionnaires and of screening programmes of various kinds needs to be constantly assessed (Walker, 1977), but on the basis of 'prevention being better than cure' it does seem to be a worthwhile exercise. The typical developmental screening tests carried out in the first 18 months of life will detect the severely subnormal child or the one with frank cerebral palsy but are unlikely to detect the minimal neurological signs and developmental delay of the clumsy child. The later birthday checks and pre-school check are more likely to pick up evidence of developmental delay. This applies particularly to the locomotor and eye and hand coordination fields of development where the five-year-old clumsy child may well fail in almost all of the test items.

Francis-Williams (1976) followed up a group of children she had assessed in the pre-school period and found that those who had had severe visuo-spatial and perceptuo-motor abilities in the pre-school years and continued to show this disability at eight or nine years had great difficulties in forming number concepts. Children who had had very low scores in the pre-school Copy Form Tests had severe reading retardation at follow-up examination. Also delayed language development was a particular indication of later learning difficulties at school.

School entry screening
It is often at the start of more formal schooling at the age of five in the UK that troubles arise, and this may be the best time to screen for 'clumsy children'. It also means that the observations of the teacher can be added to the results of any tests that are carried out. Obviously, when large numbers of children have to be examined, a test that can be performed simply and in a short period of time is essential. It may consist of a few items from scales such as Stott's test of motor impairment, the Frostig developmental test for visual perception, and the Bergès and Lézine's imitation of gestures (Bergès and Lézine, 1965). Now that so many of the nutritional and hygienic disorders of childhood are largely a thing of the past in developed countries more time can be given to searching for evidence of a variety of disabilities from visual defects and impaired hearing to delays in learning motor skills and disorders of language development. Bax and Whitmore (1973) have used a special school-entrant medical examination. This included examination for squint, hearing of the spoken voice at six feet, speech comprehensibility, facial symmetry, motor impersistence, tongue tremor, hand patting, finger-nose pointing, Bergès-Lézine items, rapid pronation/supination of the hand, pencil grip, drawing of a circle, square, and triangle, gait, heel-to-toe walking, hopping, tendon reflexes, level of physical activity and general behaviour. These tests could be included in a school-entrant examination lasting 15 to 20 minutes. Follow-up studies showed evidence of predictive value as over half the children with low scores were in difficulties three to four years later.

After carrying out a pilot survey on 279 children attending a primary school in Western Australia a larger number of children (922) aged 6 to 12 years were examined by Gubbay (1975). The methods used in the pilot survey were modified in the light of experience. These included a questionnaire for teachers (seven items), and a screening examination questionnaire (eight items). Clumsy children were identified on the basis of the number of failures at each year of age. Then the parents of the clumsy children (56) and a control group were asked to complete a questionnaire. A neurological and general examination, and an EEG, were carried out. As a result of this study the 5th to 95th percentiles of eight tests of Motor Proficiency for children from 8 to 12 years old have been scored. These items were: whistle through parted lips; five successive skips; roll ball with foot around six matchboxes; throw ball up, clap hands up to four times and catch ball; tie single shoelace with double bow; thread 10 beads; pierce 20 holes in graph paper; posting box using six shapes.

Further work (Gubbay, 1978) has shown that in fact four of these tests of motor ability are the best as a guide to the severity of the disability: throwing a tennis ball into the air and clapping hands (up to four times) before catching it again; rolling a tennis ball underfoot in a zig-zag pattern between six matchboxes lined up 30 cm apart (timed); threading 10 beads of 3 cm diameter and 0.8 cm bore (timed); and inserting six differently shaped objects into appropriate slots (timed). He gives the 5th percentile values for the four tests between the ages of 6 to 12 years.

Dubowitz and her colleagues (1977) assessed a clinical screening test in four and five year old children. The children were asked to build a tower with cubes and to name the colours. Then they had to copy designs with the cubes, and to copy designs drawn by the examiner, to count fingers and cubes, and to repeat three, four and sometimes more digit numbers. When these tests had been completed the Peabody Picture Vocabulary Test was administered. These tests which can be completed in a short space of time correlated well with intellectual function assessed on the WPPSI, and also assessed handedness, coordination, concentration and social rapport.

Elinor Jaffa (1972) investigated a group of 132 white, socially deprived children in Birmingham aged 76 to 90 months. A very comprehensive series of tests was used including pure tone audiometry, a clinical hearing test using a phonetically balanced list of words, tests for near and distant vision and colour vision and a complete physical examination. In addition, a battery of neurodevelopmental items was included which covered items under the following headings:

1. *Tests of gross motor coordination*, e.g. heel-to-toe walk, hopping, standing on one leg.

2. *Tests of fine motor coordination*, e.g. hand tapping, finger-nose test, pencil grasp.

3. *Sensory items*, e.g. position sense — kicking the examiner's hand in three different positions.

4. *Mirror movements or synkinesis*, e.g. Fog's test, walking on the lateral aspects of the feet when the hands and arms are observed for simultaneous movements such as positioning of the hands to mirror the foot positions.

5. *Motor impersistence*, e.g. inability to keep mouth open, eyes closed and tongue protruded for twenty seconds. N o

6. *Miscellaneous items*, e.g. attention span and tests of laterality, use of a preferred hand for drawing and asking the child to stamp hard on a coin on the floor pretending it was a 'nasty insect', the preferred foot being noted. right foot / right hand

Each child's parents had completed a health questionnaire and the school had screened each child by educational assessment. The results of the school screening were not known to the doctor prior to her examination of the child to avoid unconscious bias.

Her results indicated, (a) that the learning disabled children showed a significantly higher incidence of abnormal minor neurological signs, but, (b) the total population was homogeneous in terms of social disadvantage, family structure and morbidity.

A simple screening test for neurodevelopmental delay designed to be used as part of the routine school medical examination of 4- to 5-year-old children is the 'Coffee Jar' test used in the Manchester area (Table 3.1). The equipment, contained in a coffee jar, consists of five one-inch wooden bricks each with a hole bored through the centre, a reel and a length of stiff nylon lace on which to thread the bricks (Fig. 3.1). Table 3.1 shows the tests carried out and the areas of development being investigated. No detailed analysis of results is available yet, but, among 100 consecutive school entrants examined, five children (three boys and two girls) were slow at completing the tests though they eventually succeeded with help and persuasion; three boys failed the balance items and one boy could not build the brick tower. Balance items seem to prove the most difficult which is often the case when testing the older clumsy child on Stott's test of motor impairment. It is hoped that a more detailed follow-up of the children who failed items will be carried out at a later date and the test is in the process of validation. When a child fails one or more of the test items he is retested the following year and his progress in the classroom discussed with the teacher at that stage. The parent is reassured after the initial tests that normal children vary in their skills just as do normal adults. Sometimes a mother will say that she or her

(a)

(b)

Fig. 3.1 Coffee jar test. (a) Threading bricks. (b) Winding lace.

Table 3.1 School entrant screening (age 4–5 yrs) Coffee Jar Test.

Test	Area of development being tested
1. Heel toe walk across room.	} Balance and coordination. Watch for associated movements of upper limbs.
2. Come back on tiptoe.	
3. Stand on one leg (8 seconds)	Balance and coordination.
4. Unscrew lid of jar.	Can unscrew at 2 years.
5. Build tower of 5 bricks.	Eye-hand coordination – watch for tremor.
6. Build ▢◆▢▢ placing ◆◆ simultaneously.	Simultaneous movements of both upper limbs.
7. Wind lace on reel, right and left.	'Clumsy child' finds this very difficult – manual dexterity.
8. Thread bricks on lace.	Eye-hand coordination.
9. Replace things in jar and screw on lid.	Can screw back on by 2½ years.

The above order is only a suggestion, but if possible all tests should be included.

If a child fails in more than one area of the tests and if the parent confirms difficulties with a history of late walking, frequent falls, or difficulty with dressing, especially buttons, further investigation is indicated.

If hand dominance is not yet established, this suggests developmental delay.

Demonstrate each item and make sure the child understands what is wanted. The generally retarded or very immature child may fail many items because of lack of comprehension.

husband is, 'no good with their hands', and it is reasonable to assume that manual dexterity like other characteristics may have a hereditary basis. The teacher is not usually told that a child has 'failed' items as the idea of a 'test' at this age may give a pre-conceived idea of how a child will progress in class. But a general discussion between doctor and class teacher about all the class will give the teacher the opportunity to comment on any child who seems to be in difficulties. If this is confirmed by the parents' history and the developmental tests, a full investigation is justified.

Infant teacher's check list

The experienced infant teacher will soon pick out the clumsy child who may have learning difficulties, but it may be helpful to use a check list when considering individual children. The following is a suggested list to follow:–

1. *General coordination*, e.g. very poor at games, hopping, jumping. Generally awkward and clumsy, poor balance.
2. *Hand and eye coordination*, e.g. cannot catch a ball. Difficulty in learning to write or form letters and shapes.
3. *Manual dexterity*. Cannot fasten buttons, shoe laces and zips.

Difficulty in learning to use scissors. Persistence of immature grip of pencil. Difficulty in learning to use knife and fork.

4. *Uncertainty in hand dominance.* Changes hands when writing. Confuses right and left more than peer group.

5. *Very poor concentration*, e.g. easily distracted or day dreams unless in a small group.

6. *Poor speech.*

Difficulty in several of these areas should alert the teacher to the possibility of future learning difficulties. If these arise, further investigation by the clinical medical officer attached to the school and the education psychologist is indicated, so that a remedial programme and help from a physiotherapist, occupational therapist, or speech therapist may be arranged.

An alternative is the Croydon Check List described by Wolfendale (1976). It is designed for use by teachers of children, aged between 4.9 and 5.4 years approximately, at the end of their first term in school. It is based on the work of Gesell, Bayley, Griffiths and others and is designed to assess the child's readiness to learn. Results correlated well with their early learning difficulties. The nineteen items are grouped into four sections as follows.

1. *Speech and communication* (language), e.g. listens to stories with interest and organises thought to narrate experiences.

2. *Perceptual–motor,* e.g. copies shapes, can manipulate and understand the use of simple tools and constructional toys.

3. *Emotional/social,* e.g. forms appropriate relationships with peers and teachers.

4. *Response to learning situations,* e.g. eager to learn and can attend solely to the task in hand.

A young clumsy child would have problems in the perceptual-motor items in particular. The check list is related to a handbook of guidelines for teachers to use in helping the children with remedial work and exercises appropriate to the child's developmental level.

Shepherd (1973) also describes a battery of tests for the use of teachers with children at the end of their first term in school (The Shepherd School Entry Screening Test — S.S.E.S.T.). The tests are grouped under four main headings as follows.

1. *Kinaesthetic perception.* This section includes tests of gross motor skills and awareness of body image as well as tests of visual perception. The young clumsy child will readily be picked out by tests of these skills — he will be unable to throw and catch a ball, hop and skip and may have confused hand and eye dominance.

2. *Visual perception.* Copy forms test (Ilg and Ames, 1964) were used, and as in Wolfendale's work the tests were followed up with training programmes when skills were poorly developed. Frostig's (1967) training programmes were used.

3. *Auditory and language perception.* A large battery of tests is used covering both receptive and expressive sides of language development. Again suggestions for remedial programmes are given.

4. *Tactile perception.* Three tasks are used:
   a. Matching textiles beginning with grossly dissimilar textures and going on to very similar textures, e.g. cotton and linen.
   b. Haptic – visual equivalence. This involves feeling hidden objects and matching them with similar objects from a selection seen on the table.
   c. Haptic – kinaesthetic equivalence. Hidden objects are felt and then the shape drawn by the child on paper.
   Remedial programmes are given for this area of skills.

It will be seen that the full S.S.E.S.T. programme is very detailed and time-consuming. It has been used in Australia by trained personnel (not teachers) spending upwards of two hours with each child. This would not be practicable in many instances as a routine screening method. The Croydon Check List is much shorter, and the suggested Infant Teacher's Check List given above, even more so, but should still direct the teacher's attention to the clumsy child who may have learning problems. It is better to have a short test carried out carefully and accurately on every child than to attempt a very ambitious check list like the S.S.E.S.T. when there are insufficient resources of time and personnel to assess every child thoroughly.

It must be emphasised that most checklists in common use have not been shown to have good predictive value for subsequent educational outcome. They do, however, heighten the teacher's awareness of the current diverse abilities of pupils and suggest the immediate educational strategy for each particular child (see Ch. 5).

Conclusions

The problem of detecting the clumsy child has been considered, but at what age should children be screened for this condition? If it is done early, in the preschool years, the tests are more difficult to carry out and very time-consuming, and it must be borne in mind that children under the age of four show no conception of order when asked to copy a string of beads or a line of washing, and cannot make knots. They lack a mental representation of objects and the relationship of their parts. They are unaware of Euclidean properties such as number of sides, verticals and parallels (Beard, 1969). Also if performed too early in life the tests will pick out many children whose skills will improve with maturity and who do not need special help. If it is left too late, until seven or eight years of age, affected children may have struggled for two or three years in the infant school, their problems unrecognised, until maladjustment in some form or other occurs.

The best time to screen children may well be at their school entry medical examination during the first year in school. The infant teacher is probably the key person in this screening along with the clinical medical officer and it is vital for these two people to meet to discuss children whose condition gives rise to concern. Contact with the head teacher alone is not enough.

Those who work in this field and realise the importance of recognising learning difficulties in order to help the child reach his full potential and to prevent emotional and behavioural complications, are likely to develop their own examination techniques in the light of their experience.

Finally, it is not enough to detect such children at an early age: we must be able to offer a remedial programme from physiotherapist, speech therapist, educational psychologist and teacher, not at a distant regional centre, but in the child's home town and, if possible, in his own school.

REFERENCES

Bax M, Whitmore K 1973 Neurodevelopmental screening in the school entrant medical examination. Lancet ii: 368–370

Beard R M 1969 An outline of Piaget's developmental psychology for students and teachers. Routledge & Kegan Paul, London

Bergès J, Lézine I 1965 The imitation of gestures. S.I.M.P. Heinemann, London

Dubowitz L M S, Leibowitz D, Goldberg C 1977 A clinical screening test for assessment of intellectual development in four- and five-year-old children. Developmental Medicine Child Neurology 19: 776–782

Francis-Williams J 1976 Early identification of children likely to have specific learning difficulties: Reports of a follow-up. Developmental Medicine and Child Neurology 18: 71–77

Frostig M 1967 The developmental program of visual perception: teachers' guide for beginning, intermediate and advanced stages. Follett, Chicago

Gubbay S S 1975 The clumsy child. Saunders, London

Gubbay S S 1978 The management of developmental apraxia. Developmental Medicial and Child Neurology 20: 643–646

Ilg S L and Ames L B 1964 School readiness. Harper & Row, New York

Jaffa E 1977 Learning disorders in young schoolchildren: is neurodevelopmental screening of value? Public Health, London, 91: 237–247

Sheppard M 1973 S.S.E.S.T.: Sheppard School Entry Screening Test. SPELD, New South Wales, Australia

Sheridan M 1973 Children's developmental progress from birth to five years. National Foundation for Educational Research, Windsor, p 104–118

Walker C H M 1977 Pre-screening questionnaires, screening and post-screening programs. Developmental Medicine and Child Neurology 19: 241–245

Wolfendale S 1976 Screening and early identification of reading and learning difficulties. A description of the Croydon Screening Procedures. In: Wedell K, Raybould E C (eds) Early identification of educationally 'at risk' children. Educational Review, Faculty of Education, Birmingham University

SUGGESTIONS FOR FURTHER READING

Alberman E D, Butler N R, Gardiner P A 1971 Children with squints. A handicapped group? Practitioner 206: 501–506.

Bryant G M, Davies K J, Richards F M, Voorhees S 1973 A preliminary study of the use of the Denver Developmental Screening Test in a health department. Developmental Medicine and Child Neuroloey 15: 33–40

Egan D, Illingworth R S, Sheridan M 1969 Developmentsl Screening 0–5 years. London, Heinemann

Frankenburg W K, Dodds J B 1967 The Denver Developmental Screening Test. Journal of Pediatrics 71: 181–191

Frankenburg W K, Goldstein A D, Camp B W 1971 The revised Denver Development Screening Test: its accuracy as a screening instrument. Journal of Pediatrics 79: 988–995

Griffiths M I 1973 Early detection by developmental screening. In In The Youug Retarded Child: Medical Aspects of Care 11–19. Edited by Griffiths M I, Edinburgh & London, Churchill Livingstone

Griffiths R 1954 The abilities of babies. London, University of London Press

Holt K S 1974 Screening for disease. Infancy & childhood. Lancet 2: 1057–1061

Lancet 1975 Developmental screening. Lancet 1: 784–786

Moore J R 1973 Comprehensive assessmen. In: Griffiths I (ed) the young retarded child. Medical aspects of care. Churchill Livingstone, Edinburgh, p 29–51

Moore P C, and Rhys-Jones W G 1971 Routine screening of hearing and vision of 9 months old children in Shropshire. Medical Officer 125: 241–245

Orton C 1979 The Child with a Medical Problem in the Ordinary School. Home and School Council Publications, 17 Jackson's Lane, Billericay, Essex

Prechtl H F R 1967 Neurological sequelae of prenatal and perinatal complications. British Medical Journal 4: 763–767

Rhys-Jones W G 1973 Community Services. In: Griffiths M I (ed) The young retarded child. Medical aspects of care. Churchill Livingstone, Edinburgh, p 62–70

Richards I D G and Roberts G C J 1967 The 'at risk' infant. Lancet 2: 711–713

Roberts C J, and Khosla T 1972 An evaluation of developmental examinations as a method of detecting neurological, visual and auditory handicaps in infancy. British Journal of Preventive and Social Medicine 26: 94–100

Rogers M G H 1967 The risk register — a critical assessment. The Medical Officer 118: 253–256

Sheridan M D 1962 Infants at risk of handicapping conditions. Bulletin of Ministry of Health and Public Health Laboratory Service 20: 238–245

Smith V H 1969 A screening service for the early detection of visual handicap. In: Gardiner P A, McKeith R C, Smith V H (eds) Aspects of developmental and paediatric ophthalmology. Heinemann, London, p 101

Touwen B C L 1971 Neurological follow-up of infants born after obstetrical complications. In: Stoelinga G B A, van der Werff ten Bosch (eds) Normal and abnormal development of brain and behaviour. Leiden University Press, p 179–186

Wolfendale S Bryans T 1979 Identification of learning difficulties. National Association for Remedial Education, 2 Lichfield Street, Stafford

The psychologist's assessment of the clumsy child

Clumsy children are more often referred to the psychologist for reasons other than their perceptual-motor disability. The three most common guises under which clumsy children do present are learning difficulties, behaviour problems and psychosomatic aches and pains. The first category, learning difficulties, covers a wide range of specific problems encountered by these children, including difficulty in concentration ('will not concentrate'); poor reading, writing and/or spelling skills; untidy work; inability to work to a time schedule. Numeracy appears also to be a problem for some in this group (Weddell, 1967; Schonell and Schonell, 1957). Whilst these children have had one or more of the above-mentioned learning difficulties from the beginning of their school careers, often they are not recognised as needing specific help, being assumed to be of lower general ability than their true potential, or simply reluctant pupils. Fortunately for some children, eventually, parents or teachers will notice the discrepancy between his verbal reasoning ability and his written work, resulting in referral to a psychologist through either medical or educational route. This kind of referral tends to occur a few months preceding a scheduled change of school. It is of course at this time that a child's future educational needs and prospects are being most closely examined. Parents are particularly sensitive, too, regarding the type of education which will be available to their child for the next period of his school life.

If the clumsy child's learning difficulties remain unnoticed, behaviour problems often develop. Abnormal behaviour may show in one of three ways. He may give up, becoming withdrawn and apathetic, and lose interest in his school work. This kind of child will be a loner, having no close friends and rarely being chosen by other children to play with since his clumsiness will let the side down in physical team-games. He may give up trying but instead of becoming withdrawn, turn to playing the role of clown or nuisance, and constantly causing a distraction in lessons, thereby drawing upon himself the wrath of his teacher. Secondly, the child may become frustrated and hostile, with the development of aggressive behaviour. The following case history provides a good example:

John, aged nine years, was referred because of complaints from school about his poor work and violent behaviour. The school warned his parents that he was to be moved to a remedial class and that they should not expect too much from him academically. On testing, John was found to be of bright/normal general intelligence but with reading and spelling ages three years below his chronological age. He was clumsy and hated all sports and children's games. He was prone to extremely violent outbursts both at home and at school, attacking both adults and children. John was annoyed when his specific difficulties were explained to him. He had always thought of himself as being unintelligent — the 'dunce' of the class; in fact a failure in all areas. However, eventually buoyed up by the new knowledge that he was an intelligent boy, John's violent behaviour at home ceased immediately and his reading improved dramatically.

The significance of this last fact will be discussed later.

The third way in which clumsy children commonly present to the psychologist is with symptoms of non-organic pain. Head, abdomen and limbs, particularly the legs, are the most usual sites for pains to occur. Vomiting or nausea is also common. Again, psychological assessment may indicate learning difficulties associated with clumsiness. In some of these children the symptoms of pain arise from general anxiety. In others it appears to take the form of an hysterical conversion syndrome; that is, the child has learned to use the symptoms for his own advantage. Frequently this allows the child to avoid the more distressing aspects of school life such as games lessons, reading or art. One 11-year-old boy with a five-year history of painful knees had successfully avoided all physical education for virtually all his school career. He was later discovered to be a clumsy child. The phenomenon, well-known to us all as that Monday morning feeling, assumes reality for these children. Their symptoms, which are experienced as real pain or actual vomiting, occur on Monday mornings or on whatever morning the dreaded school subject occurs. Lonely, physically inept children may also be affected in this way during the holidays.

The above discussion illustrates very clearly the serious effects clumsiness may have on a child. Note that the types of children described were not suspected of being 'clumsy' until after a psychological assessment had been made. Tests used by psychologists are not infallible measuring instruments. In the main, tests sample pieces of behaviour exhibited by an individual, on request, and compare the sample with like collected from his peers in the general population. In order for clumsiness to be detected, motor coordination must be sampled. So far available tests of motor coordination are quite limited in their range and level of sensitivity. For motor coordination assessment of children of school age, probably the most useful are the Stott Test of Motor Impairment

(Stott, Moye and Henderson, 1974), and the Visual Motor Gestalt Test (Bender, 1938). The Stott test (age range from $4\frac{1}{2}$ years to 13 years) has five items at each age level. These items involve gross, complex movements and cover only very small areas of postural, balancing or manipulative faculties. Many clumsy children are clumsy only in specific areas of motor coordination, being quite adept in others. An example is the five-year-old boy, who could stand on his head, but could not hold a pencil correctly. Some clumsy children have problems with only very fine motor movement, which are not picked up by the Stott test. Lauretta Bender's Visual Motor Gestalt Test, developed in 1938, is extremely interesting to use with clumsy children. Unfortunately clinical experience shows its greatest value to be with children whose mental age is at least eight years.

Briefly, Bender's test consists of nine cards, each bearing a line drawing originally used by Wertheimer in his experimental work on visual perception. Each card is presented to the child, who copies it onto a plain sheet of paper working at his own speed. The child's reproductions can then be scored. However, the most useful part of this test is not the final score obtained but an analysis of the way in which the child actually draws his reproductions; the way he holds his pencil; how hard he presses on it; whereabouts on the paper he commences to draw; whether lines are drawn from right to left or vice versa; the order in which particular lines are drawn. These pieces of information are particularly valuable and shed far more light on the specific difficulties of the child than does the obtained score alone. It is equally useful to watch the child as he writes, to notice how he forms his letters and whether he does so in a consistent manner.

Without knowledge of the child's overall ability, it is impossible to interpret test results of motor coordination. As there is a full range from clumsy mentally handicapped children to clumsy gifted children (McKinlay, 1978) it is vital to know a child's level of intelligence. The Wechsler Intelligence Scale for Children (Wechsler, 1949) is especially valuable in the age range 7 to 16 years as it allows comparison between the verbal ability and non-verbal ability of the child. Clumsy children frequently show gross discrepancies between their Verbal and Performance IQs. They are often penalised for very slow responses in tasks involving manipulative skills. The Wechsler Pre-School and Primary Scale of Intelligence allows similar assessment of children from the age of four years (Wechsler, 1963). These two tests will show evidence of visuo-spatial difficulties but a lack of a discrepancy between the performance and verbal IQ does not exclude a perceptual motor disability, as these tests do not offer a comprehensive assessment of coordination. Equally, a good performance score does not preclude a performance problem. It is not uncommon for children with frank cerebral palsy to achieve average performance scores on the Wechsler Intelligence Scale for Children. Clumsy children appear to fall into two categories: those with visual perception problems and poor motor coordination; and those with only motor coordination difficulties. This is not surprising if one accepts Bender's description of the development of visual motor behaviour (Bender, 1933). Her experiments led her to state that visual motor patterns arise from motor behaviour that is modified by the characteristics of the visual field. Furthermore, she reminds us of Koffka's view that all motor acquisitions, even during development, have a sensory component and that movement is a necessary condition for perception.

The Frostig Developmental Test of Visual Perception (Frostig, 1963) purports to provide a means of looking specifically at visual perception in the child aged $3\frac{1}{2}$ years to $7\frac{1}{2}$ years. The test has five sections, namely: (1) visual-motor coordination (2) figure-ground perception (3) perceptual constancy (4) position in space and (5) perception of spatial relationships. However in practice it is mainly a test of visual-motor function. When particular areas of difficulty can be pinpointed, the Frostig Programme for the Development of Visual Perception (Frostig, 1973) may be used to develop the defective skill. This would be expected to be of benefit when writing difficulty, rather than reading difficulty, is the main problem.

A full psychological assessment should include the administration of reading and spelling tests (Schonell and Schonell, 1957; Neale, 1958; Pumfray, 1976; Lansdown, 1976). Many clumsy children have good reading ability, others having specific reading retardation (Rutter and Yule, 1975). A much higher proportion of these children have serious difficulties with spelling (particularly irregular words). Indeed some are so distressed by even the thought of it that occasionally it is impossible to obtain a spelling age. As with all psychological testing, the feelings of inadequacy experienced by the child during testing must be taken into account. There are many differing views about the relevance of correct spelling and whether unnecessary emphasis is laid upon it in schools. A good review of the literature on the subject is presented by Frith (1978), who points out that spelling preserves the root from which a word is derived and gives information about its history and relationship to other words. If spelling were to change with changing pronunciation, some children would have increasing difficulty with reading.

Skilled observation of the actual learning errors children make may be more useful in the long term to teachers than results of a battery of standard psychological tests alone, though the latter may be able to indicate 'general ability' in a way which is convincing to teachers, parents and children. Rough-and-ready coordination tests with Australian and American norms respectively are available in Gubbay (1975) and Arnheim and Sinclair (1975) for children aged 4–12 but no British norms exist yet.

Psychological assessment of clumsiness in infants and preschool children is very difficult. The Girffiths Mental Development Scales are helpful in infants because the child's developmental age may be calculated for each of five different areas of specific ability, namely: locomotor; personal-social; hearing and speech; eye and hand coordination; and performance. However, norms of development cover wide ranges in age and it is extremely difficult to pinpoint clumsiness in very young children. Serious deficits in the Locomotor and Performance Scales alone for example, generally occur in children with frank neurological disorder or overt physical handicap (Griffiths, 1954; 1970). However, poor articulation of speech, with good understanding of language, is a feature for the tester to look for (Francis-Williams, 1974). Other developmental scales such as the Gesell Development Schedule (Gesell and Amatruda, 1947), or the Bayley Scales of Infant Development (1968) are no more helpful than the Griffiths in the detection of 'clumsiness'.

In children aged two to five years, the Merrill-Palmer Test of Mental Abilities (Stutsman, 1931) may be of help in demonstrating specific motor coordination difficulties and in giving an overall assessment of general ability. This is primarily a performance test of intelligence for children aged from 18 months to six years.

Skilled clinical judgement is as essential as experience with test material in the assessment of these children. Frequently, it is history given by the parents, or the way the child sets about a task which gives a vital clue. In the Sequin Form Board test, for example, the three-year-old may select the correct hole for each shape but have difficulty in manoeuvering the piece into its hole. In the Little Pink Tower test, he may select the bricks in the correct order for size but be unable to make them balance in the tower formation. Buttons are pushed through their buttonholes with extreme effort and in a much longer time than the average for his chronological age. One interesting aside here is that mothers of clumsy three- and four-year-old children dress them in clothing devoid of buttons. This, apparently, is to speed up and facilitate the dressing process and as a consequence these children do not practice.

Informal observation of how children do things and finding out why they do them in a particular way is often more illuminating than standard test results. This aspect of assessment is as relevant to teachers and doctors as to psychologists. Informal observation will also reveal difficulties in concentration which may be manifested as memory problems or as difficulty in focusing attention on one thing long enough for satisfactory achievement of a particular task.

One other standard test, which can be of value in the assessment of clumsy children is the Illinois Test of Psycholinguistic Abilities. (Kirk, McCarthy and Kirk, 1968). This was developed as a diagnostic test of communication abilities. It aims to delineate specific abilities and disabilities in children in order that remediation may be undertaken when needed. Difficulties in communication, particularly of rhythm and sequencing, are commonly associated with poor coordination. A helpful discussion of the value of this test is contained in Pumfrey's text (Pumfrey, 1976).

Some children are thought to maintain their incompetence if only to retain the personal attention it brings (Stott, 1978). Certainly some children find it difficult to give up the role of being the fool or the 'dunce' when their motor coordination has improved. This may be because the child's body image has changed but not his self-image of his social worth.

Psychological assessment is helpful in three ways to the management of a clumsy child. Firstly it provides one important means of diagnosing the problem, often when unsuspected, so long as the psychologist pays attention to physical coordination as well as cognitive function. Secondly, it points out specific areas in which the child is functioning below expectation for his age, general ability level or both. Thirdly, diagnosis of ability can be of immense therapeutic value. This last factor cannot be over-emphasised. In the case of John, described earlier, his extremely violent behaviour at home ceased immediately and he began to make excellent progress in reading without any other intervention than knowledge of his own ability. He regained self-esteem and confidence in himself literally overnight. The psychologist must remember that he can alleviate distress by feeding back information regarding both ability and disability in a positive constructive way to both parent and child.

Finally, the psychologist has a responsibility to do something positive with the test results and information he has obtained during assessment. Simply communicating results to teachers, physiotherapists, speech therapists and so on, is not sufficient. In the main, psychologists spend relatively short periods of time with the children they assess, and are also somewhat limited in being able to offer teaching method advice. Many clinical psychologists have had no teaching experience at all, and most educational psychologists have had limited experience compared with the time some remedial teachers have taken to learn their craft. It is not surprising, then, that psychologists have difficulty in suggesting methods of teaching which have not occured to the teachers themselves. There is therefore an obvious need for psychologists to work in close cooperation with remedial teachers and therapists.

REFERENCES

Arnheim D D, Sinclair W A 1979 The clumsy child, 2nd edn. Mosby, St Louis

Bayley N 1968 Bayley scales of infant development. The Psychological Corporation, California

Bender L 1938 Visual motor Gestalt Test and its clinical use. American Orthopsychiatric Association, New York

Francis-Williams J 1974 Children with specific learning difficulties. Pergamon Press, 2nd edn. Oxford and New York

Frith U 1978 Spelling difficulties. Journal of child Psychology and Psychiatry 19: 279–285

Frostig M, Lefewen W, Whittlesey J R B 1963 Developmental test of visual perception. Consulting Psychologists Press, California

Frostig M Horne D 1973 Program for the development of visual perception. (Revised Edition), Follett Chicago

Gesell A, Amatruda 1947 The Gesell Development Schedule

Griffiths R 1970 The abilities of young children. Child Development Research Centre, London

Gubbay S 1975 The clumsy child. Saunders, Philadelphia

Kirk S A, McCarthy J J, Kirk W D 1968 Illinois test of psycholinguistic abilities. University of Illinois Press

Lansdown R 1976 Children with spelling difficulties. Child Care, Health and Development 2: 353–364

McKinlay I 1978 Strategies for clumsy children. Developmental Medicine and Child Neurology 20: 494–496

Mittler P 1970 The psychological assessment of mental and physical handicap. Methuen, London

Neale M 1958 Neale analysis of reading ability. MacMillan, London

Pumfrey P D 1976 Reading: Tests and assessment techniques. Hodder & Stoughton

Rutter M, Yule W 1975 The concept of specific reading retardation. Journal of Child Psychology and Psychiatry 16: 181–197

Schonell F J Reading & disgnostic tests. Oliver & Boyd, Edinburgh

Schonell F J, F E 1957 Diagnosis and remedial teaching in arithmetic. Oliver and Boyd, Edinburgh and London

Stott D H, Moye F A, Henderson S E 1972 Test of motor impairment. Guelph, Brook Education, Windsor, N.F.E.R.

Wechsler D 1949 The Wechsler intelligence scale for children. The Psychological Corporation, New York

Wechsler D 1963 The Wechsler preschool & primary scale of intelligence. The Psychological Corporation, New York

Weddell K 1967 Some implications of perceptual-motor impairment in children. J. Remedial Education 2: 5–9

Growing points in understanding and assessing perceptuo-motor problems

As so frequently happens, perhaps the main growing point in the study of clumsy children has been in the increased awareness of how little we know. This is by no means a negative outcome, since the effectiveness of providing help depends on how accurately we understand the problem. Growing points in understanding and assessing perceptuo-motor problems in relation to clumsy children may be grouped under three main headings:

1. The definition of clumsiness.
2. The relationship between defect and handicap.
3. The implications of points (1) and (2) for remediation.

Definition of clumsiness

The issues about defining clumsiness have largely been covered in the preceding chapters, which have indicated that clumsiness may occur as a quite specific defect in children. Further work on this subject has been mainly concerned with examining the educational implications of this finding — where 'educational' is understood in both the developmental and the more specifically academic senses. Two main strands of study have been followed up: research into the organic bases of clumsiness; and research into the nature of clumsy children's impaired performance.

Studies of the organic bases of children's motor deficiencies are crucial to the long-term aim of developing preventive and curative methods. It will however be apparent from the preceding chapters, that the available research has, in general, not reached the point of indicating specific measures for achieving these aims. Some research with implications for treatment is, however, beginning to appear (Harrison, 1975). Research has, on the other hand, provided indications that motor deficiencies do often have specific organic concomitants, and this has contributed to the recognition of clumsiness in children as a form of dysfunction which may occur independently of general developmental retardation, or of emotional and other problems. Recognition of a specific learning problem in children has the implication that teachers will need help in teaching them, and this leads to the second of the two strands of research mentioned above.

Some of the main advances in Special Education in recent years have been concerned with making teaching approaches more specific, in order to make them more effective (Haring and Bateman, 1977). While Special Education has long been seen as a relatively non-specific resource for helping children to cope with their learning problems, in recent years considerable progress has been made in devising teaching approaches which can act as specific resources appropriate to specific problems. One aspect of this work has been concerned with the task-analysis of those performances in which children fail, so that the skills and other prerequisites for achievement can be identified, and so be built into the teaching sequence. Such an analysis is based on psychological and other models of performance (Wedell, 1978a). Clumsy children, for example, will frequently complain as Cruickshank (1973) reports, that 'they cannot make their hands do what their eyes see'. In other words, their difficulty lies in organising movement to achieve an intended action, rather than in any difficulty in understanding what they want to do. Furthermore, their frustration in not carrying out the action they intended clearly demonstrates their capacity for accurate perception. This analysis distinguishes them from children with other types of learning problems, and indicates the lines of educational resource they need. Wedell (1973) offered a simplified model of perceptuo-motor function, which illustrates some of these distinctions (Fig. 5.1). Sensory experience depends on the efficiency of the sense receptors (receptor-efficiency), and also on the selectivity of sensory organisation (e.g. we hear only a limited range of sound frequencies, and at any point in time, 'decide' to attend only to a limited range of

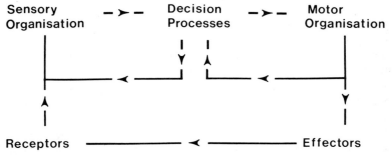

Fig. 5.1 Simplified model of perceptuo-motor function.

sound input). Voluntary action depends on a decision to act, and the organisation (motor organisation) of movements (effector efficiency) to accord with a specific intention. The outcome of this activity is then, in turn, monitored with respect to the intended action through sensory input, and so a feed-back loop is set up, by means of which the action continues to its completion. (For example, if we miss the cup in pouring out tea, we have a 'closer' look to increase the accuracy of pouring.) The model emphasises the fact that motor organisation can never be separated 'in real life' from sensory organisation, but it also enables us to define the clumsy child as one who has difficulty in motor organisation rather than in the other functions in the model. This account corresponds to the clinical neurological description given by Gubbay (1975).

Wedell and Horne (1969) attempted to isolate some of the functions included in the above model in a study of $5\frac{1}{2}$-year-old children who had difficulty in copying the figures of the Bender Gestalt test (a pencil and paper pattern copying task). This test was given to children in the first year of infant school. A group of twenty children who obtained the lowest scores and a group of twenty who obtained the highest scores were given a further set of tasks, which were intended to involve specific component skills of pattern copying. The children were asked to match and to trace a further set of six 'letter-like' patterns, and to copy the patterns both with strips of plasticine and with pencil and paper. The matching task involved identifying each pattern from among various transformations and was intended to indicate perceptual or 'sensory organisation' skills. The tracing task required the children to trace a line within double lines making up the patterns, and so to indicate any problems in 'effector efficiency'. The two copying tasks were intended to indicate aspects of motor organisation. Copying the patterns with plasticine strips allowed the children to correct their copies until they 'looked right', something which was clearly only partly possible in copying the pattern with a pencil. Wedell and Horne devised instrumentation for scoring the tracing and the two copying tasks on the same (and relatively strict) criteria, and the findings are presented in the graphs in Fig. 5.2. The low Bender scoring children (L group) are shown to include some who had difficulty in matching the experimental patterns, as well as some who did not. The higher Bender scoring children (H group) all matched at least five patterns correctly. Neither the H nor the L group children had difficulty in tracing the patterns, but the distribution of their scores on the plasticine copying task shows that most L group children were poorer than the H group children. While the L group were poorer than the H group on the pencil copying task, the rather strict scoring criteria reduced the difference between the two groups

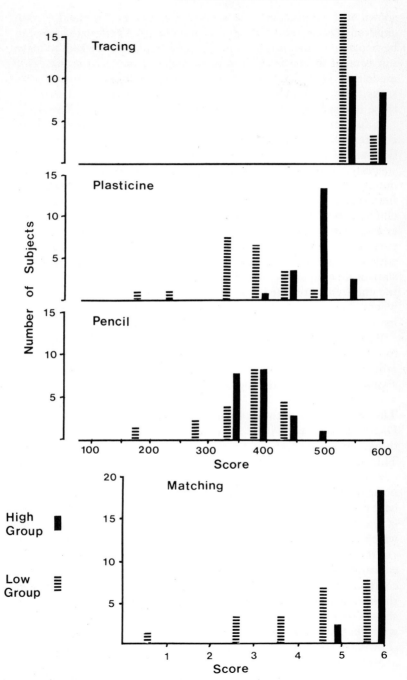

Fig. 5.2 Distribution of the scores of children in the high and low groups.

shown in their Bender Test scores. The graphs for the L group children illustrate how the various components of pattern copying can be separated out. While none of these children seemed to have impairment in motor efficiency, some could not get the plasticine models to look 'right', while others could not discriminate them sufficiently accurately in the first place. The educational needs of these two subgroups of the L group were clearly very different.

A further aspect of the motor organisation problems of clumsy children was investigated by Fenelon (1975). A previous study by Giles and Wedell (1974), which will be described later in this chapter, suggested that clumsy children depended much more on visual monitoring of their movements. In a small pilot study to follow up this finding, Fenelon asked teachers in a special school to rank groups of children aged eight and ten for their motor competence in everyday tasks and self-help and social skills. She then asked the children to perform a standard manipulatory and a locomotor task with and without restricted visual monitoring. Although not reaching statistical significance, her findings indicated that the more clumsy the children were rated, the greater the drop in their performance when their visual monitoring was restricted — in both the manipulating and locomotor tasks.

Both these studies show that clumsy children's problems are related to quite specific aspects of perceptuo-motor functions. Studies by others (e.g. Bortner and Birch, 1962; Birch and Lefford, 1967) have similarly differentiated subgroups of such children.

The relationship between defect and handicap

Demonstrating that a child has a defect in motor organisation is one thing, but establishing whether it is likely to handicap him is another. This may seem a simplistic statement, but it raises important educational issues. For example, at present many procedures are being devised for the early identification of children who are likely to have learning problems in school (Wedell and Raybould, 1976). Some of these procedures require children to perform on various tests, which are then scored on fixed criteria, usually of a normative kind. On the basis of these scores children are then categorised as being educationally 'at risk', or not. Pattern copying is a common component of these tests (e.g. Tansley, 1976). Follow-up studies of the later achievement of children identified by these procedures often show a surprising proportion of false positives (i.e. 'at risk' children who do not manifest learning problems when followed up later) (Lewis, 1978).

Most early identification batteries are validated against aspects of children's later educational achievement which are in fact unrelated to motor organisation (e.g. reading) although, as has been mentioned, the batteries may include measures of motor organisation. Attempts are now being made to predict later motor organisation difficulties in children, but an approach which seems likely to be more relevant is the construction of developmental rating scales (Evans and Sparrow, 1975). Many of these scales have been developed mainly for those working with mentally subnormal or severely physically handicapped children. The aim of the scales is to identify performances which children can be expected to master at successive stages of development. These performances are selected for their usefulness and relevance for a child at each stage, so that they can be used as goals for training those children who have not achieved them. Although the items of the scales clearly are related to the achievement expected of normal children at successive ages (and to that extent are norm-referenced) their major importance lies in their attempt to answer the question 'what does this child need to be taught next *now*?' If a child is not making progress towards achieving the next item on the scale, he is seen to need help in doing so. Developmental rating scales are designed to be used by those responsible for the daily care of children — including parents. Most include subscales of performance involving motor organisation, and some (e.g. Portage Guide to Early Education) have highly structured recommendations for helping children achieve the 'next stage up'.

One of the main reasons why the prediction of later learning problems from children's earlier performance is so uncertain, is that we do not know how much children's compensatory resources are likely to help them. Wedell (1978) has put forward the notion of 'compensatory interaction', both between the resources and deficiences within the child, and between the outcome of this and the outcome of the interaction of the resources and deficiences of the child's environment. The complexity of this interaction makes it likely that only the most severe defects will have a *determining* effect on the course of a child's development. Consequently, it would seem that the most appropriate aim for early identification procedures should be to improve the recognition of those children who are failing to meet developmental expectations. These children are, by definition, those whose defects are in fact having handicapping consequences.

Implications for remediation

Education, in its various forms, and from its various sources, clearly provides one of the main compensatory resources for children. Many programmes have been devised for children with perceptuo-motor problems, and many of these have been specifically aimed at the development of motor organisation (e.g. Kephart, 1960; Frostig and Maslow, 1970). The development of motor organisation has been seen in these programmes as an important prerequisite for children's progress in educational attainments. In other words, the programmes reflect the view that training in aspects of motor organisation will transfer to performance in reading and other educational attainments.

Over recent years a considerable amount of research has been directed at evaluating the effectiveness of perceptuo-motor training programmes, and these studies have been reviewed by Cratty (1970, 1975), Cruickshank and Hallahan (1973), Wedell (1973), Hammill and Myers (1976) and others. The general conclusion to be drawn from these reviews is that these programmes often do not improve children's educational achievement more than systematic teaching in the subjects themselves. In other words, training, in motor organisation for example, does not transfer to educational attainments in as direct a way as the producers of the programmes had hoped. This has led many to reject these programmes as of limited use.

Wedell (1973) has pointed out that it would be more appropriate to evaluate the effectiveness of motor organisation programmes with reference to motor achievement, such as performance in relevant social competence and self-help skills. This was done in a study by Giles and Wedell (1974). The aim of this study was to provide specific forms of training in motor organisation to a group of boys in a residential school for children with learning problems, who had been rated as particularly clumsy both by their teachers and by the child care staff responsible for them. The items of the scale on which the children were rated for clumsiness were discussed with the school staff, and included aspects of the children's performance on everyday tasks such as managing cutlery and crockery at table, dressing, and not bumping into furniture and other people.

The study was designed to compare the effect on this type of performance of a standard physical education programme and of a programme based on elements of Kephart's (1971) approach, which stresses the importance of developing left-right discrimination and 'body image'. The 22 boys (C.A.7–0 to 10–11, mean 9–3) were divided into two groups, matched by pairs for their clumsiness ratings. In the first four weeks, one group was given the standard motor training, and the other the special training, and in the second four weeks the allocation of training was reversed. Special motor performance measures were devised, as analogues of the kinds of performance in which the children had been rated as having difficulty. One task, for example, replicated carrying a tray between tables. The child was required to carry a tray-like frame, while walking between two long benches on which skittles had been placed to protrude into his pathway. The children's performances were assessed for speed and accuracy. Some of the tasks were also designed to allow greater or lesser visual monitoring of movement. For example, in the above 'tray' task, the children were also required to walk between the obstacles without the tray, which had had the effect of blocking their vision of the 'path' immediately in front of them.

Four tasks were devised to be measured in these various ways, and the boys' performances were assessed before and after the training programmes, and at the change of programmes. The performance of both groups of boys improved in both speed and accuracy on all tasks over the eight-week period, but there was no significant difference in the improvement attributable to either training method. Efforts had been made to equate the two training methods for interest and motivation, but the experimental design did not, of course, control for the 'Hawthorn' effect of administering the programmes as such. However, the boys' progress during training has to be seen against their previous lack of progress.

This study, although of course limited in scope, indicates that motor training can be shown to improve the performance of clumsy children in self-help skills and social competence. Neither training method specifically included the activities of the assessment tasks, and the results therefore suggest that general motor training can transfer to these specific aspects of performance. The results do not provide support for the prime importance of 'body image' development implied in the Kephart approach, but neither can they be regarded as sufficient to question it.

There is a further issue which needs to be considered in relation to motor training for clumsy children. Even if general motor training transfers to specific aspects of performance, specific training in those individual tasks with which clumsy children have difficulty might be more effective still. This issue needs to be investigated, but it is related to a practical problem involving the difference between performance on educational tasks and performance in self-help skills and social competence. The relevance of perceptuo-motor skills to educational tasks is mainly limited to the recognition, production and grouping of letter and number shapes. Consequently, specific training in these aspects is feasible. The tasks included in social competence and self-help skills on the other hand are myriad, and separate training in each would be quite impracticable. The later chapters on physiotherapy and occupational therapy will, however, indicate that the choice between specific and general motor training need not be an exclusive one. Indeed, this is a topic area where there is much scope for cooperation between these two professions and those involved in special education.

A point which needs to be stressed about specific training in everyday competence skills, is that individuals are required to be able to perform them at speed, and also often simultaneously with other actions. Training in dressing, for example, cannot be regarded as complete when the child can put his clothes on accurately by himself, regardless of the time taken. This point was forcefully brought home to me when I was filming dressing difficulties in some cerebral palsied children. One child, who had had considerable specific training succeeded in putting her cardigan on quite accurately while sitting on the floor. However, after the filming, she was put into her wheel chair, and given her anorak to put on in a hurry to return to her classroom. In this situation, she totally failed to find her way into the anorak. She was then put back on the floor, and asked to put the anorak on without hurrying, and succeeded with no apparent difficulty. The cramped space and the stress of haste appeared to have disrupted her capacity to organise her movements. Connolly (1970) provides a useful account of the way in which the organisation of complex actions may occur. He suggests that complex actions can be achieved when some of the component movement sequences come to be performed in an 'automatic' way. He refers to these sequences as 'subroutines', which are themselves then incorporated as units in more complex actions. A feature of these subroutines is that the movements within them do not have to be deliberately 'guided'. This type of explanation is also relevant to the findings about clumsy children's dependence on visual monitoring of movement in the study by Fenelon mentioned above.

The full importance of helping clumsy children in their performance on tasks which are not specifically academic has been stressed only relatively recently. Studies by Walton et al. (1962), Dare and Gordon (1970), Gubbay (1975) and Brenner and Gillman (1966) demonstrated the range of problems these children had in everyday tasks, and they also indicated the stresses which failure produced. Parents tend to be aggravated by clumsy children's mistakes, breakages and slowness, and these difficulties also affect teachers' perception of the children. Furthermore, clumsiness also affects children's performance in games and sport, and this has consequences for their standing among their fellows. This latter point was demonstrated in a study by Symes (1972). He identified a group of clumsy children in a grammar school (11 to 16 years of above average ability). Using sociometric measures, he assessed how far they were accepted by their classmates and found that the clumsy children were much less frequently chosen for games teams, or as companions for camping outings.

There has been little research specifically on the effect of clumsiness on the basic educational attainments — in contrast to the vast literature on the effect of perceptual problems. Handwriting is probably the task which is most likely to be affected by motor organisation problems. The children in the study by Wedell and Horne mentioned above, were followed up towards the end of their period in infant school, and their handwriting was assessed. The assessment of handwriting is notoriously difficult and unreliable, and so teachers' rankings of 'general quality' of handwriting were used. The lowest ranking children had all performed poorly on the plasticine pattern copying task, suggesting that poor handwriting was related to poor motor organisation. However, in line with the comments made about compensatory interaction earlier, it is worth noting that one of the children rated most highly for handwriting had scored relatively poorly on the plasticine copying task.

The effect of specific motor training on handwriting acquisition has also not been extensively investigated. A currently ongoing study by Thomas is concerned with this topic. Using video and other assessment techniques, she is attempting to analyse the handwriting of clumsy children, and to devise specific training approaches to help them in letter formation strategies and accuracy. Thomas's study is concerned with teaching handwriting to these children as a quite specific movement skill, and it is interesting to note that, while some of the children are making very accelerated progress, the improvement of others is slight. These different responses to training will hopefully help to differentiate the problems of the various children.

Clumsiness is also likely to affect children's performance in later stages of their schooling, in subjects such as handcraft, physics and chemistry practicals, and technical drawing. However, no investigations of this appear to have been made. It may be that most children with more severe motor organisation problems 'select themselves out' of these subjects.

Conclusion

At the start of this chapter, I mentioned that recent advances in the study of perceptuo-motor problems in children had shown the limitations of our knowledge, but that this was a positive contribution, because it helped us better to appreciate the diversity and complexity of the problems. Advances in definition have helped us to see clumsiness in children as a problem which needs to be recognised in its own right, as distinct from other specific learning disabilities. It is clear that children may have other learning problems in addition to their clumsiness. However, if one is concerned with planning appropriate intervention, this requires initially a careful analysis of what the child can and cannot do.

Research has made us recognise the complexity of the interaction between the resources and deficiencies within the child and his environment, and to realise how simplistic our attempts at the prediction of development have been. This has also had a positive consequence, because it has pointed to the need both for more sensitive recognition of early manifestations of inadequate developmental progress, and for making help more immediately and widely available to children, through those who are in daily contact with them. The negative outcomes of the evaluation of remedial approaches has helped to clarify educators' assumptions about the transfer of training. In this area also, the importance of carefully assessing the deficiencies in a child's present performance has become apparent, as well as the need to plan training to be specifically relevant to them. It is clear that this involves individualised teaching approaches, which, in turn, presents practical problems. Two points are relevant here. Firstly, initial advances in involving parents in helping their children show that they represent a neglected 'personnel resource'. Secondly, it is evident from the medical field, that one cannot expect to carry out effective treatment without the necessary resources.

REFERENCES

Birch H G, Lefford A 1967 Visual differentiation, intersensory integration and voluntary motor control. Society for Research in Child Development Monograph (No 2) 167
Bortner M, Birch H G 1962 Perceptual and perceptual-motor dissociation in cerebral palsied children. Journal of Nervous and Mental Diseases 134: 103–8
Brenner M W, Gillman S 1966 Visumotor ability in school children — a survey. Developmental Medicine and Child Neurology 8: 686–703
Connolly K 1970 Skill development: problems and plans,. In Connolly K (ed.) Mechanisms of Motor Skill Development. Academic Press, New York
Cratty B J 1970 Perceptual and motor development in infants and children. Collier-Macmillan, New York
Cratty B J 1975 Remedial motor activity for children. Lea & Fabinger, Philadelphia
Cruickshank W M, Hallan D P 1973 Psycho-educational foundations of learning disabilities. Prentice Hall
Dare M T, Gordon N 1970 Clumsy children, a disorder of perception and motor organisation. Developmental Medicine and Child Neurology 12: 178–185
Evans R, Sparrow M 1975 Trends in the assessment of early childhood development. Child Care, Health and Development 1: 127–141
Fenelon M K C 1975 Changes with age and degree of clumsiness in the performance of

skilled motor tasks when visual monitoring of the performing trials is restricted. MEd (Educational Psychology) Dissertation, University of Birmingham

Frostig M, Maslow P 1970 Movement education: theory and practice. Follett Educational Corporation, Chicago

Giles A M, Wedell K 1974 A comparative evaluation of training methods for children with difficulties in motor coordination (clumsy children). Paper presented at the International Federation of Learning Disabilities Conference, Amsterdam

Gubbay S S 1975 The clumsy child: a study of developmental apraxic and agnosic ataxia. Saunders, Philadelphia

Hammill D D, Myers P I 1976 Methods for learning disorders. Wiley, New York

Haring N G, Bateman B 1977 Teaching the learning disabled child. Prentice Hall

Harrison A 1975 Training spastic individuals to achieve better neuromuscular control using electromyographic feedback. In Holt K S (ed) Movement and Child Development. Heinemann, London

Kephart N C, 1971 The slow learner in the classroom, 2nd edn. Merrill, Columbus, Ohio

Lewis A 1978 The early identification and treatment of children with learning difficulties within the infants school. B Phil Ed Dissertation, University of Birmingham

Symes K 1972 Clumsiness and the sociometric status of intellectually gifted boys. Bulletin of Physical Education 9: 35–41

Tansley A E 1976 Special educational treatment in infant schools, 6½-year-old screening. In: Wedell K and Raybould E C 1976 The early identification of educational 'at risk' children. Educational Review Occasional Publications No. 6, University of Birmingham

Walton J N, Ellis E, Court S D M 1962 Clumsy children: developmental apraxia and agnosia. Brain 85: 603–612

Wedell M 1973 Learning and perceptuo-motor disabilities in children. Wiley, New York

Wedell K 1978a Investigation strategies for helping children with learning problems. Paper presented at 75th Conference of Dutch Special Education Association, Amsterdam

Wedell K 1978b Early identification and compensatory interaction. Paper delivered at NATO International Conference on Learning Disorders, Ottawa

Wedell K, Horne I E 1969 Some aspects of perceptuo-motor disability in ½-year-old children. British Journal of Educational Psychology 39: 174–2

Wedell K, Raybould E C 1976 The Early identification of educationally 'at risk' children. Educational Review Occasional Publications No. 6, University of Birmingham

Rationale for remediation

This book gives an account of many of the imaginative tactics used to help clumsy children. It would be unfair to such children not to try to help them, and the widening range of ideas for remediation is refreshing and stimulating. Yet the work is time-consuming and makes heavy demands on limited resources. The children may have to be taken out of class or may have to sacrifice leisure time to remedial activities. Insofar as many seem to catch up later on, is the intervention justified when so much of the remediation has yet to be proved effective? It is common to hear sceptical comment about the lasting value of remedial teaching or physiotherapy with the implication that the practitioners may keep their clients happy rather than achieve measurable response to specific techniques. This placebo effect might yet be worth tapping but could be practised by less highly trained personnel.

The measured performance of athletes strongly supports the belief that training and rehearsal produce better results. It may be that one coach can motivate an athlete better than another coach. But without individual attention, and the training itself, results would be poor. Just how much distance running, how much weight lifting, how much circuit-training etc. are appropriate for success depends on the sport. But athletes believe in training programmes. It would seem reasonable to expect a selective training programme to be helpful to clumsy children on the same basis if they have practical difficulties they wish to overcome.

Remediation can be effective in several ways. Firstly, the child who has experienced failure can lose confidence and become unwilling to risk further failure. Thus tasks potentially within the child's capability may be avoided. By starting afresh with a new teacher with different methods, or with a new structured physical style of management such as that offered by therapists, the child may be motivated to try again. This process, involving individual attention, may account for the relatively rapid improvement made by some children after beginning remedial education or a course of therapy, devised according to the particular needs of each child.

Secondly, the learning experiences of children vary considerably. Simple lack of experience may depress performance and cause a child to appear clumsy. High rise flats, lack of safe play space, watching television instead of exploratory play, large families, and parents who shun physical contact are examples of the factors which could delay the development of a normal child. The general experience of infant school will compensate for many such children but for others a course of individual attention may lead to catch-up.

Thirdly, a clumsy child, reacting to frustration and disappointment may show conduct which threatens the relationship with family and teachers. The fresh approach created by a new assessment and involvement of a new sympathetic team may create another climate. A child can share remedial activities with parents alerted to his problems, and the shared experience of improvement can come as a relief and a pleasure. It is true that this does not always work out easily. As with teaching a relative to drive a car some parents may have difficulty avoiding tension in treatment sessions at home. Part of the responsibility of therapists and teachers is to judge how much responsibility to put on parents. It is possible to select leisure activities such as swimming rather than formal exercises when appropriate.

So far as specific treatment is concerned it is reasonable to suggest that body image training could lead to better use of body parts. It is also possible that some of the benefit from remediation derives from training of cross-modal pathways. It is also likely that activities which strengthen the shoulders will stabilise the arm for finer activities such as writing. People learning to play musical instruments sometimes notice an improved general facility in hand function after practice (e.g. of the left hand in guitar players). It thus seems reasonable that fine activities can be practised, within reasonable limits, with some benefit. The activities chosen should of course be interesting to the child. Repeatedly practising tying shoe laces would not be appropriate for many such children, being excessively frustrating and laborious. Yet the same child might find pegboard games or magnetic board games amusing and be willing to persist in mastering them.

In general, remedial education in schools concentrates on teaching reading, sometimes to the neglect of spelling and writing. Some clumsy children catch up on reading fairly quickly after a slow start but continue to perform poorly at maths, spelling and writing for which little help may be available. Readiness to learn may be improved by introducing a physical component to the child's remediation under the guidance of a therapist, trained teacher or physical education expert. Whether this can be done on the basis of a weekly session or whether it requires maintenance by daily activities at home or at school remains to be proved but research on these lines is beginning.

A child who has struggled to keep up with his classmates and siblings may easily feel that everyone else is out of step. Individual attention may be encouraging as well as an opportunity to devise prescriptive remediation, so difficult when dealing with large groups. It also provides a means of reviewing whether or not a change of method is required in the light of response. To say that a child is receiving remedial teaching or therapy is not enough. What teaching? What therapy? What effects? Yet, above all, a sympathetic teacher or therapist who communicates confidence and optimism to a child may be creating a good climate for learning.

Many skilled remedial teachers have commented on how important it is to offer an undistracting structured basis for learning for such children using the sensory modalities through which the child can learn best. This might involve kinaesthetic training and touch (e.g. sandpaper or plastic templates for letters), detailed verbal description of the task, visual memory or colour clues in a child with weak auditory skills. Not only may the child learn better by these means but the variety involved in multisensory teaching is more likely to be an interesting process. Rhythm and rhyming ability, commonly weak in such children, is likely to be susceptible to teaching, to be enjoyable and be of general benefit to the child.

In older children, formal exercises are less likely to be acceptable than general activities, e.g. dancing, swimming, karate, riding, yoga, cycling, cooking, music, hill walking, etc. To a certain extent, the approach to the older child includes more acceptance of and adaptation to difficulty than in the younger child whose potential is less certain. Nonetheless, our department's experience includes some children, thought to be educationally subnormal, whose potential only declared itself in teenage years. There may then be a case for continuing education beyond the anticipated school leaving age for selected children.

Adaptation to difficulty requires skilled advice. Typewriters, calculators, tape recorders and modified clothing all have their place but careful selection and appropriate teaching are required if the child is to use something different from his classmates. The clinic doctor's bright idea is often not acceptable to the child or a suitable teacher may not be available. This is not to say that resourceful use of technology should be rejected. For example, a boy of 11 with superior general intelligence, whose thirst for information could in no way be met by his laborious, inaccurate reading, found selective use of talking books, radio, T.V. and a tape recorder satisfying and stimulating. Some children with illegible writing have done well with typing or tape cassettes. But many cannot or will not use them and others should not. Gadgetry offers no panacea.

Because therapists and remedial teachers are keen to help children by any possible means there is a tendency to offer a wide range of ideas and to drop those which are unacceptable or which do not seem to 'work'. If only in making life more interesting and stimulating for children with uneven development the remediation process can be justified. Perhaps there is a need to clarify further the aims and means of remediation before evaluating them critically. But the development of an extending repertoire of remedial ideas has provided a good basis for research.

SUGGESTIONS FOR FURTHER READING
Kinsbourne M, Caplan P J 1979 Children's learning and attention problems. Little, Brown & Co., Boston

Physiotherapy

With more emphasis on the identification of clumsy children it is inevitable that demands on therapists to devise means of helping clumsy children should increase. It is not an easy task, requiring concentration during assessment and resourcefulness during treatment. A well-organised programme can lead to warm rapport and measurable improvement with satisfaction for all involved. There can also be periods of frustration, little progress and poor cooperation requiring a change of style, new activities or a rest. Clumsy children present to their therapists great (and diverse) challenges but also great rewards.

Physiotherapists take referrals from all sorts of agencies through a registered medical practitioner, and with diagnoses which may or may not describe the nature of the motor disorder. A child with frequent falls may be thought to need flat foot exercises or a session with the orthotist. Another may be in an assessment class or playgroup because of indistinct speech. Some are in special schools because of learning difficulties or fits. Though a major problem for any of these children may be in the organisation of movement, this may not have been fully appreciated. Conversely the child may have unrecognised potential abilities. Competent physical assessment depends on knowledge of the range of normality at any age, as well as experience of abnormality. This may be easier to acquire in community services than in hospital practice. However, the therapist must be able to offer an informed independent opinion if the interests of the child are to be served. The therapist may also be willing to consider acquiring a repertoire which extends beyond her usual range as there may be no occupational therapist available to advise on the development of manipulative skills or self-care skills (e.g. dressing).

The session with the child should be quiet, unhurried, punctual, based on available information and systematic. The general purpose should be explained to the child and at each stage it is important to know that the child understands the instructions given. A child with language comprehension difficulty may need the help of diagrams or the therapist as a model, either supplementary to, or sometimes in place of spoken instructions. Spoken instructions should be unambiguous.

It is our practice to examine the child in a sequence of positions and activities with parents present. Parents may not have observed their child undressed for some time and may recognise, possibly for the first time, that the child does have physical difficulties as the assessment unfolds. However, any discussion must include the child in a sensitive way if he is within earshot.

When and where does the therapist see the child?
It is advisable to see the child regularly, at least twice weekly at first, then gradually to tail off to twice- and then once-monthly visits until a six- or twelve-month evaluation, check up or counselling session is all that is required of the therapist. It has been found most useful to have, and to review with the family at these sessions, audiovisual as well as written recordings of the child performing certain activities.

The frequency and number of treatment sessions is dependent upon the amount and efficiency of parental and teacher cooperation and upon the child's own ability to cooperate with them. Age, home and school conditions and demands, must all be taken into consideration when designing specific programmes or planning department attendance.

The therapist will initially assess and work with the child in a distraction-free room before his graduation to a group situation. A group may be held in a therapy department or school gymnasium. It is important to note that the therapy room, be it in a hospital, clinic or health centre is an abnormal setting to the child and that, as soon as possible, the suggested activity routines and management strategies should be incorporated into the normal school and home life of the child.

Introduction to group work should be gradual, initial work being carried out in pairs on a self competitive basis, with group size and competitive elements gradually brought in as confidence and ability become established.

Points to observe during assessment and therapy sessions

1. The length of time taken to change into the gymnastic kit or to dress.
2. Whether a parent automatically goes to help the child dress or undress.

3. If the child shows balance or spatial disorientation whilst dressing, e.g. whilst eyes are covered up.
4. Note if he wanders around the room aimlessly or seems to be day-dreaming and delaying the dressing process.
5. Watch if the clothes are put on wrongly or fastened oddly or left undone.
6. Throughout all activities note any associated movements, primitive or abnormal movement patterns, lack of equilibrium or saving reactions, limitation or hypermobility in joint range, increase or decrease or intermittent changes in muscle tone, lack of body symmetry or an unawareness of position or parts of the body.
7. Having presented all work materials to the midline of the child, take note if he consistently moves the work over to one side or the other and if he always bends his head down to one side or uses one eye for preference, taking that eye down to the work surface and whether there are frequent shifts in hand use.
8. During performance of any gross, fine, self-help or communication activities note should be made if there seem to be initiation, organisation, production or sequencing disorders.

Assessment procedures

Check of gross motor skills
Basic motor skills, postural organisation and control, body and spatial awareness, movement sense, joint range, muscle tone and strength can be detected by asking the child to assume and hold various positions for a few seconds.

Supine lying
Ask the child to lie with hips and knees fully flexed (*a*), arms around the knees; have him extend first one leg and then the other (*b*), always keeping the other leg fully flexed on to the trunk; extend both legs (*c*), raise head and both arms forward to an arm reach position (*d*); ask the child to roll over onto his face from supine to prone lying.

Prone lying
With both arms extended by his head, have the child raise his head to look upwards (*e*), then take both arms down to the sides of his body placing both palms flat on the floor (*f*); flex and then extend first the right and then the left knee whilst keeping the hips down as flat as possible (*g*); note if there is hip flexor tightness; tell the child to first raise his upper trunk by supporting himself in forearm lean position (*h*) and then on fully extended arms (*i*) keeping his face vertical, trunk

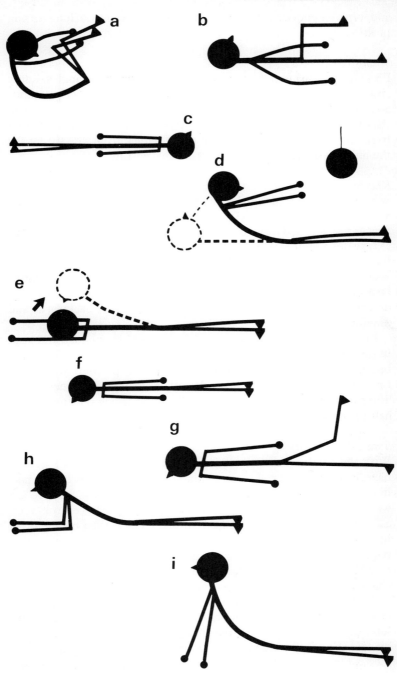

and hips extended; ask him then to roll over into a long sitting position.

Sitting

From long sitting with hips abducted and flexed at right angles, knees straight, lean forward to hold ankles (*j*), keeping the knees straight; assume a side sitting position with weight first on one hip and then on the other (*k*, *l*) with upper trunk straight, arms relaxed and moving from one side to the other without use of hands; from side sitting ask the child to assume a four-point kneeling posture.

Kneeling

Whilst kneeling on all fours (*m*) with hips, knees, shoulders and wrists at right angles, back and elbows straight, ask the child first to lean forward to take body weight on his hands and then to rock backwards to take the weight with buttocks resting on his calves; having resumed the four-point square kneeling position have the child raise and extend in turn each of the four limbs separately and the opposite limbs (arm and leg) together followed by the same side arm and leg together; observe the child on four-point crawling, forwards, backwards and moving sideways.

From an upright kneeling position (*n*) with hips extended and head in midline, arms by his sides, ask the child to knee walk forwards, backwards and sideways; from a half kneeling position (*o*), weight first on one knee and then on the other, maintain balance whilst lifting and placing to hold the forward foot in varying positions; from half kneeling, ask the child to stand up straight.

Standing and walking

With the child standing erect on a small base of both feet together, have him swing his arms forwards and backwards (*p*); get him to take his weight first on one and then the other forwardly placed leg (*q*), with forward knee extended, pelvis and trunk aligned over front foot; ask the child to bear weight first on one leg and then on the other holding it in mid-stance (*r*) with rear leg raised without hip flexion; request him to hold a heel strike (*s*) position with rear leg extended and externally rotated, heel of the forward foot down and toes raised, then change to the other heel placed in front.

Walk the child along a nine inch wide strip (two lines of masking tape), then have him heel-toe walk along a single line, walk along the same lines, first on the inner borders and then on the outer borders of his feet (Fig. 7.1), followed by walking on his heels and then on tip toes . On the spot jumping, jumping forwards, backwards and

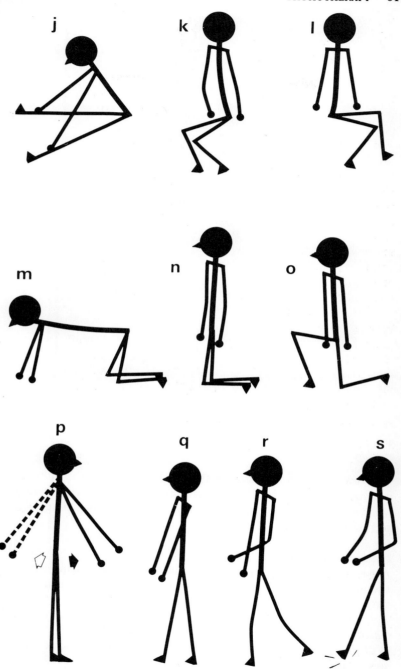

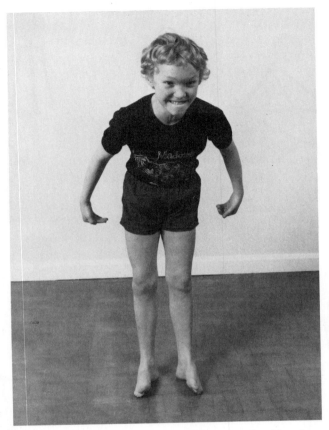

Fig. 7.1 The Fog test. Walking on the outside borders of the feet. Note the associated movement of the arms and face — marked for nine years.

sideways to specific commands and rhythms, hopping on either leg and standing still with weight on one leg should be observed, together with running, kicking a ball, dribbling and aiming a ball, single step and stair climbing.

Postural check
A postural check of spinal mobility, leg and foot girths and lengths should be carried out if joint and muscle inadequacies or irregularities have been demonstrated by the above examination.

Check of fine motor skills
With the child well seated at a table use some or all of the activities suggested in the 'coffee jar' test (Grimley and McKinlay, 1977). This

is elaborated on page 26. The movement difficulties demonstrated by this assessment may show undue developmental lag in gross and/or fine motor skills, increase or decrease in muscle tone; possibly associated limb or trunk movements, rigidity or tremor, abnormal movement patterns, joint instability, poor postural musculature, perceptual or motor learning problems with poor self awareness, lack of self-help and social skills.

For example: a ten-year-old boy, asked to stand on one leg, may show that:

1. He cannot stand on one leg.
2. He does not know his left from his right side.
3. He cannot tell up from down nor front from back.
4. He has lack of body symmetry, poor limb girdle organisation, fixation and control.
5. He has immature or poor balance and equilibrium reactions.
6. He has excessive associated movements.
7. He has increase or decrease in muscle tone.
8. He has auditory memory or sequencing difficulties (count the number of commands given to him: stand/on left/leg/hold/right/leg/up/behind/count 8!).
9. He shows a sense of failure through a refusal or attempting to distract the examiner.

Aims of treatment

NB

The long term objectives in physical therapy for the clumsy child are to gain effective body and object control, together with an improvement in emotional control, learning and social skills, social interactions, self concepts and self esteem.

The immediate aim of physical treatment is to give the child experiences which will, through sensations and movements themselves, improve motor response and skill, enhancing perceptions and thereby learning.

Through the experience of movement, perceptions are formed. The sensory input from movement plays an important part in perceptual development. Improvement and development in gross motor skills stimulated by therapy can serve as a basis for more complex perceptual motor learning and the acquisition of fine motor skills. Ayres (1972) emphasises the importance of sensory experience in promoting efficient movement.

The programme, having been tailored for the individual needs of the child, should offer a rich and varied but controlled experience of all types of stimulation, the activities being modified according to the results, i.e. if too excitatory or inhibitory depending upon the child's sensitivity or arousal threshold (Lewis, 1978).

Design of individual, as well as class programmes, should be along usual exercise class lines; general activities, specific postural and sensori-motor tasks, dynamic movement work, game or skill activities followed by a quietening down session.

The therapist should at all times remain in charge of the situation, controlling, stimulating, encouraging, demanding acceptable behaviour and, if need be, firmly discouraging unacceptable behaviour.

Programmes of movement experience should incorporate activities which demand of the child differing amounts of control through time change or physical effort, change of direction or stress in light and heavy movements, and quick or slow motion within all the dimensions of movement as described by Abbie (1978).

Tasks should be clearly explained or demonstrated, the child initially being assisted, advised and thereby encouraged to perform. Close observation of performance leads to further analysis of difficulties or skill gains. If one needs to correct, it is best to correct only one fault at a time. Demands made by the therapist are constantly adjusted to the results obtained. Tasks are initially broken down into the components of an activity in logical sequence, then gradually bringing the whole action together until there is satisfaction in achievement of a complex skill. Children may be introduced to joint activity sessions on a sharing but still self-competitive basis until it is found that competition can be tolerated and constructive.

Regular reassessment of movement, possibly using preferred notations (Abbie, 1974), and evaluation with subsequent programme modification serves to adjust to changes in the child. Through discussing the results of such evaluations with the child, his parents and teacher and with the child's increasing sense of self, he, and others concerned can be more realistic in their expectations. Following such ascertainments they can accept or design needful circumventions, e.g. extended exam time, tape recorders, typewriters, velcro fasteners, slip-on shoes, cross country running (instead of ball games).

Motor programmes in physical therapy

One may draw from the many excellent activity programmes suggested by workers in this field (Arnheim and Sinclair, 1975). The child gradually learns to move and adjust more normally from increasingly accurate integration of sensory experience. It will probably be found needful at first to take the child back to early levels of movement experience where he may acquire an awareness of spatial relationships and of his body through using movement education.

Solving the problems of sequential movement calls for more creative rhythmic activities and introduces propulsion in all directions of the body or other objects. Once gained, these skills in throwing, catching, running and hitting can be followed by improved participation in rhythmic actions as in dance, games and sports activities.

The former programmes are often best undertaken in the therapy situation, the latter or second level activities within the school curriculum.

Activities to be used may include those for the following purposes.

1. Relaxation and release of tension

Deep breathing, yoga, remedial drama, active alternate tensing up and relaxing of muscle groups are useful. Rhythmic punching of a 'mad bag' (sponge off-cuts or rags inside a pillow case suspended from a hook or clothes line) not only serves to release tensions all round but is useful for target skills and body strengthening. Both boys and girls often find tension release in bread-making. Eating it may be reward in itself!

2. Body awareness

This can be gained through tactile, auditory and visual stimulation, e.g. giving initial skin sensations as in rubbing the body all over with a rough towel, fur, sponge, brush, velvet or pan scrub. The parts being rubbed and their position in space are looked at and described by the child. This does help particularly a tactile defensive child who can be encouraged to do the rubbing himself, name and become more aware of his body parts through feeling and tolerating his own self-stimulating actions. If these are then reinforced by the gradually introduced assisted action of a parent it can literally be a means of bringing child and parents back in touch with each other.

Body awareness can also be improved through using bending, stretching and twisting actions.

3. Body alignment

Once the child is aware of his body parts and acquires postural sense and control, he can then be conscious of, adjust and hold his position in space. He can become aware of body weight, and parts, and the direction of movement by having the limb placed by himself or another and holding that position; and once moved again, learn to regain and hold the first position. The child may learn to copy the placing of limbs on one side of the body through active movements of the limbs on the other side in mirror fashion.

It is essential to make clear points of reference for the child: midline, up/down, right/left, front/back, on top of/underneath, through/over, near/far. Through use of hoops, tunnels, mirrors, ropes, mimic and semaphore cards one can incorporate the spatial and directional aspects of effective movement into the experience of the child. Angels-in-the-snow is an excellent activity with which to work on body alignment, correction and awareness of posture and position in space. Tactile, visual and auditory clues are often necessary to reinforce this type of learning activity (Kephart, 1971).

4. Locomotion and balance
With controlled use of large therapy balls, balance and spring boards, gait ladders, rings and chinning bars, ropes and climbing frames, the child can learn to propel, transfer, bear and receive body weight more efficiently (roll, creep, crawl, walk, jump, hop, run, climb, pull up, hang, swing and land).

5. Rhythm, temporal awareness, rebound and airborne activities
These are stimulated and achieved through such actions as tapping, clapping, skipping, jumping, marching and trampolining. Translating auditory clues or commands into body movements which are echoing the given rhythm can not only be enjoyable but relaxing. He becomes more efficiently synchronised as he learns to control himself in actively gaining a sense of timing for movements.

In a group situation, marching, rhythmic action songs and well taught country dances are often enjoyable experiences.

Trampoline activities must be carefully controlled, bearing in mind the needful safety aspects, but, if properly used, the trampoline proves one of the most useful tools in the treatment of the clumsy child (Fig. 7.2). An excellent description of rebound and airborne activities is given by Arnheim and Sinclair (1975).

6. Projectile management
To acquire this skill, the child can practise throwing, catching, pitching, striking, kicking, dribbling and bouncing various types, shapes and sizes of objects through, onto, under, over, around or at targets (Fig. 7.3). Catching or hitting projectiles helps train eye-hand or eye-foot coordination, and depending upon the size of the object to be caught or thrown can improve bilateral or unilateral skills and strengths.

The therapist should carefully design a positive and gradual

(a)

(b)

Fig. 7.2 Use of the trampoline. (a) Front drop. (b) Knee drop.

Fig. 7.3 Target practice: throwing the bean bag.

success-orientated regime for these activities in projectile management, as the clumsy child is well aware of his failures. Conversely though, it might happen that he is unrealistic and over-enthusiastic about his prowess at games such as football and is hurt when not selected by his peers or teacher for team activities. Careful counselling and skilled direction into other hobbies may have to be advised.

7. Manipulative dexterity, eye-hand coordination

Enhancement of these skills can be gained through practice in sorting, grading, threading, lacing, texture and shape feeling and matching, shape and size sequencing, model building with bricks, lego and meccanno (large), clay modelling, working with sand or plaster or papier mâché (Fig. 7.4).

The child can use large body movements, maintain balance, work on eye-hand coordination as well as on shape, number and letter recognition by drawing large shapes, figures or letters on the chalk board, formica wall board, on a table or the floor. Further tactile experience may be gained by drawing with the whole hand, fingers or feet using finger paint, soapy water, shaving or crazy foam on a tiled floor or wall.

Fig. 7.4 Selection of equipment used for manipulative and perceptuo-motor training for younger children.

This increase in tactile learning, using the body and arms at differing angles to the writing surface also gives visual and motor learning sensations and can prove a good introduction to a systematic remedial writing programme.

8. Eye-foot coordination

These are skills which may be gained through experience and practice in toeing a line, line walking on straight, curved or angular lines (these can be in the form of shapes, numbers or letters) and balance board walking (gradually introducing either higher or narrower boards as balance is gained and confidence appears). Lines and boards can be walked forwards or backwards or sideways in either direction. The child may step alongside or over, between or around objects such as in dribbling a football around an obstacle course or even taking himself through, over, under or on to obstacles.

9. Body fitness, strength and endurance

These may all be promoted in a therapy room and elsewhere by such activities as static bicycling, controlled use of weights and pulleys, trampolining and well-taught swimming. This latter, and horse riding, if well instructed, promotes self-confidence as well as balance and physical well-being. Weight lifting, trampolining, swimming, judo and karate are useful activities to selected clumsy children. They are often available under qualified supervision at the Sports and Leisure centres which in the UK at least are becoming more accessible. Many Riding for the Disabled groups accept the clumsy child for tuition.

One finds that the older child is much happier at attending such a centre for his 'training' programme rather than having to be different from his peers by attending a hospital or clinic.

10. Hobbies

The child and his family should be actively encouraged to design or discover hobbies which are not only therapeutic but also enjoyable and which permit family participation (particularly the young lad in conjunction with his father) although not competition between each member.

Also useful are: canoeing, rowing, archery, fishing, kite-flying, sculpting, clay modelling, pottery, tapestry and counted thread work, bread making, gardening, hill climbing, fell walking, orienteering and cross country running.

These and similar activities can be enjoyable, take the pressures off the anxious non-achiever and give him guidance to a lifestyle which can be interesting and more worthwhile than any he has yet experienced.

Example case history

B.S., born 20.7.68, average intelligence, first referred at age of six years six months; then attending local primary school, 40 children in class.

At referral, reported to be a child who fell a lot, bumped into everything, tripped over curbs, poor at ball catching, buttoning, lacing and tying. Assessed as described above and found to have: very poor upper limb organisation, fixation and coordination with poor postural musculature; difficulty in unilateral weight bearing; increased associated movements on effort; positive Fog test; slight tremor; poor spatial orientation, shape and tactile recognition with confusion in body image, laterality and directionality.

Initial programme (Gordon and Grimley, 1974)

Designed in conjunction with parents and mainly carried out at home, in order to improve: body awareness, body image, postural organisation and strengths, limb girdle fixation, spatial orientation, locomotor skills, coordination and manipulation and attention span.

Initial towelling of the whole body for tactile stimulation reinforced knowledge of the body parts of the side being rubbed, as the child verbally repeated which part or side of the body was being stimulated. Controlled rolling over and over in specific directions (best done in sand, on carpet or coconut matting) was used to reinforce tactile input for directional sense, as well as teaching muscular organisation and strength, when he had to push or resist being pulled by another. Assuming, relaxing and reassuming good postures when lying, sitting, kneeling or standing, together with holding these positions against varying resistance, encouraged limb girdle and postural musculature fixation. Resisted crawling and directional crawling to a rhythm reinforced this. Angels-in-the-snow became a favourite activity particularly as it increased in complexity, e.g. the child, lying on his back, arms and legs in midline positions, had both arms and legs passively and rhythmically taken out to the side (fully abducted) simultaneously and then returned to the midline. This was followed by the child repeating the command before the therapist again passively moved the limbs (one, two or any combination of all four limbs). Having repeated the command once more, the child then performed the action and looked to check limb positions before returning to the starting position. The complexity of this activity was therefore gradually increased. It proved to be an enjoyable activity when talcum powder was sprinkled under his hands and feet (sand or flour would do) which showed the 'angel' shape when movements had taken place. This helped in acquisition of body image, laterality and directionality.

Back extension exercises, press-ups, pole work, chinning bars, punch ball and static bicycle work helped generally in his initial programme for strength and endurance, whilst practice in floor line walking, low plank and obstacle course and football dribbling assisted eye-foot coordination and balance.

Eye-hand coordination, manipulative skills and shape and tactile recognition were encouraged by finger painting, clay modelling, sandpaper letter feeling and drawing, kite flying, bean bag target throwing at and into a bucket, as well as throwing and catching a large ball.

Therapy department attendance was once monthly for twelve months. After two years nine months from initial referral, improvement was marked in:

1. Whole body coordination (three-year improvement)
2. Manual dexterity (two-plus-year improvement)
3. Simultaneous movement control (three-year improvement)

as shown on the Stott test for Motor Impairment. Spatial relations showed a three year three month improvement but persisting problems at this stage were: visual perception, eye-hand coordination and balance items.

Five months later, having undergone a further specific sensori-motor programme, he showed gains in laterality and directionality awareness, unilateral standing balance and dressing skills with generalised improvement in body image and distance judgment; but persisted in right and left confusion despite further improvement in spatial orientation.

Belonging to a single-parent family and requiring a very structured learning situation, B.S. showed home and school behaviour problems when moved to an open plan classroom with 40 classmates and another 40 in the adjacent section of the building. He did not appear to make any good peer group relationships. A remedial class was suggested and within six months the behaviour problems, tantrums and school refusal had been eliminated, but it was now evident that B.S. needed extra attention for school work in sequencing, visual and auditory memory and spatial awareness for writing, copying and reading skills.

A joint physiotherapy/occupational therapy programme is currently being carried out between school and therapy staffs whilst suitable memory games such as lotto, pairs, etc. are encouraged for home use. Mother and child both receive support and counselling.

ACKNOWLEDGEMENT

The author would like to thank the members of the Physiotherapy Department staff at the Royal Manchester Children's Hospital, in particular Mrs Sheila Grundy, M.C.S.P., and Mrs Paddy Sykes, M.C.S.P. for their invaluable contributions to discovering and designing the 'Clumsy Programmes' described in the text.

REFERENCES

Abbie M 1974 Movement notation. Australian Journal of Physiotherapy 20: 21–69

Abbie M 1978 Laban Notation and its application to treating clumsy children. Developmental Medicine and Neurology 20: 110–114

Arnheim D D, Sinclair W A 1979 The clumsy child, a programme of motor therapy, 2nd edn. Mosby, St Louis, Ch 3, 20–33, Ch 10, Ch 15, 142–148

Ayres A J 1972 Sensory integration and learning disorders. Western Psychological Services, California Ch 3: 36–37

Gordon N, Grimley A 1974 Clumsiness and perceptuo-motor disorders in children. Physiotherapy, 60: 311–314

Grimley A M D, McKinlay I A 1977 The clumsy child. Association of Paediatric Chartered Physiotherapists p 14

Kephart N C 1960 The slow learner in the classroom 2nd edn. Merrill, Clumbus, Ohio Ch 9: 221

Lewis B J 1978 Sensory deprivation in young children. Child Care, Health and Development, 4: 229–238

SUGGESTIONS FOR FURTHER READING

Adams S 1978 The ball games book: A collection of games to play in your garden. John Adams Toys, Wargrave, England

Bartel N R, Hamill D D 1971 Teaching Children with learning problems. Temple University, Philadelphia, Pa

Bentley W G 1970 Learning to move and moving to learn. Citation Press, New York

Bowley A H, Gardiner L 1972 The handicapped child 3rd edn. Churchill Livingstone, Edinburgh, Ch 2

Cruickshank W 1961 A teaching method for brain injured and hyperactive children. Syracuse University Press, Syracuse, New York

Frostig M, Horne D 1964 Teachers guide to the Frostig programme for the development of visual perception. Follett Educational Corporation, Chicago

Frostig M 1969 Move grow learn. Follett, Chicago

Holle B 1976 Motor development in children. Normal and retarded. Blackwell, Oxford

Marshall L 1978 Yoga for your children. Ward Lock, London

Montessori M 1912 The Montessori method. Frederick Stoke, 1965 Bentley, Cambridge, Mass

Vallett R E 1967 The remediation of learning difficulties. A Handbook of Psychoeducational Problems. Fearon Press, Palo Alto, Calif

Van Witsen B 1967 Perceptual motor training activities handbook. Teachers College Press, Columbia University, New York

Occupational therapy

Introduction

Children referred to the occupational therapist as clumsy usually have difficulties in one or more of the following areas; fine motor and eye/hand coordination, specific learning or perceptual difficulties and self-care skills. They also often need advice on hobbies and leisure activities.

The degree of involvement in any particular area of treatment will vary from one department to another, depending on the availability and interests of other members of the remedial team and the occupational therapist should be willing to adapt to the needs of the child within the team in which she works.

A similar attitude of flexibility is needed in respect of the actual treatment programme. There is no value in having a 'treatment programme for clumsy children'. Each child needs his own individual programme based on an assessment of his specific difficulties. Similar activities may be used with many children, sometimes with a different aim for each child, and it is important that the therapist is always clear about their purpose, even if it appears to be 'only a game'. The programme is adjusted as progress is made so that all activities remain relevant.

Anything which an occupational therapist has to offer is of little value in isolation. A good relationship with parents as well as with the child is important, as is liaison with other members of the treatment team. The occupational therapist should be familiar with the approach and terminology used by the doctor and psychologist so that parents are not confused. Contact with the physiotherapist and speech therapist is also vital so that treatments do not overlap unnecessarily and the occupational therapist is aware of difficulties in other areas. Shared treatment sessions with other therapists are sometimes valuable. Contact with the teacher may be made directly or through the psychologist.

Assessment

The child usually comes to the occupational therapist having been through at least one assessment procedure, the results of which the therapist should be aware. A school report or discussion with the teacher is helpful, as is discussion with parents. The latter may best be done out of the hearing of the child, who is usually very conscious of his failures in relation to himself and his family.

Although previous explanations about reasons for the child's difficulties may have done much to relieve anxiety, these should be reinforced and an explanation given of the purpose of an occupational therapy assessment.

The child should be reasonably comfortable before starting the assessment; not too hot or cold, not hungry, thirsty or wanting to go to the toilet and preferably should not have been kept waiting, as all these situations may contribute to distractibility or anxiety.

Eye/hand coordination
Eye fixation: fixing on one object such as a moving suspended ball.
Building: using blocks graded in size, related to the age and ability of the child.
Threading: graded from large wooden blocks to small glass beads. For older children, threading a needle.
Dot-to-dot drawing: joining two dots with a straight line, graded in distance, using chalk and board or paper and pencil.

Manipulation
Using scissors: cutting along a short straight line, graduating to cutting out a complicated shape. (Children can normally manage scissors from about the age of three years.)
Lacing: threading a cord in an organised way in and out of holes in a board, graduating to a card and fine lace.
Screwing: turning door handles, undoing the lid of a jar, turning a tap. For older children, using small screws, possibly with a screw driver, e.g. dismantling/reassembling an electric plug.

Body image
Draw a man: indicates the child's awareness of body parts and their relationship to one another and also pencil grip and control.
Imitation of posture: indicates child's awareness of position of body in space, ability to control limbs and copy body position.
Laterality: does the child know left and right? can he cross the mid-line in large drawings, etc.?

Perception
Spatial awareness: does the child know the spatial relationships of

one object to another e.g. inside, behind, underneath, etc.? Can he copy a 'bridge' of blocks? *Yes*

Grading and sequencing: can the child recognise large and small and fine gradations, to put objects in order of size? Can he put cards in logical order from left to right?   *Yes*

Shape recognition: graduating from a simple form board to a more complicated jig-saw. Can the child copy designs, from vertical and horizontal lines (from about the age of two) to geometric shapes and letters?   *Yes*

Sorting: can the child sort for colour and shape or texture; has he established conceptual thought; can he focus attention on one object on a confused background?   *Yes*

Independence in self-care

Eating: can the child manipulate a knife, fork and spoon successfully? Does he cause an unacceptable mess when eating? Can he chew adequately?

Dressing: can the child organise the correct sequence in which clothes are put on? Can he recognise top and bottom, inside and outside and back and front of a garment? Can he monitor the movements of his limbs adequately in relation to the garment, particularly if his eyes are covered? (e.g. by a sweater). Is his coordination and manipulation adequate to cope with buttons, zips, press-studs, ties, shoe laces and buckles? Does he dress himself at a reasonable speed or is he unacceptably slow?

Leisure activities

Because leisure activities are so important for the building of confidence, it should be discovered whether the child has hobbies and interests which are appropriate for his age and skills, which provide enjoyment and companionship with his peers.

Treatment

Having completed the assessment, a treatment plan can be drawn up. In doing so, the degree of interest shown by the parents and their willingness to carry out a home programme should be considered, as this will affect the content of the treatment session and probably frequency of attendance. The amount of time being lost from school must always be considered in relation to the possible value of treatment. Practical considerations such as length of journey and ability of parents to bring the child must also be taken into account. It is often found that about an hour (depending on the attention span of the child) once a week is the most practical, although not necessarily the optimum, time for treatment. It is usually helpful to establish a regular time for the treatment session, choice of which may be discussed with the teacher in order to provide the least disruption to the school timetable.

When planning the programme, consideration needs to be given to the room to be used. Clumsy children can be divided into two groups, the more usual highly distractible, overactive children, and those who are withdrawn and possibly understimulated. If it is possible to provide a fairly stimulus-free room for the first group, they may show improved concentration. However, as the programme progresses there is some value in moving on to use a room with more distractions because the child ultimately has to learn to focus his attention despite distractions, as at school or in the home. The more withdrawn group may benefit from bright, attractive rooms containing interesting toys and games. Care should be taken that they do not become overwhelmed by too great a choice and the treatment session must be equally carefully controlled.

The importance of establishing a good relationship with the child cannot be over-emphasised. The explanation of his difficulties which he has been given often helps to establish a willingness to cooperate with activities which should be enjoyable and attractively presented. However, although the sessions should be enjoyable, it is sometimes necessary to make clear that the therapist is in control, especially with those children who have learned to compensate for their difficulties by 'clowning'. These children usually respond well to quiet but firm handling, often needing to have limits set for them as they are poor at monitoring their own behaviour appropriately.

Parents are almost always included in the treatment session so that they are aware of exactly what their child's difficulties are, and what is being done to help. They should be told that much of what the occupational therapist will do is simply to practise, in various ways, the skills the child finds difficult, or to give advice on ways of overcoming or avoiding problems.

Parents often need to discuss ways of encouraging their child, and sometimes need reassurance when the child will attempt activities with the therapist which he refuses to try at home. This is often simply because of the lack of emotional involvement or perhaps because a more able sibling is not watching his attempts.

A programme to be continued at home may be given to parents but care should be taken that their attitude is appropriate, so that the child is not subjected to stress. However, practice at home is invaluable because short, frequent periods of work are of much greater value than the infrequent therapy session. In some cases parents may carry out most of the remediation, supervised by the therapist. They are often very imaginative therapists and should not be undervalued. Toys or equipment needed for home programmes can often be acquired from a toy library and exchanged as progress is made.

Many children respond very well in a 'one-to-one' situation because they enjoy individual attention, but occasionally they need competition and small groups of two or three children may be treated together. If this is the intention, the therapist should be careful in her choice of grouping so that one child does not dominate all activities. Meeting others with similar problems is often very reassuring as the child may be the only one with such difficulties in his class or school. Parents may also appreciate the opportunity to compare experiences and exchange advice.

The treatment programme should be varied to retain interest, the activity being changed just before the child's attention is lost if possible. It seems preferable to reward good attention with a few minutes free play of the child's choice, than to lose his concentration entirely so that the session becomes rather negative and the child possibly rebellious.

Eye-hand coordination

Eye-hand coordination begins to develop when the baby learns to fix his gaze on one object. He then has to learn to move his hands appropriately in order to grasp the object, and then learns more complex skills involving good coordination between eye and hand. It is difficulty in this area which often earns the child the 'clumsy' label because he knocks over and drops objects as well as having difficulty with many of the normal aspects of play such as building, construction, etc. Because he lacks the confidence to attempt activities needing good coordination he will lack experience and practice and as he becomes older he appears increasingly inept. Although as an adult he may be able to choose to avoid almost all activities needing good eye-hand coordination, throughout the school years he will find this difficult and, therefore, some attempt at remediation is worthwhile. He may even find subsequently that he has no need to avoid such activities!

Eye fixation

The ability to keep the eyes fixed on one object is perhaps the most basic requirement for coordination. Activities designed to improve this skill may include that used for assessment, watching a 'marble run' or watching a ball rolled along the floor. This can be made more difficult by involving a further skill as in using hammer and pegs, playing marbles, 'conkers' (when one chestnut suspended on string is swung to hit that held by the opponent), using the ring and wire toy (Fig. 8.1) or target games. In these activities, one object is stationary

Fig. 8.1 Eye fixation. Use of the ring and wire toy made for the department by North West Region REMAP (Rehabilitation Engineering Movement Advisory Panels).

and the child must move to hit it. A further difficulty can be introduced by having the object to be hit moving, as in table tennis, tennis, table football, etc. In order to achieve many of these activities, the child may need verbal reminders to 'watch the ball', etc. and at first it may be necessary to wait until he has focused on the object before starting the game. Verbal reminders should gradually be decreased and the child taught to 'remind himself', either verbally or in thought.

Constructional activities

Children who have great difficulty with building blocks because of poor coordination may benefit from the use of large lego blocks or stickle bricks which will fit together firmly without the need for fine coordination. The use of these blocks will increase confidence and enable other learning (e.g. perceptual and spatial awareness) to take place.

Older children may use meccano, do simple woodwork or use clay or plasticine in a controlled situation.

Bilateral activities

Clumsy children often have more difficulty with activities requiring the use of both hands in a coordinated way. Perhaps the simplest activity with which to approach this difficulty is using water which is poured from one container to another without spilling. This can be complicated by asking the child to pour to a certain level in different containers, and may be made more enjoyable by the use of coloured water.

Another nursery based activity which requires bilateral coordination is bead or block threading. This should be graded according to the age and ability of the child and can range from large coloured blocks with a fairly stiff plastic thread, to small glass beads and fine, floppy thread, or threading a needle if more appropriate.

Tracing and drawing

These skills may start with finger painting or tracing shapes in the sand tray as they have the added advantage of greater sensory feedback. The child may then progress to joining dots with chalk on a blackboard, or with paper and pencil. It is possible to obtain books of 'dot-to-dot' pictures which are good practice for eye-hand coordination. Wooden shapes to be traced round may be useful as are colouring books which encourage the child to keep within lines when using crayons (Fig. 8.2).

Fig. 8.2 Tracing round a wooden shape. Note associated mouth and tongue movements.

Manipulation

Practice in these skills seems to need to be specific. It does not seem to be adequate to hope for a 'halo' effect from a general improvement in coordination. Children who have poor coordination are sometimes not taught skills such as using scissors because they are thought to be unsafe. The therapist should find out whether the child has experience of using scissors when doing her assessment and then either teach the child or give help when required. Scissors specially designed for left-handed people are available and should be provided when appropriate. It is usually more satisfactory to use sharp scissors rather than the plastic nursery ones which do not cut well. Provided that the child is adequately supervised, sharp scissors are not particularly hazardous and their use decreases the frustration engendered by poor cutting blades. If the child has severe difficulty, training scissors (Fig. 8.3) may be used initially until the movement

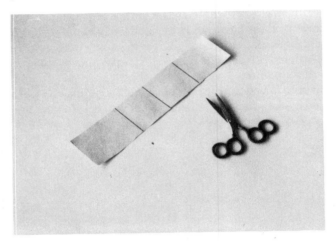

Fig. 8.3 Training scissors.

pattern required is established. When using these the therapist is positioned behind the child with her arm parallel to his, so that he can still see what is being cut.

Early practice in cutting can consist of short, straight lines across a narrow strip of paper (two to three inches wide). The child should be encouraged to follow a line when cutting as soon as the basic movement has been learnt. The line to be followed should be clearly marked, perhaps with a felt tipped pen. It is sometimes helpful to stick cardboard to the back of the paper as a guide for the scissors to move between. When progressing to cutting geometric shapes, coloured lines may be used to remind the child of a change of direction.

Cutting out should progress as soon as possible from straight lines to geometric and then more interesting shapes. As early as possible the exercise should have a creative purpose such as making a collage. It is always important to remember that stiff paper will be easier to handle at first because it holds its shape. Also when choosing items to be cut out, children with difficulties of figure-ground perception may have additional problems in focusing their attention on the shape to be cut around and material should be chosen accordingly.

The ability to thread laces is directly related to dressing skills. This skill not only involves eye-hand coordination and manipulation but good motor organisation. Many children find extreme difficulty in following the sequence of holes and tend to approach the hole from the wrong side, causing confusion. Practice should be graded, starting with a coarse, fairly stiff thread and a board with large holes, then progressing to the finer lacing card or shoe laces. Older children may be able to cope with coarse thread embroidery, especially if it is held in a frame.

Occasionally a child may need to practise unscrewing and screwing up lids of jars of various sizes. A few sweets inside a glass jar often improves motivation to try this task. Older children may be given tightly wrapped sweets inside the jar, as some will need help with unwrapping some of today's sophisticated packaging. They often need to be reminded of the need to look at the packaging and decide how best to open it, as they may have the required skill but do not approach the task in an organised way. A screwing rod may also provide useful practice.

Some children may need practice in turning taps on and off and this can be incorporated into other activities needing water. If possible, they should be introduced to different types of tap so that they learn to cope in a variety of different situations. One of the problems is often not realising quickly enough how and when to turn the tap off to prevent a flood! In order to avoid recriminations from parents and teachers they may need to be taught to turn taps slowly as they often tend to rush at all activities. (The value of pulling out the plug should not be overlooked!)

Other specific manipulative skills may need to be taught or practised. The therapist will discover these from the child or his parents.

Perception

In many situations the occupational therapist will be involved in this area of treatment, particularly with younger children before formal teaching has begun. Perceptual problems not only contribute to specific learning difficulties at school, but also to problems with dressing and other skills.

Body image
Development of body image starts with the baby's contact with his mother through touch, movement and the sensory feedback received from these stimuli. In clumsy children the development of body image often seems to be delayed and the child remains unaware of the relationship of one part of his body to another, or of himself to his environment. This contributes to difficulties with dressing and generally organising himself and his work.

The training of body awareness is closely related to work which the physiotherapist may be doing, of which the occupational therapist should be aware. Activities used to improve body awareness may be an extension of those used for assessment.
Draw a man.   There are various activities which may encourage the child to draw a more mature image of a man, indicating his improved awareness of body image (Fig. 8.4). Direct interference with drawing

Fig. 8.4 Draw a man: use of chalk and blackboard.

tends to result in a distorted image and in any case would only demonstrate improved copying, not necessarily an improved body image.

Life sized drawings are enjoyable to do and encourage awareness of the relationship of one body part to another. The child is asked to lie down on his back on a large sheet of paper and the therapist draws round him. He then has to fill in the details of body, face and clothes (Fig. 8.5).

To encourage awareness of facial expression the child may be asked to identify and then draw for himself, a series of faces looking happy, sad, angry, surprised, etc. This may also be done by picking them out of a book or magazine.

Other useful activities are completing puzzles of faces or figures and indicating what body part is missing on an incomplete drawing. This can be developed into a game with first the therapist and then the child drawing an incomplete figure which the other must complete.

Imitation of posture.   It is important to be sure that the child knows and can point to all the body parts, on himself and someone else. He may also be asked to close his eyes and say which part of his body was touched. Some children become confused if asked to do these exercises while lying on the floor, so this should be included and, if necessary, practised.

There are many singing games which involve identification of body parts which are useful, especially in a group or for practice at home.

The child may then be asked to imitate the position in which the therapist is standing. The game of 'Simon says do this' is a more interesting way of practising this skill. Alternatively a robot man may be used which the child either puts into the same position as himself, or imitates the position of its arms and legs.

If it is possible to set up an obstacle course which includes crawling through a barrel, stepping over an object, walking between two chairs, getting through a hoop, etc., this is enjoyable and very useful for encouraging body awareness, especially if there is a small reward for completing the course without touching anything.

Laterality.   Clumsy children are often slow to establish hand dominance and this may contribute to difficulties in learning left and right. If the child has not established a firm knowledge of left and right this may need to be taught. It can be practised by asking the child to show his left hand, right foot, etc., or in a more complicated way by asking him to follow instructions, e.g. take three steps left, take one step to the right, etc. There are also various games involving the ability to put left and right feet on certain coloured squares, etc. The game of hopscotch may develop an awareness of positions of the left and right foot.

Knowledge of left and right can be constantly reinforced verbally in other activities, and games may be played with the family to encourage this, such as counting houses on the *right* while travelling in

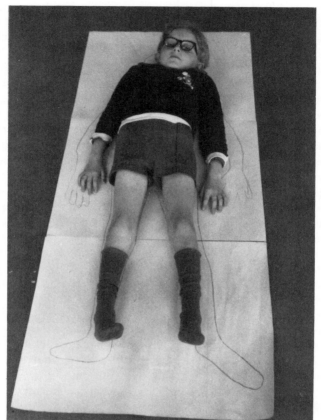

(a)

(b)

Fig. 8.5(a) Life size drawing of the child's outline. (b) Filling in the outline.

a car. Older children can take part in a 'treasure' hunt involving instructions to turn to the left or right.

Spatial awareness. Many children do not know the spatial relationships of one object to another and, therefore, cannot recognise whether an object is inside, outside, behind, in front, underneath or on top, in relation to another. Work on this ability can be included in body image training, as the child may need to experience these positions himself first, before he can relate them outside himself. Initially, games involving putting objects into these positions may be played, perhaps in sand, or using commercially made toys. He may also enjoy estimating the distance or number of steps from himself to an object.

This can be made more difficult by using a pegboard to provide patterns which the child must copy or patterns which have to be copied using coloured blocks. The ability to translate from a card into a three dimensional pattern may also be involved here. The child may also be asked to identify relative positions of people in a picture book, or cards made for the purpose.

Grading and sequencing. The child may need practice in recognising different sizes, especially in fine variations. Various games may be played which require the ability to recognise and match for size, such as the wooden eggs and matching cups, sorting different sized buttons or cards or sorting out pencils to go into a box of correct size. Sequencing skills are likely to be dealt with by the speech therapist or teacher but cards which tell a story are useful, as are games such as 'Scrabble' or 'Lexicon' for the older child.

Shape recognition. There are many commercially available toys and games which may be used to develop this skill. Younger children may use simple form boards or posting boxes and older children will enjoy dominoes based on shape recognition, snap or pelmanism. The latter game also involves good visual memory as the player turns over two cards which, if a matching pair, he keeps, otherwise he places them back leaving the next player to have a turn, but trying to remember where that shape was. Another similar game is 'Double Match' manufactured by MB Games.

The child may also need practice in drawing or copying shapes. An enjoyable way of doing this is to make a dice with a different geometric shape on each face (Fig. 8.6). The child then throws it, not knowing what shape he will have to draw. The element of surprise seems to overcome reluctance to practise this skill.

Sorting. Clumsy children who have difficulty with shape recognition or focusing their attention on one object in a confused background may need practice in sorting. This can be done using assorted plastic geometric shapes, different sized balls, buttons or pins.

Fig. 8.6 Dice for practice in copying shapes.

He might also be asked to 'tidy' the toy farmyard, putting all the pigs in one pen, all the horses in the field and so on. A dolls' house or garage could be used for the same purpose. At home he might be asked to tidy the cutlery drawer or sort groceries which not only gives practice but increases his self-esteem in the home.

Writing.   The occupational therapist may become involved in the provision of equipment to help with writing. This may be as simple as a piece of clay round the pencil as a reminder for a good grip, the provision of a clipboard to hold the paper still or as complicated as the discussion about the provision of a typewriter. Children are sometimes referred to the occupational therapist specifically for assessment for a typewriter. It is often rather difficult to decide at what stage, if at all, the provision of a typewriter should be recommended. However, it is worth considering the following points: the child should not use this as a method of avoiding learning to write manually (i.e. it should not be provided too young); he should have adequate basic skills for learning to use the machine, such as letter recognition and the ability to isolate finger movements; he should be provided with proper tuition, *not* left to learn on his own; he should be positively motivated towards learning this skill. It should also be remembered that it is often possible to be allocated extra time in examinations, and that a typewriter has somewhat limited use because of the inconvenience of transporting it, and the noise it makes. The latter problem may be overcome by combining its use with that of a tape recorder. If it is decided that use of a typewriter is appropriate the child should learn to use it before the pressures of examinations increase, probably around the age of 12 to 14 years.

Training may need to be given in isolating finger movements and the occupational therapist may need to do this before an adequate assessment for use of a typewriter can be made. Games such as finger football with marbles, flicking paper, finger printing, etc. may be used (not only for this purpose but also for a child who wants to be able to do the cub scout salute!). Parents often ask about the value of playing the piano and this too may be useful as long as it does not cause too much frustration. The occupational therapist is sometimes involved in training writing patterns, but this is usually done by the remedial teacher and is dealt with in Chapter 11.

Independence in self-care

Close cooperation with parents is important when trying to help the child to become more independent in activities such as eating and dressing. Usually parents are anxious to establish early independence but on occasions when there is a degree of over-protection, it may be necessary to see the child without parents and at a later date, demonstrate independence.

Eating.   Children who have difficulty using a knife and fork are often not allowed by parents to use a very sharp knife. This, however, often contributes to the difficulty and a sharp or serrated knife often helps to solve the problem. Such children sometimes prefer to cut all the food first and sometimes need help with this. Practice during play may be obtained by cutting thin plasticine pancakes with a knife and fork.

In order that they do not miss the opportunity to practice, but can still eat a meal while it is hot, it is sometimes useful to persuade the child to cut just one piece before accepting help, and gradually increase the number of pieces he cuts. A piece of non-slip material under the plate is unobtrusive and may prevent the plate sliding around on the table. Apart from finding a mug or cup with a handle which particularly suits an individual child, there seems to be little that can be done to overcome the problem of spilling while drinking. A fairly heavy mug sometimes helps and the child should be taught to monitor his own movements sufficiently to prevent spilling. Discussion with parents is useful as in some households the standard of table manners required is much higher than in others and this may contribute more to the child's distress than the actual difficulty which he has. Clumsy children are usually very unwilling to accept 'aids' to eating, probably quite rightly.

Dressing. If a child needs practice at dressing, a realistic situation should be created which requires him to undress. It is unfortunate that after a swimming session he is often slightly damp and clothes are not as easy to put on. Cooperation with a physiotherapy session may be the ideal situation. As far as possible the reason for the child's difficulty should be pinpointed as this will affect the approach adopted. Problems related to perceptual difficulties may improve as the child's ability to identify top and bottom etc. improves. It may be necessary to practise such identification on garments and sometimes to practise dressing a doll. It can be useful in cases of extreme difficulty, to start by pulling rings or loops over the limbs, as practice. Various 'dressing up' games may also be useful and regarded as fun. These can be encouraged at home. Some children benefit from a colour-coding system where a small tag stitched at the back and top of the garment, for example, will identify it.

Body image games, especially with the eyes covered will help in training awareness of position of body in space which should help dressing. Verbal reinforcement by the child himself may also be useful (e.g. put my arm in the sleeve). It is obviously necessary to establish first that the child can identify both body parts and parts of garments and, if he cannot, to teach them. Extra practice at coping with laces, buckles and buttons can be provided by the use of lacing cards or a practice board which may consist of a picture made of felt which, to be completed, demands the ability to do up buttons, and zips and tie bows. The 'double loop' method of tying shoe laces is sometimes easier to learn (Fig. 8.7) and loops on zips may make them

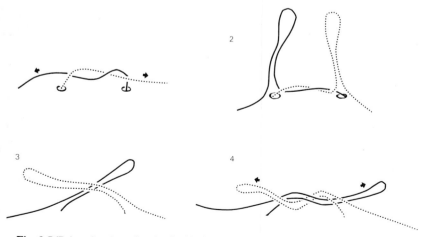

Fig. 8.7 Tying shoe-laces by the double loop method.

easier to cope with. It may also be helpful to provide a selection of size graded buttons and matching button holes for use before the child attempts them on his own garments. Tying a tie often needs practice especially if the school uniform includes a tie. This may be attempted with the child standing in front of a mirror, with the therapist behind the child. The child and therapist can then see what he is doing and the therapist's hands can guide him. If this fails a tie attached to a piece of elastic round the neck may be used, at least as a temporary measure, until he has learnt to tie his own properly.

In order to overcome the general disorganisation often exhibited by the clumsy child he may need to be taught a routine sequence in which he dresses. He should also be encouraged to be as tidy as possible, as this will decrease the chance of frustration over a lost garment and may help him in achieving the correct sequence.

Discussion with parents about suitable choice of clothing may be helpful. It is best to choose clothes which are not too tight and which do not have small buttons or open zips which are difficult to align. Sometimes it is possible to find sweaters which have a distinctive pattern on back or front which will help in orientation. It may seem preferable to choose shoes without fastenings, as an aid to independence, although the child should still be taught to cope with laces and buckles. Elastic shoe laces or gussets may be useful in gym shoes until he is able to tie laces quickly. These look normal but eliminate the need to tie laces quickly before a lesson.

The child who is very slow at dressing may lack practice because of the necessity for speed on school mornings. If parents feel that it really is impossible to provide the time for the child to practise independence, then care should be taken to make the opportunity for him to undress at night, and to dress himself at weekends. A chart which the child completes (supervised by parents) is sometimes a useful incentive to achievement.

Hobbies

Because the child may be under pressure from parents and teachers, the way he uses his free time may be of considerable importance for establishing self-esteem and self-confidence. Parents who are aware that they have a child who has problems sometimes seem to feel guilty if they encourage that child to join a club or organisation which will take them out of the home. This can, however, be a welcome break, perhaps once a week, for both parents and child. There are many youth clubs or organisations, ranging from the scout/guide movement, to specific interest groups. The therapist should be aware of those available in the area and suggest them where appropriate.

Occasionally, discussion with the group leader may be appropriate to avoid misunderstandings over the child's difficulties.

The child should be encouraged to follow up any area of particular interest and suggestions may be made as to how these can be extended by keeping diaries, scrap books, etc., which may also be a useful method of practising other skills which are more difficult. It is often helpful to suggest that a child develops a skill which is perhaps unusual at that particular age as this may add prestige and thus increase confidence. Examples are horse riding, carpentry, photography, gardening or amateur dramatics. The confidence of one child increased greatly when allowed to make a film using his father's cine camera. Unfortunately many such hobbies depend on the financial or material resources which the parents can make available, but there are other possibilities such as baking, cooking, bird-watching, hill walking, swimming, camping, listening to music, car mechanics, growing plants, etc. which perhaps depend more on parental interest than on finances. The older child may choose an activity related to possible future employment and may develop confidence by helping, for example, at an old people's or children's home or at a kennels, or by taking a part-time job delivering newspapers. It seems that unless a child is determined to succeed at a leisure activity which involves a skill which he finds difficult, then it is preferable simply to encourage him to find an interest which will increase confidence and give him enjoyment. It may be that his interest will extend to skills which he needs to practise, and at least he will be well motivated to do so.

Sources of treatment materials in Britain
James Galt & Co. Ltd., Brookfield Road, Cheadle, Cheshire.
E. J. Arnold, Butterley Street, Leeds, LS10 1AX.
Taskmaster Teaching Aids, Taskmaster Ltd., Morris Road, Leicester, LE2 6BR.
ESA Creative Learning Ltd., Pinnacles, P.O. Box 22, Harlow Essex, CH19 5AY.
Anything Left Handed, 65 Beak Street, London, W1A 4SL.
4 to 8, Medway House, St Mary's Mills, Evelyn Drive, Leicester, LE3 2BT.
Learning Development Aids, Park Works, Norwich Road, Wisbech, Cambs, PE13 2AX.
Philip and Tacey (Learning Resource Material), North Way, Andover, Hants.
Living and Learning, Church Walk, King's Cliffe, Peterborough.
Games to Develop Reading Skills, 2nd edn. (1973) J. McNicholas & J. McEntee, N.A.R.E.

REFERENCES

Bergès J, Lézine I 1965 The imitation of gestures. The Spastics Society M.E.I.U. Clinics in developmental medicine 18: Heinemann, London
Goad M M 1977 A picture approach to typewriting. Special Education: Forward Trends 4: 14–16

Holt K (ed) 1975 Movement and child development. Spastics International Medical Publications. Clinics in developmental medicine 55: Heinemann, London

Illingworth R S 1972 The development of the infant and young child, normal and abnormal, 5th edn. Churchill Livingstone, Edinburgh

Jarman C 1979 The development of handwriting skills. Blackwell, Oxford

Kephart N C 1960 The slow learner in the classroom 2nd edn. Merrill, Columbus, Ohio

Sheridan M 1968 Developmental progress of infants and young children. HMSO, London

Stott D H 1977 A strategy for remedial handwriting. Special Education: Forward Trends 4: 20–22

Tansley A E 1967 Reading and remedial reading. Routledge & Kegan Paul, London

Physical education

INTRODUCTION

Since the end of World War II, physical education has undergone radical change at all levels. In the schools there are now better indoor and outdoor facilities and also more varied equipment. As a result, a more challenging programme of creative and skilful activities is offered in schools.

One change that is not yet so prevalent is the appearance of specialist physical educationalists in pre-secondary schools (i.e. schools which teach children aged 5 to 13 years). Whilst virtually all secondary schools have at least one specialist on their staff, it is far less common to appoint one to junior (8- to 11-year range) and middle schools (9- to 13-year range). It is rare in England to find such an appointment in first or primary schools (5- to 8- or 9-year range). This is an unfortunate position because the early school years are a time of rapid physical development in the child. Specialist teaching during this period might be valuable.

In schools without specialists, the task of teaching physical education involves the class teacher. During her teacher training, she will have received some element of physical education training but this may prove inadequate when she is faced with a problem such as that posed by a clumsy child in the classroom or gymnasium.

If the teacher recognises that this child is suffering particular and understandable problems, then the danger of ignoring him as being 'no good at games' may be avoided to some extent. Physical education provides an opportunity for him to learn requisite skills. By teaching clearly and concisely and by progressing through the hierarchy of skills in a logical manner, the teacher will be able to give the clumsy child some of the support he requires without penalising the rest of the class.

If the child has been diagnosed clinically as clumsy, he may be receiving some form of therapy and it is important that the teacher is aware of what he is doing in those sessions. For instance, physiotherapy techniques may be supported and usefully extended by activities in the physical education lesson.

It must be remembered that the child will not want to be identified as 'clumsy' and so the help he is given must not be too obvious. Equally, the class must not suffer from undue attention being paid to one member. The clumsy child must learn to adapt to the class just as they, too, must adapt to him and his problems.

NEEDS OF THE CLUMSY CHILD

One problem appears to be that he has failed to acquire 'basic' skills of balance, coordination and anticipation and thus is unable to progress to more sophisticated skills. The clumsy boy who cannot dribble, kick or catch a ball suffers a worse handicap than an obese child who can do these things but cannot move fast. Thus the clumsy boy is the one most likely to be ignored when selection of teams occurs. Yet he needs to achieve recognisable standards: recognisable both to him and also to his peers.

The teacher's threefold task is:

1. To teach the basic skills and encourage further development of these.
2. To help the clumsy child to learn to adapt to the demands made upon him by his participation in class activities.
3. To ensure that he experiences some degree of recognisable success.

APPROACHES TO TEACHING THE CLUMSY CHILD

1. Whole-part-whole method

The skill is taught as one unit but is reduced into discrete parts when necessary. For instance, the skill of *throwing*.

The throw is a single fluent action but the components which might be identified are:

a. Sideways stance
b. Movement from body through shoulder, elbow, wrist and fingers.
c. Moment of release — timing.
d. Point of release — position.

Having worked on these points, the whole action can be tried again.

A 'high-spot' technique may be useful. This entails identifying salient moments in any particular chain of movements and stopping the child at those moments. Thus attention is focused on the 'feel' of a specific position. For instance, the 'high-spots' in the throw that could be demonstrated with the child are:

a. Moment of preparation: shoulder back, elbow high.
b. Moment of release: hand high, arm extended.
c. Position after follow through.

2. Logical development

The simplest of skills are taught first and then are developed and incorporated into more complex movement patterns. For example, in *gymnastics* the logical progression in the development of the concept of balance might be:

a. Lie flat on the stomach — relax.
b. Tighten muscles to raise head, shoulders and arms.
c. Combine these to bring about stomach balance. Maintain tension.
e. Balance on other gross body parts (thighs, seat).
f. Reduce area of balance (four points of contact with floor; three points; two points).
g. Eventually a sequence of movements which leads from one balance position to another can be developed.

It is the ordering of the activities that will help the clumsy child in particular. He will not learn faster, necessarily, but he will be given opportunities to experience the logical progression of skill acquisition.

3. Rhythm

The clumsy child often appears to lack a clear sense of rhythm. The teacher can use rhythm in her voice and actions in order to help the child to recognise and use the innate rhythms of movement.

4. Apparatus

To direct the child's attention to the most relevant cues in the environment, certain aspects can be emphasised.

For instance, alterations to colour, texture or sound of equipment can aid selective attention to its position in relation to the child. Changes in *colour,* for example, could involve the use of bright or fluorescent paint on apparatus (balls, quoits, ropes, benches).

THE PHYSICAL EDUCATION PROGRAMME

The activities in which the child is most likely to encounter in the physical education programme are:

a. Pre-games and games activities.
b. Gymnastics and dance.
c. Swimming.

PRE-GAMES AND GAMES ACTIVITIES

During the pre-secondary school years a very wide range of activities is introduced. These fall into three main stages:

a. Activities for infants: emphasis laid on individual skills.
b. Activities for lower juniors: emphasis on cooperative activities.
c. Activities for upper juniors: emphasis on cooperative and competitive activities.

The emphasis on physical education changes from concentration on personal skills in the youngest age groups to group work in the older age range. Table 9.1 illustrates these stages and some of the activities that may be experienced during them.

In the early stages, with much concentration on individual skill development, the teacher will be able to ensure that each child has adequate opportunity to work on specific skills. As he progresses up

Table 9.1 Methods of developing games skills.

Stage	Activity	Apparatus
Infants	Individual skills: catch, throw, bounce, aim, strike. Some small group work.	Small, medium, large balls. Bean bags, bats and balls. Quoits, hoops and individual ropes.
Lower juniors	Principles of cooperation. Individual and group skills. Passing and receiving, striking, propelling, fielding, marking. Small-sided games.	Large, medium, small balls. Various bat, stick and racket implements.
Upper juniors (up to 13 years old)	Principles of competition and cooperation. Introduction to formal games through competitive situations: small-sided games, e.g.–	
	a. Striking games: hockey, shinty, rounders, softball, cricket.	Bat, sticks, balls, goalposts, targets.
	b. Net games: tennis, volleyball, table tennis, badminton.	Bats, nets, variety of balls, shuttlecocks.
	c. Running games: football, mini-basketball, netball, athletics.	Variety of balls, goalposts and targets.

the school, he will have to participate in the increasing range of group activities even though he may encounter severe problems in this. However, there should always be opportunity for the child to continue to concentrate on individual skill improvement since any lesson will always contain a section on a particular relevant skill. For instance, a rounders or softball lesson for upper juniors might have a format such as that outlined in Table 9.2.

The lesson outlined in Table 9.2 shows that, even with reasonably advanced rounders or softball, players who have already progressed to a six-a-side game still have ample opportunity for individual development and help. However 'advanced' a class may appear to be, there is always need for basic skills work.

REPETITION AND COMPETITION

The teacher must ensure that adequate opportunity is given for frequent repetition of the most basic of the pre-games skills for all the

Table 9.2 Typical rounders or softball lesson for upper juniors.

Theme: Improvement of throwing technique — leading up to a six-a-side game.

Introductory activity:

Individual	— throw and catch rounders ball on the move.

Skill development:
Individual work:

1. Throw ball at near target	— i.e. to hit a bucket/post emphasisng: sideways on shoulder back elbow— wrist — fingers movement.
2. Throw ball at distant target	— Same teaching points. Alter moment of release of ball.

In pairs:

3. Throw and catch N.B. Good catch depends on accurate throw.	— Take one step *away* from each other with each successful catch. Step *towards* each other if catch is dropped.
4. Throw to moving partner	— Judge speed and aim ahead. Confine area of activity.

In threes:

5. 2 versus 1	— 1 thrower. 2 catchers. Catchers start together and one sprints to get away from other, indicating for direction of throw.

Climax: Six-a-side rounders or softball game.

class but particularly for the clumsy child. Repetition of skills is highly acceptable within a competitive framework. Obviously problems arise here for the less able child. However, if the competition is individually based, all the class will benefit. Any skill eventually breaks down under a 'stress' situation. If the teacher devises self-demanding tasks, stressing any one particular skill, then each member of the class can function at the most appropriate individual level.

Development of individual work into small-sided games is important. This can be done gradually through two versus one, three versus one, three versus two situations. The clumsy child's inclusion can be guaranteed either by working in a 'side' of two where he must contribute or in a 'three' where each must pass to the other in order to score a goal or point. These small-sided games can be developed towards six-a-side games (e.g. rounders, cricket, shinty, football). It is important that every games or activity lesson should always finish with a climax game. By retaining 'mini-sides', the teacher can ensure that all the children are fully involved and are contributing to the game.

PRE-GAMES SKILLS

An enormous variety of small games apparatus is available to pre-secondary schools. Full use of such equipment will aid skill development. Segregation of materials into 'infant' or 'junior' should

Fig. 9.1 Examples of the wide variety of size, shape and texture of games balls.

be avoided since the clumsy child and probably other members of the class will benefit from experiencing activities with a wide variety of equipment.

Ball handling skills

This term covers handling of quoits and bean bags as well as various types of balls (Fig. 9.1).

Work should start with large, slow balls and gradually progress to smaller, faster balls. Alternatively, progress can be made through weight, whereby light balls are used initially and are gradually replaced by heavier balls. (See Tables 9.3 and 9.4.)

Table 9.3 Development of ball handling skills using balls of differing sizes.

Size	Type of ball
Large	Giant inflatable balls. Plastic beachballs. Medicine ball — for rolling only.
Medium	Football, basketball, waterpolo ball, netball.
Small	Airflow ball, sponge ball, rubber balls of various types, tennis balls, plastic balls, Medau ball.

Table 9.4 Development of ball handling skills using balls of differing weights.

Weight	Type of ball
Light	Medau ball, tennis ball, various rubber and plastic playballs, airflow balls, sponge balls, beach balls.
Heavy	Medicine ball, basketball, football, netball, waterpolo ball, hockey ball.

'Cue' alterations to equipment
(a) Colour: Brightly coloured; self-coloured; multi-coloured
                 Fluorescent — dots, stripes, totally fluorescent.
                 Black — for use against a different coloured
                         background. i.e. white walls.
(b) Texture: Coat balls and quoits with glue and roll them in
                 wood chips.
                 Paste strips of sandpaper, velveteen, hessian or
                 velcro on equipment.
(c) Sound: Bells, wooden beads or plastic pieces can be
                 inserted into airflow balls. Some rubber balls can
                 be opened and resealed.

Softballs (materials of felt, sponge or cotton stuffed with rags) can be made.

Add a 'squeaker' or a soundbox that works when inverted.

Suggested activities

Activities should be appropriate to the demands of the class. Overly easy tasks can alienate a group. However, successful sessions can be built around a very simple task if it involves some challenge or if it is part of a demanding whole. The activities mentioned here can be used in a variety of teaching sessions either on their own for individual improvement or as early stages in development of throwing, catching and striking skills.

Depending on the age and stage of the class, these tasks can be graded from 'easy' to 'difficult' by altering the size and weight of the ball, bean bag, etc.

1. *Aiming:*   Hand rolling at target (skittles, boxes), or throwing at circles and shapes on the walls. Rolling along 'tunnels' made by benches placed on their sides — progressively narrow the gap.

2. *Kicking:*   Dribbling along lines on the floor. Dribble around an obstacle course. Kick along 'tunnels'. Kick through 'goals' to partner.

3. *'Trapping':*   Stop balls, bean bags or quoits travelling along the floor with hand or foot. Emphasise watching the object and getting in line with it in order to stop it.

4. *'Giant marbles' game:*   (Jack = a large ball.) The child throws, rolls or skims a ball/bean bag to move the jack. This can become a team game by aiming to move the jack over a particular 'goal-line'.

5. *Bouncing:*   Use either hand, both together or alternate hands. Follow patterns and courses laid on the floor. Bounce into and around hoops laid on the floor.

6. *'Mini-basketball':*   Use bounce, skim or roll. Use containers as goals. (Wastebins or buckets at floor level or five-a-side lacrosse nets above floor level). The ball must be dropped in these in order to score a point.

Gradually increase the complexity of the game by:

a. Change in weight, size or colour of the ball.
b. Allowing travel with the ball.
c. Raising the level or changing the size or colour of the 'goals'.

Many simple yet challenging games can be devised using these ideas. No child is responsible to another despite the group situation. Thus the clumsy child can participate more easily at his own level.

Coordination skills
Throw, catch, strike.

Throwing skills
The breakdown of the skill into discrete units will help with its acquisition. But in order to avoid an unattractive and inefficient movement, the complete throwing action must be retained. Rhythmic verbal patterns can be used.

Underarm throw.   This is basically a swing and release action so that a chant of 'swing down-up-release' will fit the appropriate backswing, forward swing and release. Emphasis on the use of the fingers as a means of flight direction is essential. Practice of the skill will be facilitated if the individual can throw a large number of balls one after the other rather than waiting for alternate turns with a partner. The partner can act as collector and feeder of balls.

Overarm throw.   The same idea of rhythmically identifying the discrete components within the skill may help the child who apparently 'cannot' throw. Thus emphasis will be on:

1. Sideways stance.
2. Movement through shoulder, elbow, wrist, fingers.
3. Transference of weight.
4. Rhythm of the action.

Other passes.   Chest, overhead and bounce passes can be introduced using the same method.

Suggested activities.   Throwing skills can be developed in the following ways.

1. Aiming at coloured patches and shapes on the wall. (Use coloured cartridge paper or fluorescent paper from which the class can make and colour their own 'targets'.)
2. Aiming through hoops suspended from other apparatus (beams, high-jump stands and poles). Tie on strips of bright coloured paper or material. Work in pairs.
3. Throw ball/bean bag onto a sounding board. Stiff cardboard braced in a climbing frame or on wall bars makes a loud snapping sound. Aim for specific marked areas on the board.
4. Use return boards: a piece of wood resting on a fulcrum with a bean bag placed on the far end. The child hits the near end of the wood with his foot and the seesaw action throws the bag up into the air.
5. Use a dustbin lid flat on the floor. A group of children with a tennis ball can use this as a 'comeback' device with an added erratic factor due to the flutings on the lid.

Catching skills

Emphasise the basic points concerning 'watching the ball'; getting in line with the flight path, stretching out for the ball and yielding into the catch.

Three distinct stages can be followed with catching:

1. Self throw and catch.
2. Self throw and catch against wall.
3. Catch from partner.

The teacher, from the earliest stages, can teach that the thrower and the catcher are in partnership and can help each other.

Fielding can be introduced by the use of rolling or skimming objects along the floor. The recipient must crouch down and place his hands in line with the approaching object.

Striking skills

These can be subdivided into four types:

1. Stationary object — stationary child.
2. Stationary object — moving child.
3. Moving object — stationary child.
4. Moving object — moving child.

The first is the easiest and thus to be concentrated on until confidence and a degree of skill are achieved. Limit demands at first and then increase complexity by introducing moving ball, and eventually achieve 'moving child — moving ball' games situations (e.g. hockey, football).

Rhythmic verbal instructions can be used again. Other relevant teaching points can be introduced when the basic skill is mastered.

Suggested activities.   The following activities will help to develop striking skills.

1. Using a ball suspended on string from beam or other apparatus. Strike and be ready for return. Work individually or in twos. Various commercial 'come-back' type games are useful and copies can be constructed without too much difficulty, using a ball suspended on strong elastic.
2. Traffic cones are ideal 'tees'. Balance ball on top and strike with an implement: plastic bat, padder bat, plastic rounders bat, etc.
      Develop variations on rounders or softball games.
      e.g. Person to pick up free ball is next hitter.
      e.g. Ball must be passed (handed over), thrown or rolled to each member of team whilst batter runs his 'rounder'.

3. Small 'hockey' game using arms to hit a giant ball. Always play small-numbered teams; two-, three- or four-a-side.
4. Shinty/hockey type activities. Dribbling, pushing or hitting ball/bean bag along a course or around obstacles. Use feet, or any of a variety of short or long handled bats with which to propel the ball.

GYMNASTICS AND DANCE

In this section on gymnastics and dance, the basic factors underlying movement are pointed out. Emphasis is laid on the importance of rhythm in the acquisition and execution of skills.

The major task of the teacher in these aspects of the physical education curriculum is to develop an awareness of the rhythm innate in all movement. With this she will teach a range of balance, coordination, functional and expressive skills. There is no doubt that the essential prerequisite to efficient, successful or creative performance is a well established set of 'subskills'.

Development of body awareness is the first stage in both dance and gymnastics and the child should understand the communality of movement principles in these two areas and in his everyday life.

Gymnastics is primarily a functional activity concerned with body management whilst confronting and solving problems posed by a particular situation or set of equipment. It involves mastery and development of the 'maturational' skills of walking, running, leaping and rolling. When the young child first enters school, he will have had experience of these skills but through gymnastics he is given the opportunity to develop and integrate them into highly skilled movement.

The clumsy child whose experience will have been less adequate will need a breakdown of skills to those original maturational skills which he should have experienced prior to school entry. Through the gymnastics lesson he can be re-introduced to experiences of balance, coordination, simple flight and basic body management.

Innate to all movement is rhythm. Whilst gymnastics demands a degree of rhythmic awareness, rhythmic skills are the main priority in 'educational' dance. The clumsy child appears to have an absence or relative unawareness of rhythm in movement. Through dance, he can experience a range of movements which involve simple or complex rhythmic patterns. This approach can be developed by the teacher through emphasis on the innate rhythms in other aspects of movement. For instance the rhythmic patterns involved in a throwing action can be expressed as 'Swing back-up-and chuck'. These patterns are as relevant in the dance situation as in a games activities lesson.

FACTORS UNDERLYING MOVEMENT

The majority of teachers who have undergone some form of physical education teacher training will have been introduced to the work of Rudolf Laban. Using his thematic approach to movement it is possible to develop both the maturational and rhythmic skills basic to all movement.

Laban presented sixteen 'movement themes', each of which 'represents a movement idea corresponding to a stage in the progressive unfolding of the feel of movement in the growing child, and in later stages to the development of his mental understanding, of the principles involved' (Preston-Dunlop, 1963).

The sixteen themes divide into four groups, each of which is concerned with one particular aspect of movement. These are common to both 'educational gymnastics' and 'educational dance' and all must be experienced since it is not feasible to develop one aspect alone.

The four aspects are concerned with:

1. Body
2. Effort
3. Space
4. Relationships.

Body

What moves?
Gymnastics.   Body awareness involves knowing what is moving, why it is moving and what results from the movement. This awareness is known as the kinaesthetic sense and tends to be poorly developed in the clumsy child.

The types of action through which bodily awareness can be developed are:

1. Actions emphasising use of particular body parts, e.g. legs and feet — for flight. Discovering the different types of jump that result from different take off and landing patterns (flight from one foot to the other foot is a long leap, flight from one foot to the same foot is a hop), e.g. use of elbows, hips, knees to lead the body into twisting movements.
2. Twisting, turning, stretching and bending. These involve

awareness of where the different body parts are. They are movements basic to all gymnastic actions.

3. Body symmetry and asymmetry. For the clumsy child with his poor sense of balance, this aspect is a way of emphasising the difference between deliberate off-balance and controlled on-balance. Symmetrical movements — using both sides of the body simultaneously — will demand conscious efforts of control and balance. Many basic gymnastic skills will be experienced through experiment with symmetry and asymmetry, e.g. handstand and headstand (two-foot take-off), forward rolls, handsprings.

Asymmetrical movements occur when one side of the body is stressed. This leads to a more mobile, unbalanced, action. By learning to control asymmetrical movement the clumsy child will develop 'normal' movement patterns.

Examples of asymmetrical movements are: twisting, turning and any action which involves these, e.g. running and swinging on a rope so that a change in direction is brought about.

4. Body shape. There are four basic shapes that the body can assume: rounded, long and stretched, wide and stretched, and twisted. These shapes alter depending on the ongoing actions, and a clear feeling of what the body shape is, or should be, at any moment is essential. For example, a sequence of movements such as 'run — jump — land — roll — shoulder balance' may demand a wide jump, a tight rounded roll and a long stretched body shape in the shoulder balance. By stopping or 'holding' the sequence at various points or 'high-spots', the child can be made aware of his body shape.

Dance. The 'body' themes in dance are also centred around the need to develop a kinaesthetic sense. Material used will cover:

1. Use of the body as a whole unit.
2. Movements with emphasis on different body parts.
3. Symmetric and asymmetric use of the body.
4. Instrumental use of the body — which uses many 'gymnastic' actions.

Through these aspects the clumsy child can be encouraged to develop a deeper awareness of his own body, its potential and actual movements. Activities will include stepping, running, skipping, leaping and turning. The ways in which different body parts can initiate these can be the cause of much interest and experiment. Children can create their own rhythmic movement patterns and phrases stressing different body parts.

Effort

How does one move?

There are four fundamental motion factors in effort:

1. Time
2. Weight
3. Space
4. Flow

The interaction of these brings about the different qualities of movement. Again, the innate rhythms particular to specific actions can be exploited as through effort training the child develops an awareness of the dynamics of movement.

Time factor in effort

Gymnastics.   Movements can be fast or slow, can accelerate or decelerate or may vary between these. Variations in speed develop a rhythmic pattern which in its simplest form may be:

fast – – – – – – – – – slow – – – – – – – – – – fast
e.g.   foward roll — forward roll — forward roll.

Using only one gymnastic action, rhythm has been established. This can be developed so that vaulting, flight, twisting, turning, movements in and out of balance are all experienced at different speeds.

The teacher can help the clumsy child particularly with rhythmic use of her voice, emphasising the qualities of movement sought or expected.

Dance.   The terms 'sudden' and 'sustained' are used to describe the qualities of time. 'Suddenness' in movement brings a sense of urgency, abruptness, excitment and of released energy. 'Sustaining' emphasises the slow, calm, continuing quality of movement. By creating situations within which the child can experience the contrast between these qualities, the teacher can help him understand them and the rhythmic relationships that they create. An example of a theme that might involve these qualities is that of 'fireworks'; demanding sudden, sharp firecracker movements and the slower, sustained movements suggested by the burning out of a 'Roman Candle'.

Weight factor in effort

Gymnastics.   The weight factor involves the degree of tension used in movement. Strong movements include gripping, pulling and thrusting. Examples of this quality are illustrated in the degree of strength demanded in vaulting where an explosive and powerful take off is needed to thrust the body through the air. Lightness is often associated with, for instance, the actual moment of flight when there is less resistance to the movement. It is often stressed that 'heaviness' and strength are not synonymous and that strength and lightness are active bodily states which the child himself controls.

For the clumsy child who fails to differentiate between these states, often epitomised in his exceptionally tight grip on a pencil or racket handle, experience in contrast is again essential in learning to control muscular tension.

Dance. Changes in quality of weight bring about either 'firm' movements which are powerful, energetic and gravity centred, or 'fine touch' movements which are delicate and light. Where neither quality is present, the muscles lack tension and the child seems heavy and ungainly.

The teacher must ensure that awareness of firm or fine touch is not limited only to the limbs but that the centre of the body is involved. For the clumsy child, emphasis on the hips, thighs and legs as firm, balancing, strong body parts and on the upper body, arms and heads as the lighter, buoyant elements, is the first stage to differentiating weight qualities. With mastery of this, he can be introduced to qualities of lightness in lower limbs and of firm strength in the upper body.

Space factor in effort

Gymnastics. A body can move in a 'direct' manner through space or in an 'indirect' flexible way. The former is epitomised by leaping, rolling, stepping and swinging whereas the latter is used in turning, twisting and sequences of movement that involve change of direction.

Dance. The two space qualities of 'direct' and flexible movements are important components in the experience of effort in dance. The former demands a definite and restricted use of space whereas flexible movements utilise space to the full.

Flow factor in effort

Gymnastics. The flow of a movement can be 'free' or 'bound'. Free, flowing movement is difficult to stop, whereas any action capable of being stopped and held shows bound flow. Bound flow is more commonly encountered in gymnastics because of the emphasis on control and balance. Free flow is more difficult to attain but if the teacher helps the child to develop sequences of movement using (for instance) rolling, falling, leaping, landing and travelling without pause it can be experienced.

A clear differentiation between these two qualities of movement should help the clumsy child to be more aware of his own type of movement and indicate how he might adapt in order to gain more control over it.

Dance.   The two flow factors can be more fully experienced through dance. Together they can be built into sequences of movement which run from one to the other. Preston-Dunlop (1963) suggests that the dramatic link between bound flow and stone statues and between free flow and water or fire is a starting point for dance drama development.

The teacher can convey the idea of flow qualities through the rhythmic use of her voice which will match the rhythm of the movement.

Time — weight — space — flow

Combination of the qualities of these motion factors can be made with stress laid on one factor, two factors, three factors or four factors. These combinations offer an infinite variety of movements which can enlarge and enrich a child's movement repertoire. However, such developments take many years and it is not feasible to introduce the pre-secondary school child to much more than the basic effort actions that result from combinations of time, weight and space. But mastery of these is essential for good movement. For the clumsy child it is even more essential to learn to express himself with controlled effort. For instance by experiencing:

Action	Time	Weight	Space
Thrusting	Sudden	Firm	Direct

he also encounters the compensatory quality of:

Action	Time	Weight	Space
Floating	Sustained	Fine	Flexible

Likewise he experiences other effort actions, their opposites and the rhythmic alteration from one to the other.

Space

Where movement occurs

Gymnastics.   Personal space, the 'kinesphere', can be explored to its limits by extending the body in various directions: up, down, forward, backward and sideways, and at various levels, high, medium or low. Bending, stretching, twisting and turning actions use these directions and levels.

Beyond the kinesphere is 'general space' through which the body can leap, roll and run. Again a variety of directions and levels, on the floor, in the air and on and off apparatus, exists.

For the clumsy child with his poorly developed sense of spatial awareness, this is an opportunity to gain a clearer understanding of the relationship between body and environmentt.

The teacher can ask him to devise a pathway around the gymnasium, under or over apparatus that incorporates specific levels or directions.

Dance.   Through dance the child learns to explore and to use space. He experiences 'above', 'below', 'in front', 'behind' and 'beside', steadily clarifying his image of himself and his relationship to his surroundings.

Work can be based on the use of 'patterns' on the ground and in space. Drawing shapes or 'writing' in the air develops the child's appreciation of patterns, symbols and their relationship to each other and to him. Following similar patterns on the floor aids acceptance of the concept that patterns (e.g. the letters of his name) do not alter in meaning or relationship despite a change in size and position in space.

Relationships

With what or whom movement occurs

In the pre-secondary school syllabus, group relationships in gymnastics and dance are not of prime importance.

The child's first work in relationship will be with himself: one part of his body relating to another. But gradually the necessity for a relationship with one other child becomes obvious. 'Work in couples' is used throughout all activities and this entails a degree of social adaptation. Through the medium of partner work, the child learns to watch, assess, anticipate and react to another child. This can be introduced through 'question and answer' work where one child answers the other in movement: in shape, level, quality or rhythm. Alternatively, one child can copy the other, mirroring the actions or matching them. The emphasis is on the two performers building an understanding with each other. A secondary benefit for the clumsy child is the development of visual movement memory through the necessity of watching and closely copying a partner. For the clumsy child there is a social value in this approach since the teacher can help him learn to work with others and to help others work with him. Adaptation to another person and respect for his work are prime objectives.

Use of apparatus

Gymnastics. In the early years of pre-secondary schooling the apparatus usually consists of benches and a junior climbing frame. In middle and junior schools, there are usually various pieces of vaulting apparatus and a form of 'Southampton Cave' (see Figs. 9.2a and b) apparatus; a combination of climbing frame and ropes. Other schools have gymnasia with wall bars, beams and a large variety of vaulting apparatus and benches (Fig. 9.3).

Certain changes can be made to apparatus which may be useful. Basically these consist of using strips of fluorescent or coloured materials placed on the edges of the equipment, thus defining its limits more clearly. However, over-use of this will reduce its value as the class will either habituate to the colour or, with older children, will resent the changes.

The most efficient way of helping the clumsy child to work happily with apparatus is to introduce pieces thoroughly. Do not simply put out all the apparatus and allow 'free activity' on it. Keeping initial apparatus schemes simple, yet setting several challenging and fairly specific tasks graded to individual or group ability, will benefit not only the clumsy child, but any child.

Dance. Dance apparatus involves a variety of muscial aids. Piano, tape recorder and record player are all useful, but over-use leads to dependency on musical stimulation which detracts from spontaneous movement.

Percussion instruments are an excellent way of accompanying movement. The class derives much benefit from learning to sound its own rhythmic patterns. The clumsy child can start with the simplest two or four beat stamping rhythm accompanied by drum or tambour and, through experiment, can gradually develop an understanding of more complex rhythms.

SUMMARY

The basic format of dance and gymnastics lessons is:

1. Introduction.
2. Movement training/skill development.
3. Climax/apparatus/dance composition.

In the introduction, the previously learnt skills are practised, bodies are limbered up and prepared for the following lesson. All children work individually. In the skill section there may be some individual work and some partner work. This is the time for learning through direction, example, and experiment. Whilst emphasis is on the

(a)

(b)

Fig. 9.2a and b The Southampton Cave apparatus offers a variety of opportunities for climbing, twisting, balancing, travelling and swinging for different levels of ability.

Fig. 9.3 Trapeze emphasising the strong developed shoulder girdle of the normal child.

movement approach to activity, directed teaching has a major part to play in skill acquisition. This is particularly so when there is a 'clumsy child' in the class.

Complex skills must be built up carefully and logically from the basic maturational skills. At each stage, the class must have an opportunity to experiment with the skill in relation to the floor, to simple apparatus, to each other and to other skills already acquired. This means that the teacher must know how the hierarchy of skills is built up from the most basic skills, and also how to use this knowledge.

SWIMMING

Of all the areas of physical education, swimming is the one most likely to offer the clumsy child a degree of success as well as developing his general strength and coordination. In water he cannot fall, cannot trip and does not experience the other problems he encounters on the sports fields or in the gymnasium.

If the teacher has sole control of the class at the pool, he must remain on the poolside throughout the session. If he can obtain help from experienced swimmers (senior school pupils, club swimmers) or by assisting an instructor, the class can then benefit from some low-ratio individual teaching. This will be of especial use with the clumsy child who can rarely be given the attention he requires.

The main areas of activity within a swimming scheme are:

1. Water confidence and competence (pre-swimming skills).
2. Survival techniques
3. Stroke techniques

WATER CONFIDENCE

The normal learn-to-swim stages are well described in the many excellent swimming test books that are available. However, it should be borne in mind that the clumsy child has especial need to develop confidence in the water. It is worthwhile spending considerable time playing 'water games'. These are best learnt in shallow, warm learner pools with wide step entry into the water. Some defensive children may take some time to accept the sensation of water on the face and the noise level of the swimming class. 'Crocodile' is a good first stage. The child places his hands on a step and allows his body to float up on the water. He can then 'walk' along the step. Encourage gently kicking until this lifts the hands from the step. This activity combines flotation with face submersion and is a simple yet effective way of starting a non-swimmer in the water.

Other activities will concentrate on the various factors that are involved in swimming:

1. Face submersion.
2. Breathing out under water.
3. Kicking — prone and supine.
4. Floating — prone and supine.
5. Total submersion.

Suggested activities

1. Blowing bubbles. This introduces the idea of exhalation into the water.
2. A game of 'blow football' with a light beachball can introduce face-wetting and strong exhalation without fear. Alternatively, moving the ball by splashing the water with either hands or feet is a useful practice.
3. Floating. This can occur in contact with the steps or side, or can be experimented with freely in the pool. The clumsy child has an

unparalled chance here to relax and learn to feel the buoyancy of the water, experiencing movement without tension. In the shallow learner pool it does not matter if he moves too rapidly since he will simply find he reverts to a standing position.

There are many flotation aids available. Arm bands are commonly used but the child must not be allowed to become dependent on them. It is advisable to ensure that they are removed for part of the swimming session. As an alternative aid training floats can be used. If the supine child tucks one under each armpit, he is in an excellent position to either float or kick around the pool.

More advanced activities
Once the child moves into a larger pool the range of activity increases because there is greater depth of water.
1. Tumbling.   Learning to somersault in the water, both forwards and backwards. The action is similar to that in gymnastics so that the clumsy child will experience similar disorientation problems. However, if he stays tightly curled up as he spins around the horizontal axis, he will achieve the correct movement. Success with this in the water will be of inestimable value in the gymnasium. It is a skill basic to advanced swimming for all the class, since it forms the basis of the tumble or spin turns used in competitive swimming.
2. Sculling.   The ability to move either forwards or backwards whilst on the back, using the hands for propulsion. Keep the hands close to the body and keep legs together and straight.

When this skill is mastered, it can be made more difficult by holding one leg clear of the water whilst sculling.
3. Water polo.   Played with a large beach ball, small 'activities' ball or quoit. Rules vary according to ability of swimmers, e.g. the more experienced swimmers must keep feet off the pool bottom when throwing.

Goals can be scored when every person in the team has caught and thrown the ball.

SURVIVAL TECHNIQUES

Before learning to swim it is essential to teach water survival techniques. Drown-proofing can be taught to non-swimmers and is in fact a good introduction to learning to swim. Drown-proofing both precedes and overlaps survival swimming. Many of the techniques are similar but survival swimming is usually the system encountered in schools.

Drown-proofing

Drown-proofing is a set of skills that will keep a person alive in water whether or not he can swim.

The essential skill in drown-proofing is the ability to remain on and at the surface of the water for an indefinite time. The early stages which are simple to acquire should be learnt in a warm and shallow pool. The suggested sequence is:

1. Duck down under water, eyes open or shut.
2. Duck under water, eyes open. Exhale through nose.
3. Inhale above surface through mouth, duck under water, hold breath then exhale through nose. Continue this rhythmically.
4. Inhale through mouth, whilst chin is on water surface. Drop head and arms forward and allow feet to drift off pool bottom. Exhale through *nose*.
5. As above but continue for several cycles.

Systems vary but this is the essence of drown-proofing and is, incidentally, an excellent way of initiating swimming. Success is easily achieved and this is a prime aim with the clumsy child and any other problem swimmer in the group.

Other survival skills

Various survival skills are described in 'drown-proofing' (Lanoue, 1964), for example:

Scissors kick.   This is the next stage after the easy drown-proofing system described. Arms and legs hang down whilst the body floats vertically. To take a breath, arms are brought to the horizontal whilst legs open and scissor together gently. This raises the mouth above the water.

With the clumsy child, it is especially important to stress the relaxed manner of performance. The degree of tension often shown when he attempts to perform an action, must be lowered.

Travelling.   Using the same scissors kick, the child can travel easily whether or not he is wearing clothes.

Floats made from clothes.   There are a variety of ways of making floats. Essentially it involves trapping air in an article of clothing. However, the clumsy child faces a major problem with this skill because it usually involves taking off the garment that is to be made into a float. The clumsy child's problems with buttons, belts and general dressing skills may preclude swift removal of clothes.

The teacher can solve the problem, albeit temporarily, by providing garments from the poolside when necessary.

When the child is ready to learn to undress in the water, the teacher must ensure that the child completely understands *how* to remove articles efficiently (e.g. removal of a jumper: gather it all up at the back of the neck and then pull it off over the head in one swift movement).

Always emphasise the need to relax.

Survival swimming awards

The Amateur Swimming Association offers four awards for proficiency in personal survival (Bronze, Silver, Gold and Honours Award). It is necessary to be able to swim a minimum of 440 yards, to surface dive and to undress in the water for the Bronze award. But if the clumsy child can achieve these requirements, the psychological 'uplift' he will gain from being awarded a proficiency badge is enormous.

STROKE TECHNIQUES

There are four recognised strokes:

1. Breaststroke
2. Backstroke
3. Front crawl
4. Butterfly

Once the child is confident and mobile in the water, his swimming strokes should be made as efficient as possible. It must be remembered that individuals vary considerably and, whilst the fundamentals of the stroke are constant, allowance should be made for personal variations.

The child should be introduced to all four strokes, although a degree of proficiency in front crawl is useful in learning butterfly.

Teaching a stroke involves work on:

1. Body position
2. Arm action
3. Leg action
4. Coordination of 1, 2 and 3
5. Breathing — breath control

The teacher should remember that, whilst the clumsy child's problems are largely alleviated by the water buoyancy, he still faces certain problems. These include difficulties in coordination and also lack of strength in the upper limb girdle. He must ensure that, as in all other physical education situations, he is able to teach the discrete parts of the skill as well as conveying the whole skill.

Through swimming, the clumsy child can develop strength and stamina as well as experiencing a pleasing and perhaps unfamiliar sense of achievement. It is suggested, therefore, that swimming, which is a desirable part of the physical education programme, is especially suitable for the physical and psychological development of the clumsy child.

REFERENCES

Amateur Swimming Association 1974 The teaching of swimming. Educational Publications, London

Arnheim D, Sinclair W 1979 The Clumsy Child, 2nd edn. C V Mosby, St. Louis.

Carroll J, Lofthouse P 1969 Creative dance for boys. MacDonald & Evans, London

H.M.S.O. 1972 Movement: physical education in the primary years. Department of Education and Science

Lanoue F 1964 Drown-proofing. Jenkins, London

Lawther J D 1977 The learning and performance of physical skills. Prentice Hall, New Jersey

Mauldon E, Redfern H B 1969 Games teaching. MacDonald & Evans, London

Morison R A (1969) movement approach to educational gymnastics. Dent, London

Pallett G D 1965 Modern educational gymnastics. Pergamon, Oxford

Preston-Dunlop V 1963 A handbook for modern educational dance. MacDonald & Evans, London

Robinson C M, Harrison J, Gridley J 1970 Physical activity in the education of slow learning children. Arnold, London

Russell J 1965 Creative dance in the primary school. MacDonald & Evans, London

Ryan F 1977 Gymnastics for girls. Penguin, Harmondsworth

Whiting H T A 1975 Concepts in skill learning. Lepus Books, London

Speech therapy

Some clumsy children present with speech (i.e. spoken language) problems. These may be obviously related to the overall condition in that the difficulties experienced in the organisation of movements may be present in the fine coordination required for speech, resulting in articulation problems. However, other speech difficulties may exist which are less obviously related to the clumsy syndrome. The child may experience difficulty in putting his thoughts into words, seeming to need to 'find' the words before he can organise them into coherent sentences. Thus he appears almost reluctant to use speech. Indeed, the very young child may present with virtually no speech. There may be abnormalities also in intonation and stress patterns, and the child's intelligibility may vary from day to day. Some children have problems attending to and understanding speech commensurate with their age. Any of these difficulties may be present in varying degrees in one child.

All these children need help. At present very few controlled studies have been published regarding the effectiveness of remedial methods. It is difficult therefore to prove the efficacy of therapy and that maturation is not responsible for any improvement in the speech of a child who happens to be receiving therapy. Researchers have concentrated on the conditions necessary for the development of speech and on examining the oral abilities of children with normal speech and those with speech problems.

Lisker *et al.* (1962) emphasise the importance of laying down sensory-motor patterns (kinaesthesis) not only in learning to talk but especially when learning to understand speech. The formation of these patterns is believed to be as important as the development of auditory perception when learning language.

Berry (1969) emphasises the importance of early kinaesthetic feedback in the building of body image as an essential basis upon which to build the complex patterning involved in speech. Various researchers have reported upon the apparent inability of some people to organise this complex patterning which manifests itself in limited expressive language patterns and/or unintelligible speech. When there are no 'hard' neurological signs present and the condition has been apparent from the onset of speech, it is known as 'developmental dyspraxia'. Ferry *et al.* (1975) described 60 such patients who had a wide range of intelligence and refer to the very poor improvement in speech with 'conventional' speech therapy.

Edwards (1973), discussing developmental dyspraxia, considers it 'may be thought of as an impairment of sensory processing and in particular of proprioceptive input, with an ensuing failure to programme, to organize and to carry out movements necessary for expressive speech'. McNutt, (1977) studied a group of children with normal articulatory patterns and another group with articulatory defects and concluded that the two groups differed in various aspects of oral sensation and motor abilities — the children had to distinguish shapes and to articulate repetitive patterns involving the front and back of the tongue. Canning and Rose (1974) quote norms in British children with normal speech, for the speed of silent tongue movements and repetition of consonants, and comment that a child 'who gave a fast performance usually had good rhythm. The younger children tended to lack rhythm and had poorer breath control and this reduced their speed'. They emphasise that articulation is not dependent on motor competence only.

Yoss and Darley (1974) examined a group of children with moderate to severe defective articulation and identified a sub-group by their significantly poor ability to perform voluntary oral movements both in isolation (e.g. blowing, whistling) and in sequence (e.g. puckering lips then wagging tongue from side to side). They state that the 'group performance lends substantial support to the use of the term "developmental apraxia of speech" as descriptive of their articulatory problems'.

Putnam and Ringell (1976) studied the speech patterns of two adults with normal speech development, talking naturally, and under the influence of nerve block anaesthesia affecting the oral region. In the latter situation they demonstrated a lack of precision in both tongue and lip movements and an alteration in jaw movements. If adults with long established speech patterns lose precision immediately upon loss of sensory feedback one can ask how difficult must it be for a 'clumsy' child to lay down normal speech patterns if he is unable to organise his kinaesthetic feedback.

Initial presentation of children with speech problems

Comprehension may be on a continuum from normal to severely retarded. Expressive speech may consist of abnormal phonatory patterns, a few single words, or a limited number of short phrases.

Clumsy children may have difficulty with neuro-muscular coordination and/or with the linguistic aspects of communication.

Neuro-muscular coordination
i.e. the inability to organise consistently peripheral and central neuromuscular patterns at an involuntary level, in the absence of paralysis or paresis.

At respiratory level.   The speaker may experience lack of control of the breathing cycle and be unable to talk due to lack of breath. His attempts to speak without breath may sound as if he has a 'block stammer'. Difficulty in controlling volume of speech may also be experienced.

At laryngeal level.   (a) The speaker may not always be able to produce voice at will; (b) the pitch of the voice may vary abnormally resulting in either varying levels during connected speech, or (c) the use of two voices at different times, or (d) the speaker may be unable to signal consistently the difference between voiced and voiceless sounds e.g. 'p' and 'b'. Intonation and stress may also be affected.

At the pharyngeal level.   The speaker may lack control of the musculature of the throat and palate, resulting in hyper or hypo-nasal speech.

At oral level.   Articulatory defects may be evident due to tongue and/or lip misplacements resulting in omissions, distortions, etc.

Linguistic aspects
Edwards (1975) summarises the characteristics of a developmental verbal dyspraxia to include the following points:

Phonology.   Word-by-word testing may reveal no gross disability, although ongoing speech may sound unintelligible. Articulatory features may be deviant in terms of placement. There may be sequential difficulties in words.

Prosody.   Speech may vary in speed, with inappropriate stress and intonation.

Syntax.   Clause structures may be incomplete, due to the omission of the subject or object, etc. Verb tenses may be used inconsistently; sentences may contain intrusive structures irrelevant to the subject; or speech may be 'telegraphic' with only key words used.

Semantics.   The ability to organise thought processes and express them verbally may be impaired.

Assessment and multi-disciplinary approach
A child who has any of the above difficulties needs to be assessed by a speech therapist so that all aspects of his speech can be looked at in detail and the results discussed with his family, his school and any

other professional worker who comes in contact with him. They need to know his level of comprehension of speech so that they either use language he understands, or demonstrate visually the meaning of their requests. They must also be sensitive to the limitations of his expressive language, as these can be misconstrued as lack of cooperation. All workers, particularly physiotherapists and occupational therapists, carrying out assessments or remedial programmes with 'clumsy children' will find the work of Ward and Platt (personal communication) of interest. They tested the hearing of six grossly handicapped cerebral palsied children and found four of them showed a variation of 20 dB between each of three postures, i.e. lying down, sitting up and standing up with support. After a remediation programme, the differences between hearing thresholds in the different postures decreased significantly. Another group of similarly handicapped children showed wide variations in threshold levels of hearing, differing when they were not engaged in any activity and when they were carrying out simple tasks — most children's thresholds rose to around 80 to 90 dB in the latter situation. These variations in ability to attend to sound can perhaps be linked to the levels of attention and concentration laid down by Cooper *et al.* (1978) and should be borne in mind by those asking the child to concentrate on two different modalities at the same time. Perhaps any new physical activity should initially be purely imitative. As the child becomes familiar with the body postures and movements, the relevant language patterns can be 'latched on' and, hopefully, bonded to:

1. His body image.
2. His own movements in space.
3. General activities in play and therapeutic situations.

This is following normal developmental behaviour. Britton (1971) refers to the work of Piaget and Bruner showing that young children understand the world initially in terms of 'perception-cum-movement' and that these two modes are well established before speech becomes operative.

Many people now consider that kinaesthetic speech patterns help to 'fix' the meaning of words so that the integration of meaningful speech into physio- and occupational-therapy programmes at the relevant point is of the utmost value.

Remedial help for the young child with little or no speech

1. General considerations
2. Developing attention control

3. Training auditory perception and memory
4. Developing oral awareness and control
5. Practising sounds used in speech

General considerations
It is important that all initial remedial work takes place in a structured environment. This entails a room that is in quiet surroundings. It should be decorated and furnished with plain as opposed to patterned materials; visual stimulation should be kept to a minimum so that the child's attention is not distracted. These conditions are important because the clumsy child has difficulty in distinguishing and concentrating on the important, meaningful 'foreground' information and ignoring unimportant 'background' information, both in auditory and visual fields.

Developing attention control
The 'clumsy' child frequently has attention difficulties. Concentration upon any subject for more than a few moments may be impossible, his fleeting attention being constantly attracted by fresh stimuli. Parents say 'he doesn't sit down long enough to listen' or 'he is too busy doing things to learn to talk'.

Cooper, Moodley and Reynell (1978) examined the hierarchical levels of concentration both visual and auditory in a child's development. Their programme designed to develop attention control is of fundamental importance and is reprinted below (by permission of the authors and publisher):

(a) Stage 1. With children showing high distractibility (level 1), the teaching is directed towards helping them to focus and hold their attention on anything that interests them, so gradually moving them on to level 2. By observation of the child's free activity, and discussion with the parents, it is possible to find the materials and activities most likely to interest the child. Then a plan for using this material is worked out, so that a short task with quick success is achieved. The task, whether it is listening, or a practical activity, or a combination of the two, must be intrinsically rewarding to the child, so that he sees it as worthwhile to carry through. Once his interest is lost, it is no use at this stage to force it back. It is better to repeat the process with whatever is his next brief interest, quickly turning it into a rewarding exercise. This needs plenty of ingenuity, and parents need to be convinced of its importance if they are to make this effort at home. They need constant reassurance that this work on attention is basic to language development, and that direct work on language will follow later when the child is ready. If they are mainly concerned about the failure to 'talk' they may not immediately see the relevance of work on listening and attention for themselves. The therapist can pick out examples of the child's interests, during the session, and relate these to similar situations which may occur at home, which could be used for sustaining attention. At this stage the teaching situation should be as free as possible from unnecessary distractions, such as constant bombardment of sound from radio and television. By judiciously enhancing the interest of whatever the child chooses to do, and reducing other distractions as far as the situation allows, parents and teachers may

structure the environment to help the child. He may, for example, show a momentary interest in the soap at bath time. His mother may be shown how this interest could be sustained by helping him to rub the soap on his skin, and feel the smoothness and pleasant scent it imparts, moving from one part of his body to another. This is better learning for him than quickly moving on to splashing water over him, which only acts as another distraction.

   (b) Stage 2.   This is the stage at which the child's attention is held rigidly and inflexibly by whatever he decides to do. He cannot integrate, or even tolerate any sort of adult participation. Successful teaching depends on the therapist, parent or teacher making the directions and reward become part of the task itself, so that learning can be achieved despite the child's inability to integrate to an adult's attempt to modify the task. Directions at first need to go alongside the task, as an incidental accompaniment. For example, if the child is building a single straight tower, the teacher may sit beside him and build herself a double tower, without actually interfering with the child's own construction; or a verbal commentary may be introduced such as 'one brick, another brick, and another one on top'. This may gradually help him to integrate other aspects of his own task without a direct attempt to modify it, which he could not yet accept. Children at this stage of attention control may be seen in class as 'good' children who will concentrate for a long time, but close observation shows the activities to be repetitive and rigid, which actually blocks further learning unless help is given in the ways suggested above. All adaptations must be with the adult at first. The adult must become part of the task, and only very gradually introduce slight modifications by allowing the directions (verbal or visual) to go a little ahead, instead of the earlier stage of going alongside the task. When the child can adapt to this he is moving towards stage 3.

   (c) Stage 3.   This is a slightly easier teaching stage, but still one at which the adult needs to be very much in control. To make the most of the emerging ability to adapt to directions, the child needs constant help in transferring the focus of his attention. Parents and teachers need to be aware of the part they can play at this stage. Two examples will illustrate this:

(i) Towards the end of a session with the speech therapist, James was standing looking out of the window watching children in the playground. His mother said to him, 'Do you want an orange juice?' James appeared not to have heard this as his visual attention was fully absorbed elsewhere, and nobody had helped him to switch the focus to listening to his mother. The therapist then went up to him, turned him round to face her, and then said 'Do you want an orange juice?' The message was immediately understood as the speaker now had his full and undivided attention, and the response was very positive. This made a good teaching example for the mother, as to how to help his attention focus at home.

(ii) In the classroom Janet was playing in the sand. An adult passed and said 'Make me a castle'. Janet took no notice. The teacher then went up to Janet, turned her face round so that she could see the teacher's face, and gently prevented her hands from fiddling with the sand. Then when she had Janet's full attention the teacher said 'Make me a castle'. The teacher helped her to transfer her attention focus immediately back to the sand so that Janet was able to understand and respond to the request.

If this sort of training is to be effective, the situation must be rewarding for the child. He must see it as worthwhile. The orange juice was the obvious reward in the first instance. In the second example the child was rewarded with a smile for looking at the speaker, and then praised for the castle she made. The children should not be told to 'look at me' only to be given a reprimand for inattention. This is clearly both unrewarding and a failure to understand the developmental stage of attention. This needs to be carefully explained and demonstrated to parents.

   Constant training of this sort leads to the child gradually taking over the control of his own attention, so that he spontaneously gives his full attention to directions, provided that it has proved rewarding for him to do so during the learning stages.

(d) Stage 4.   At the beginning of stage 4, the child's control of his attention focus may be rather slow, so that it is important he should be allowed time to stop what he is doing and look at the speaker, and then allowed time to transfer the directions to the task. A preliminary alerting signal may be needed such as calling the child's name, 'listen Johnny', or 'look at this', so that he has time to adjust his full attention before the directions are given.

As he moves towards the stage of integration (level 5) he can assimilate the first part of the message while carrying on what he is doing, and he then looks at the speaker for completion of the directions. Once this control of attention focus is with the child, direct teaching is no longer necessary in order to achieve the subsequent stages. However, it is still very important to adjust communications to his level of attention control. Constantly overloading his attention at this stage, or failing to allow enough adjustment time, could cause a regression to earlier stages and habits of inattention. If anything is made too difficult for a child, with no hope of success, he will soon cease to try.

(e) Stages 5 and 6.   These are the stages of integrated attention. As far as teaching is concerned, the children can now respond to 'class' directions, and comply with simple instructions without having to interrupt a task. It is still important for teachers and parents to understand the limitations in terms of the sort of directions they are giving. If a child is doing up his shoelaces (a very difficult task for a five-year-old) he is unlikely to take in a complicated verbal message at the same time; but if he is drawing a picture, and the teacher says, 'put your pencils away, it's play time', the message will be understood despite the fact that the child was visually occupied with a drawing. Again, no direct 'attention teaching' is needed at this stage, but rather an understanding of the limits and an adaptation of the communications.

Level 6 is the stage of well integrated and well sustained attention. This is the ultimate aim for this aspect of development in the developmental language programme. This stage is not achieved by all infant-school children, whether they are handicapped or not. Children who have attained this level of attention control are more than school ready in this area of development.

Training auditory perception and memory

It is important that the child's attention is drawn to sound sources.

1. Meaningful sound.   Sound must be shown to be meaningful before any interest is taken in it, and its source demonstrated, e.g.

i. When the door-bell rings, take the child to the door so that he opens it to find the visitor/postman/milkman on the step. Then let him ring the bell so that he connects the sound of the bell with the act of pressing it.

ii. Make certain that he sees the activities connected with familiar sounds at home, e.g. meal preparations.

2. Increasing sound awareness.   The child is asked to listen and indicate when he hears a particular sound — the level of the sound should be varied in order to maintain his interest and ensure that he does not habituate to a particular volume. Musical instruments can be used — drum, chime bar or whistle, or noises made by common objects.

3. Location of sound.   Ask the child to close his eyes or blindfold him and then make sounds (on the instrument or with the objects) in various parts of the room — behind or in front of him, high up or low down; ask him to indicate the direction of the source of the sound.

4. Sound discrimination. (a) Environmental sound: have two identical sets of objects that make noises: clocks, keys, hooters, bicycle bells, etc. Let the child handle the objects and listen to the sounds they make. Then lay one set on a table in front of him, lay the other set out of his vision, make a sound with one of your set and ask him to make the same noise with the corresponding object. (b) Have the sounds of objects on an audio-tape (e.g. the noise of a car engine starting up: a door banging; an aeroplane; water running out of a tap, etc.) and have a set of pictures of the objects that make the noises. Ask the child to point to the pictures when he hears the relevant sound.

This type of training helps the child to increase his attention to various aspects of non-speech sounds, improves his general listening skills and is fun to do. However, for auditory work relating to more specific language skills, the help of a speech therapist should be sought.

5. Auditory memory and sequencing. In order to understand speech a child must be able to remember the words themselves and the order in which they come in the sentence to give a particular meaning, e.g. in the sentences: 'the dog chases the cat' and 'the cat chases the dog', exactly the same words have been used but the meaning of the two sentences is very different.

In order to help the child, the following activities may be useful:

a. Have a pile of objects between the adult and the child — can he select one/two/three objects on request?

   Have a delay of two seconds between asking and selecting — slowly lengthen the period of delay. Can he give the objects in the correct order?

   Repeat — using pictures.

   Hide the objects round the room, allowing the child to see where they are hidden — can he remember which object he is looking for and where it is?

b. Give him one command, build it up slowly to three commands:

   Give me the ball

   Put the ball in the box . . . leading to:

   Put the brick under the table, the ball in the basket and the pen in the corner.

c. More conventional games can be adapted to improving auditory memory:

   Lotto: working from the usual game of turning over one card at a time to turning over two together so that both objects have to be remembered and looked for.

   Dominoes: when he can play the conventional game, vary it by having to remember the required number/picture at *both* ends of the shape.

I went to market and bought . . .

Simon says 'Stand up . . . touch your head', etc.

Kits to develop these skills of auditory perception and memory are commercially available in some language programmes e.g. GOAL (see Language Programmes, p. 134).

Developing oral awareness and control

During the first few years of life, a child slowly develops an awareness of his own body image, including his speech musculature. All the oral activities in which the baby indulges play an important part in this development, such as putting his fingers and toys in his mouth, crying, licking, sucking, biting and swallowing. These activities are instrumental in helping the child develop awareness and perception in the oral areas, as well as exercising involuntary control over breathing patterns, that are the bases for the infinitely more finely coordinated speech patterns. Some clumsy children do have feeding problems and these generally need to be resolved before normal speech patterns mature. (Various publications are available giving help in this field, see list of suggestions for further reading.)

Even though some children develop normal feeding patterns, they do seem to need extra training in developing their oral perceptions. Some drool without apparently being aware that they do so, and without frank weakness; they seem unaware that they have a tongue and are unable to carry out voluntary tongue or lip movements on request.

Some of the following suggestions may be useful in developing oral awareness and control:

Stroke the child's face, varying finger pressure from very light to medium. Ask him to close his eyes and see what degree of pressure is required before he is aware of touch on his face and/or his body. Ask him which part of his face is being touched. He may be comparatively insensitive: alternatively he may over-react even to a very light sensation. In the latter case it would be desirable to contact a speech therapist for a desensitisation programme. Vary the stimulus — use diverse textures (feathers, fur, brushes of different fibres), vary temperatures. Encourage him to feel his own face so that he begins to incorporate both hands and face into his body image.

Sit in front of him and see if he can imitate such movements as:

1. Opening his mouth wide
2. Closing his mouth
3. Half opening his mouth — can he appreciate the difference between 1 and 3?
4. Pushing lips forward.

5. Pulling them back (as in an artificial smile).

Can he maintain a lip-seal — i.e. can he keep his lips together? Is his mouth normally open or closed when he is not talking? If the former, encourage him to keep his lips closed, starting with very short spells of one or two seconds. Stroke his lips together (the top one down and the bottom one up) to help his experience of what it feels like to have his mouth closed. Say to him 'close your mouth' — a very simple but surprisingly effective reminder. If he drools, tell him to swallow and gently stroke under his chin moving towards his neck — this will make him swallow automatically. If he has very little or virtually no movement in his tongue, push it around in his mouth with a finger or spatula. Encourage the child to push it around himself — he may become very interested in his own tongue. Sit side-by-side, looking in a mirror, so that he can see his own face, and see if he can imitate the following movements:

Let his tongue come beyond his lips, encourage him to:

1. Move it up towards his nose.
2. Move it down towards his chin.
3. Move it from side to side.
4. Stick it straight out, resting on his lower lip.

Repeat 1 to 3 keeping his tongue inside his mouth.

Make it a game so that it is amusing for the child; for example,

Mr Tongue came out one day (stick tongue straight out) . . .
He looked up to see if it was raining (raise tongue towards nose)
He looked down to see the grass (point tongue down towards chin)
Then he looked up and down the street to see if his friends were
    around (move tongue from side to side) . . .

Remember to perform all these movements slowly at first. When he can copy them easily, speed them up to increase agility.

Stimulate his tongue with different types of food. If it has very limited movement, rub an ice-cube on it — this may increase sensitivity. If the ice-cube is flavoured, the child will be very keen to repeat this exercise! Use foods of various textures — crunchy, sticky, grated, chewy; of different tastes — sweet, savoury, sour; and differing in temperature. Encourage him to lick favourite foods off the outside of his lips.

Practising sounds used in speech

Some children need to practise speech sounds because they have no idea how to produce them. If they have passed the stage in language development when the particular sound would be spontaneously produced, they may need specific help.

Speech sounds can be practised in syllabic form in play situations. Take a consonant-vowel syllable and link it to a specific activity:

e.g. La la la   — make up a tune or use a 'pop' tune. A microphone adds fun to this activity.
Shi shi   — rock the doll to sleep.
Fu fu fu   — imitate a motor bike.
Pe pe pe   — imitate the sound of water running out of a bottle.

Vary the speed, the intonation and rhythm at which the syllables are presented (these aspects are discussed in more detail on page 130). If the child cannot imitate a sound, say it slowly for him and accept his attempts. Often, over a period of a few months, a child will begin to imitate the sound correctly without an issue having been made of it. Similarly, do not expect a child to be able to incorporate a sound he says correctly in play into a word when he uses it meaningfully. Because he can say 'shoo' after you when it does not mean anything, do not expect him to be able to repeat 'shoe' when you point to his shoe, if he usually says 'doo'. If you insist on him saying 'shoe', he may end up saying 'shdoo' and this will be extremely difficult to correct. It is better to wait for the sound to be incorporated naturally into speech.

Normal versus abnormal aspects of speech and articulation development

In normal development, a baby uses very rudimentary speech sounds; over a period of years, the combinations of sounds (i.e. words) change slowly as they are modified to resemble the adult forms, the words increase in number and the sounds in the words also mature. Vocabulary and length of utterance increase in a specific progression although the age range within which it is normal to reach a certain stage of development is extremely wide. All young children's language and articulation is immature by adult standards but may be quite normal for their age. Thus, even children who have not had any problems with speech do not use all speech sounds at an early age. Sounds mature at different rates, some tending to come earlier than others e.g. 'w', 'm', 'p', 't' and 'd' will probably be early, whereas 's' and 'ch' will be later, and 'th' and 'r' may not develop until about seven years of age. Consonant blends, e.g. 'pl', 'cr' and 'spl' will develop later than when the sounds are used individually, e.g. 'lay' and 'pay' will develop earlier than 'play' and 'splay'. Some children, however, do take a little longer than the majority to start to talk or to move from one stage to the next. Their speech may be termed 'delayed' — the structure and sounds would be quite normal for a younger age group but the child will need accelerated progress to catch up with his peers. In a very few cases, speech is pathologically delayed or 'deviant'.

Similarly, other children may use words in the wrong order or use grammatically correct speech which is not relevant to the situation. Vowel sounds may also be distorted, often with accompanying problems of pitch and intonation.

As the child's speech develops, it is important that it becomes a useful tool with which he can manipulate his environment, i.e. 'make things happen'. The desire to ask a child to say a word out of context must be resisted — speech is meaningless unless purposeful. When development has been delayed, as opposed to deviant, it usually follows the normal progression from single words, to two and three word sentences, etc., although it will lag behind that of his peers for a considerable period. Make sure that the developing language can be used to describe both things (ball, big ball, mine, my ball) and actions (gone, ball gone, daddy gone, daddy work). Children are sometimes stimulated with names of objects but verbs are ignored. They need adult intervention to develop a comprehensive linguistic structure.

When a child uses immature forms of speech he can be helped by supplying the correct form and adding to his vocabulary: 'we seed the dog' — 'yes, we saw the dog — he was in the field', 'two sheep' — 'yes, there are two sheep in the wagon'.

Many children with normal speech development go through a period when they think more quickly than they can articulate or find the correct words. This frequently results in repetition of whole words, or first sounds or syllables of a word. Some adults think the child is stammering, but to the speech therapist this is such a normal phase of development that we call it 'Normal Non-Fluency'. Do not draw the child's attention to it — it generally resolves itself. If the child becomes aware of it, seek the advice of a speech therapist immediately.

It cannot be stressed too strongly that whenever there is concern about a child's speech and language development, the advice of a speech therapist should be sought who will pin-point the lack of development, keep a watching brief on the problematic case, or reassure the family that speech and language are developing along normal lines. She will take an active part in the treatment of children whose language is developing abnormally or whose articulation is so deviant that it causes embarrassment. Regular help from a speech therapist may not always be necessary. She may be able to advise on general language stimulation, on an appropriate language programme for a child who has lacked linguistic experience, or devise a programme for a child who needs help in specific areas, which can be carried out in his normal environment.

Remediation for children who have developed language patterns

The majority of this chapter has been concerned with helping children in the very early stages of language acquisition in the hope that early recognition of the clumsy child's difficulties, and subsequent parent guidance and therapy will help communication to develop normally. Thus the distress clumsy children frequently experience at a later stage due to inability to communicate both in social situations and in learning situations in school should be overcome. However, some clumsy children's problems are not recognised until they are older, when most of them will have developed language patterns. In some of these cases the child may have abnormal articulation patterns which make his speech difficult to understand. In other cases, the child's continuous speech is unintelligible, although he may be able to say single words correctly. In these cases his problem may be due to abnormal prosody i.e. stress, intonation and rhythm and it is in these areas that the non-specialist can help.

Prosodic features of speech

Intonation and stress are features of spoken English which can change the implied meaning of a sentence. Consider the variations of implied meaning in the sentence 'Where is my hat?' when different words are stressed and intonation patterns varied accordingly:

Where is my hat? (i.e. I'm surprised you say it is in that place)
Where *is* my hat? (i.e. I've looked everywhere and can't find it)
Where is *my* hat? (i.e. not your hat)
Where is my *hat*? (i.e. not my coat)

It is these features which intensify the meaning of English. The speech of a foreigner who uses correct vocabulary and grammar but who cannot incorporate the prosodic features of English into his speech may not be immediately intelligible. Wallwork (1969) discusses the importance of these features for both native English speakers and foreigners learning English.

Similarly, the clumsy child sometimes has difficulty in organising and reproducing these features in his own speech so that rhythm, which is a combination of stress and intonation, and subsequent intelligibility are diminished.

Exercises to develop prosodic features

1. Stress patterns. At a very simple level, any nonsense (i.e. non-meaningful) consonant-vowel syllable can be used to vary the stress patterns within a phrase. Use a syllable the child can repeat easily, e.g. ba.

Encourage him to copy it: ba ba ba
Add stress to one syllable: **ba** ba ba
                                      ba **ba** ba

Link the syllables to coloured bricks:
e.g. a black brick = a stressed syllable **ba**
     a white brick = an unstressed syllable ba

Now the pattern can be visually presented to the child and he can translate it into an auditory one. This is usually easier for him than trying to copy an auditory pattern which cannot be held constant. The use of bricks was suggested to me by Kellatt (personal communication)

These patterns can be made longer and more complicated as the child becomes more expert.

2. Rhythmic patterns. The spacing of the bricks can be varied to indicate different rhythmic sequences, the white bricks remaining the unstressed beat and the black ones being stressed.

These syllabic patterns can be presented slowly in the beginning, illustrated by widely spaced bricks:

then presentation can be accelerated, this being demonstrated visually:

3. Intonation patterns.   Exercises to help the child to develop wider patterns of intonation can also be visually demonstrated and integrated into therapy. The stressed syllable of a word is usually dependent on the meaning being conveyed. Start with nonsense syllables, illustrating rise and fall of the pattern with bricks as previously:

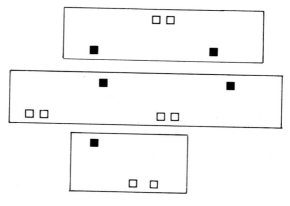

Space the bricks widely to emphasise the difference:

When the child can copy the visual display easily, introduce polysyllabic words for imitation, illustrating with the written word if the child can read:

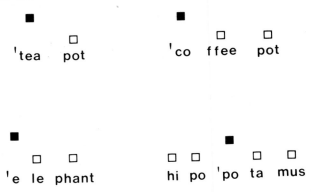

The difference in meaning can now be illustrated by the variations in stress and intonation patterns:

Pe	ter's	swim	ming	down	the	ri	ver	Implications of the variations in stress/ intonation
■ □	□	□	□	□	□	■	□	– Not John, but Peter
□	□	■ □	□	□	□	□	□	– he's not in a boat
□	□	■ □	□	□	□	■	□	– This is highly un- likely, 'are you sure of your facts?'

In this way stress and intonation which combine to give English its rhythmic patterns can be worked on individually at first and then in an integrated form as the child becomes more proficient.

Summary
In a chapter of this length, it has only been possible to highlight the speech and language problems that may affect the clumsy child and indicate some remedial approaches for the non-specialist in speech therapy to carry out.

Each child has his own individual problems and not all methods referred to here will be appropriate to every child. Whenever difficulties are encountered it is advisable to refer the child to the local speech therapy services, if this is possible.

Acknowledgements

I am indebted to Deirdre Birkett, Area Speech Therapist, Stockport Area Health Authority and Brenda Kellatt, Area Speech Therapist, Manchester Area Health Authority (Teaching) for their constructive help in the preparation of this Chapter.

I also thank Margaret Edwards, Area Speech Therapist, Nottinghamshire Area Health Authority (Teaching) for her ideas and comments in the initial stages.

REFERENCES

Berry K F 1969 Language disorders of children — the bases and diagnosis. Appleton-Century-Croft. Meredith Corporation, New York

Britton J 1971 — in the introduction of 'Speech and the Development of Mental Processes in the Child' by Luria and Yudovich. Penguin Papers in Education, Harmondsworth

Canning B A, Rose M F 1974 Clinical measurements of the speed of tongue and lip movements in British children with normal speech. British Journal of Disorders of Communication, 9: 45–50

Cooper J, Moodley M, Reynell J 1978 Helping language development — A developmental programme for children with early language handicaps. Arnold, London

Edwards M 1973 Developmental verbal dyspraxia. British Journal of Disorders of Communication, 8: 64–70

Edwards M 1975 Perceptual processes and language disorders. Paper 'The Seven Ages of Man' Vol 1, 7th National Conference — Cardiff; College of Speech Therapists

Ferry P C, Hall S M, Hicks J L 1975 'Dilapidated' speech: developmental verbal dyspraxia. Developmental Medicine and Child Neurology, 17: 749–856

Lisker L, Cooper F, Liberman A M 1962 The uses of experiment in language description. Word, 18: 82–106

McNutt J C 1977 Oral sensory and motor behaviours of children with S or R misarticulation. Journal of Speech and Hearing Research December, 20: 694–703

Putnam A H B, Ringell R L 1976 A cineradiographic study of articulation in two talkers with temporary induced oral sensory deprivation. Journal of Speech and Hearing Research 19: 247–266

Wallwork J F 1969 'Language and linguistics' — an introduction to the study of language. Heinemann Educational Books, London, ch 4

Yoss K A, Darley L D 1974 Developmental apraxia of speech in children with defective articulation. Journal of Speech and Hearing Research 17: 386–398

SUGGESTIONS FOR FURTHER READING

Binns R 1978 From speech to writing. A teaching technique for use with slower learners. Scottish Curriculum Development Service, Moray House College of Education, Holyrood Road, Edinburgh EH8 8AQ

Bindley W, Griffiths R 1976 In: Edwards R (ed) Listening and speaking, games and activities to develop language skills. National Association for Remedial Education, London

College of Speech Therapists Material for language stimulation. The College of Speech Therapists, Harold Poster House, 6 Lechmere Road, London NW2 5BU

Gallagher M 1977 Let's help our children talk. O'Brien Press, Dublin

Lee V (ed) 1979 Language development. Open University, Croom Helm

Nash-Wortham M 1978 Take Time. A programme of activities for children with language problems, coordination difficulties and impaired sense of rhythm. Available from the author, 2 College Close, East Grinstead, West Sussex RH19 3YA

Ryan M 1975 Feeding can be fun. Spastics Society, London

Seglow D, Millar C 1976 Feeding the child with cerebral palsy (Tape and 36 slides for sale or hire, available from The Medical Recording Service Foundation, P.O. Box 99, Chelmsford CML 5HL, England)

Tough J 1976 Listening to children talking. A Guide to the Appraisal of Children's Use of Language. Ward Lock Educational London (Schools Council Publication)

CATALOGUES CONTAINING SECTIONS ON DEVELOPING LANGUAGE SKILLS, ETC

Books for Primary and Middle Schools. E. J. Arnold & Sons Ltd., Leeds, England

Taskmaster Aids. (Includes section on developmental learning materials) Taskmaster Ltd., Morris Road, Clarendon Park, Leicester, LE2 6BR, England

Materials for Children with Learning Difficulties. LDA, Park Works, Norwich Road, Wisbech, Cambs., England

S.R.A. Materials. Sciences Research Associates Ltd., Newtown Road, Henley-on-Thames, Oxon, RG9 1EW, England.

Tebbs T 1978 Way and means. A resource book of aids, methods, materials and systems for use with the language retarded child. Somerset Education Authority

LANGUAGE PROGRAMMES

Language Activities Kit for Beginning Levels and Handbook. *Also* Sense and Tell: Teachers Guidebook and Kit. Scott, Foresman & Co., Glenville, Illinois 60025, USA

Peabody Language Kit. Test Division, N.F.E.RR., 2 Jennings Buildings, Thames Avenue, Windsor Berks. SL4 1QS, England

GOAL — Language Development Programme. L.D.A., Park Works, Norwich Road, Wisbech, Cambs., England

Learning to Listen. L.D.A., Park Works, Norwich Road, Wisbech, Cambs., England

Herbert D, Davies-Jones G A classroom index of phonic resources, 2nd edn. National Association for Remedial Education, London

Reading, spelling and writing problems: research on backward readers

Many clumsy children seem to experience reading and spelling difficulties, but these difficulties are not exclusive to them. Before considering the particular problems of clumsy children, it is necessary to look at the general question of research on reading backwardness. Children are complex inidividuals; and reading, spelling and writing are very complex, learned tasks, requiring competence in the use of language, as well as the development of perceptual, cognitive and motor skills. Research into difficulties experienced by children in the acquisition of these skills has continued on parallel lines in the medical, psychological and educational fields, but not often with recourse to the interdisciplinary cooperation and judgements so obviously needed (Reid, 1969). Different disciplines have looked at the problem according to their own academic specialities. Often the numbers of backward readers in studies have been too small for groups with similar problems to be identified, considering the obviously heterogeneous nature of the reading retarded population. The design of studies comparing backward with normal readers has traditionally compared children of the same age and intellectual level, the only difference between the groups being in how far they have learned to read. The trouble with this traditional design is that any difference which is found between the groups might just as well be the result of the former group's limited experience in reading. This problem could be overcome by comparing groups of backward and normal readers of normal intelligence for their age who are reading at the same level (Bradley and Bryant, 1978a). The results should be more conclusive and useful to us.

Naidoo (1972), following the intensive medical and psychological investigations with her groups of dyslexic boys, who had shown signs of early clumsiness, said that the only thing they had in common was their reading and spelling difficulties. Studies from different disciplines which concentrate on this observable handicap have yielded some interesting results:

Nelson and Warrington (1974), suggest that children with specific developmental spelling disabilities fall into two distinct sub-groups, who tend to mis-spell words in different ways, and for different reasons, and that the isolation of distinct groups, with their own particular patterns of difficulty, implies distinct and particular cognitive deficits underlying these spelling and reading difficulties. Frith (1976, 1978) distinguished between children who were bad at both reading and spelling, and children who were good at reading but bad at spelling. She suggests that the latter group spell differently from other bad spellers, and read differently from other good readers. They seem to prefer to write by ear, and read by eye, possibly, Frith surmises, because they do not connect the two strategies.

Boder (1973) describes three distinctive patterns of reading and spelling among dyslexic children. The dysphonetic group recognise whole words visually, but may not be able to identify the component letters of the words they read. When they see a word that is not in their sight vocabulary they are unable to decipher it. They are unable to sound out and blend the component letters and syllables of a word. Reading in context they can make intelligent guesses. Spelling is by sight, and not phonetic. Often they cannot identify the words they have written. The dyseidetic group have difficulty learning what the letters look like. They may be said to be 'letter blind' or 'word blind'. They read laboriously, by 'ear', through a process of phonetic analysis and synthesis, as they cannot perceive words as visual gestalts. They have a good auditory memory. Spelling, though poor, is usually phonetic. The third group have both disorders and are the most severely handicapped.

There is little statistical evidence to support the existence of these clinically defined sub-groups. Cotterell (1970) also gives a clinical description of visual and of auditory dyslexics, and of children with both problems. She has spent many years evaluating and producing suitable teaching programmes for the children she describes (Cotterell 1973).

Research suggests the possibility that there are different groups of backward readers whose problems with reading and spelling are different from one another. But it is also possible that we do not read and spell in the same way, and that reading and spelling involve different processes. Bradley and Bryant (1979) investigated the independence of reading and spelling in backward and normal readers. The two skills were surprisingly independent in both groups in that they could read words which they did not spell, and spell words which they did not read. This discrepancy was greater in the backward readers.

Our own evaluation of the needs of the child we hope to help will depend on our own experience. But we can learn from the literature to begin without pre-conceived ideas. Each study manages to group some children, but there are always the children who cross the boundaries, who fit into more than one category. So we must look at each child afresh — *his* home experience, *his* school experience, *his* development, *his* attitudes — and how these have affected *his problem* with reading, spelling, and writing.

CLUMSY CHILDREN

There are several possible reasons why clumsy children may not receive early and appropriate help with written language problems. The first is probably the result of clinicians holding a 'maturational lag' hypothesis ('wait, and they will grow out of it'). Certainly there may be a lag, but not necessarily a general one. Nelson and Warrington (1974) argue, on the basis of the results of their 1974 study, that spelling and reading retardation are best regarded within the framework of developmental anomalies in *different* cognitive systems. Certainly clumsy children are often referred so late, usually for behavioural or school failure problems, that their clumsiness does not attract the consideration it warrants, but is considered as secondary to these other problems.

Secondly, many clumsy children, referred late, are coping with reading. This is the criterion on which many judgments are based. When referred for help, a child is found to be able to read. Therefore, he is thought to have no problem, and he is sent away again. The fact that he cannot write his ideas down, or that he cannot spell, or that writing is so difficult that he cannot take notes, is not considered important. He can read, and that is said to be all that matters! Current research on spelling may show that he does indeed have a problem, and that he does need help.

Informal assessment

History
Eyesight and hearing must be checked. Establish whether progress has been hampered by developmental or environmental anomalies. Did he walk/talk late (MacKeith, 1977)? Middle ear infections during the developmental language period may be relevant to current auditory perceptual difficulties. Long illness may have meant absence from school.

Poor relationships within the family, with siblings or with peers, are relevant. Families in which communication is poor, or in which both parents are working, may mean that the child is deprived of basic experience in the use of language. Warm and secure relationships are especially important.

Language

Does he listen? Does he attend? Does he understand, use language meaningfully, 'lose' the word he wants, mis-use words, articulate clearly, speak rhythmically? Does he know some rhymes or nursery rhymes, puns or jingles?

Imagine that although you can recognise words, you cannot remember what they look like when they are not there. If you think about trying to write a word that you have not written before, and perhaps have never seen written down, you will see how important these points are. Suppose you decide to write 'psychologically'. First, you must listen and hear the word correctly. Then you will probably say 'psychologically' to yourself. If you don't 'subvocalise' it correctly, you will use the wrong letter associations when you write it down. You need to know the correct letter associations for the sounds, and have these symbols correctly orientated when you write them down. You need to say the word rhythmically so that you don't miss out any of the syllables, or get them in the wrong order. You must be able to remember the wole word, and to 'hold' each consecutive section, in the correct order, as you write it. You may need to think of other words you know or have seen that sound similar, to be able to decide what combination of letters makes the first 'psy' sound, or even to be able to work out what the word means. A knowledge of some spelling rules — every syllable must contain at least one vowel; when to use 'c' or 'k'; when to double 'l', that an 'i' or 'ee' sound at the end of a word is 'y' — would be helpful when alternatives seem possible (Cotterell, 1969).

This sounds as if writing words is a complex business. To many children and adults it is. For, to write most words that you do not know you need to follow a similar procedure, even with a simple word like 'cat'.

Whilst we can teach the child rules and strategies for spelling (Cotterell, 1969), he must first be able to specify which words he wants to spell. Furthermore, to be able to write down what he wants to say, he must use language meaningfully. Some clumsy children have difficulty in articulating or in producing speech. Some seem to get in a muddle when they are talking, particularly if they talk at length. '*Conversation*' will help the child to structure and organise what he wants to say. This 'structuring', by intervention, can gradually be withdrawn as he becomes more adept at expressing himself efficiently.

Movement

The clumsy child is likely to have problems with organising his movements, attention, concentration, what he wants to do and what he wants to say. He may also have difficulties with structure: the ability to put what he wants to do, say, or write into a format or order. He often does not know 'where to begin' when writing, and has particular difficulty with spelling.

Some clumsy children seem unable to sit still. They move around, stand up and sit down, or wave their arms around, and sometimes their behaviour seems disinhibited or bizarre. It is necessary immediately to help the child organise his behaviour. In order to concentrate on reading, spelling, and writing, and be able to direct his attention to these tasks, he must first sit still. Neither is fidgeting to be tolerated. It may be necessary to remove all distracting objects and pictures. Firm but kindly insistence usually produces a good and productive working relationship.

One consistent problem for clumsy children is handwriting. Writing is usually taught at the same time as reading, and it is through writing that the child is most likely to develop a knowledge of the structure of words. In a chapter on handwriting, Spalding (1957) says: 'The teaching of writing should precede reading. This is fundamental!' Peters (1970) writes 'Teachers must also teach handwriting. It must be swift and effortless . . . The swifter the writing, the better the spelling. This is only be be expected, since the child that writes swiftly is accustomed to writing familiar strings of letters together and there is a high probability of certain strings occurring and recurring in English.'

It is probable that the clumsy child will not want to write. (This may sometimes be because he cannot spell and so does not know what to write.) He will need sympathetic understanding and reassurance. Many children who have found manipulation of crayons and scissors difficult when they were younger have avoided using them since that time, and will need to be encouraged to begin again. Ingenuity may be called for. Many a time a clumsy child has 'talked' his way through one subject after another to avoid having to 'do' anything. But enthusiastic involvement in the child's interest will quickly provide opportunities for him to draw, make, and even to label anything, from an African tribal mask to sausages in a pan. However, as studies have shown that training in visual discrimination between shapes does not improve word recognition (Gorelick, 1965; Rosen, 1966; Beck and Talkington, 1970), the sooner he can be persuaded to write letters, the better.

Handwriting must be taught (Jarman, 1977). Often, the clumsy child has no idea how to hold a pencil. He must be shown how to sit comfortably, holding the pencil correctly in his writing hand, supporting his weight with the other. The teacher should sit on the right side of the left handed child so that movement is not impeded, and so that she can see what he is doing. He must learn to start and finish each letter in the correct place, so that the letters will join naturally one to the other. When letters are joined up in a plain 'cursive' script, words are seen as visual gestalts, and the spaces fall automatically between the words. Individual letters that use the same movement patterns can be taught in groups. The child says the name and the sound of the letters, and then 'talks' his way through the movements, so 'd' would be 'around, right up, and down'. The reversible letters are taught in different groups and are rarely confused. Some children confuse phonemes that sound alike, for example t, d; c, g; p, b; or letters that look alike, for example n, r, h.

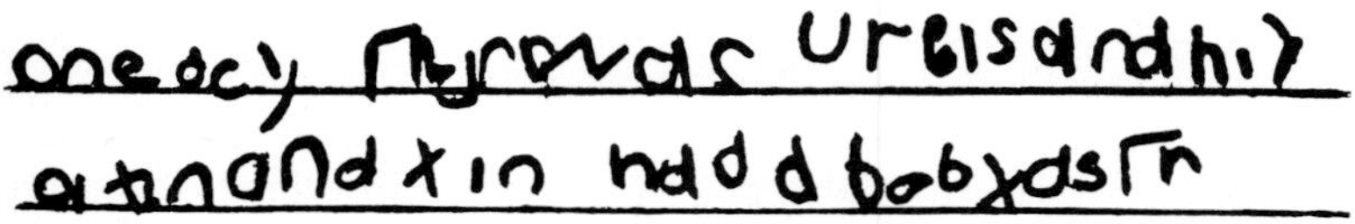

Fig. 11.1 Writing by a boy aged eight years. Amongst other problems, the child's writing shows lack of spacing between words. When cursive script is used, words are seen as visual gestalts and the spaces fall automatically between the words.

The small changes in position of mouth, tongue and throat when voicing the vowel sounds 'a, e, i, o, u' make differentiation between them particularly difficult. Learning to write the letters correctly, whilst naming them, will help him to make these discriminations and associations. It is often easier for a child to discriminate between the 'names' of letters than between the 'sounds'. Most clumsy children, taught correctly, make more progress using handwriting to help them learn words, but a typewriter can enable a child to produce work he can feel proud of if he is continually depressed by his handwritten efforts. It can slow down the child who works carelessly, giving him more time to think. It can motivate the reluctant child to write, just as recording his own thoughts on the tape recorder encourages the reluctant talker to speak, or the child who cannot write to organise his thoughts to produce stories, or poetry.

For children who have great difficulty in remembering the sound/symbol associations, and in differentiating between letters that look alike, the Alpha-beta plastic script letters* may be particularly

*Alpha-beta, No. 2 set script. Trexo Plastics. Available from toy shops.

helpful. They feel different from each other — a, e, i, o, u, are tactually quite dissimilar and they are non-reversible and colour-coded. They are invaluable for teaching reading. The intangible word becomes concrete. The number of letters in the word becomes finite. They can be arranged until they are correct before the word is written down, eliminating the humiliation of failure.

Fig. 11.2 Use of plastic script letters. The rack is not essential.

For the child who cannot recognise rhyme each word is a unique entity. Because he does not hear that words sound alike, or see that they look alike, he can not generalise, but must attempt to work out each new word without connecting it to those he may already know. Research has shown that this difficulty in categorising sounds could be an important cause of reading failure (Bradley and Bryant, 1978a). Using the plastic letters, the child can make a word that he knows, such as 'and'. He can then be encouraged to think of other words that rhyme with 'and', and can add and subtract letters to make the new words. In this way he can learn that words that rhyme, though different, often have letters, and sounds, in common. He will use words that are within his own experience. Once he has worked out his word 'group' he can record it in a word group book. All the words in his book will be meaningful to him. The letters are ideal for word building. The vowels are all one colour, so it is easy to see whether each syllable contains at least one vowel. The most resistant 'non-starters' succeed using these letters. They precede the writing, but do not replace it.

Rhythm in movement is important. We develop 'patterns' of movement in writing words (Peters, 1970). Often the clumsy child's mind is moving faster than his hand. Words and letters may be omitted. He does not learn the correct pattern. He does not practise it. Therefore spelling does not develop as an automatic motor memory. Each word has to be recalled anew. Memory for movements made while tracing over shapes or letters may help visual recognition (Hulme, unpublished data). Many remedial methods are based on this premise. (These methods have been clearly described by Cotterell (1970). The original texts are often difficult to obtain.) Thus the clumsy child is at a distinct disadvantage, and it is not surprising that his spelling is usually poor.

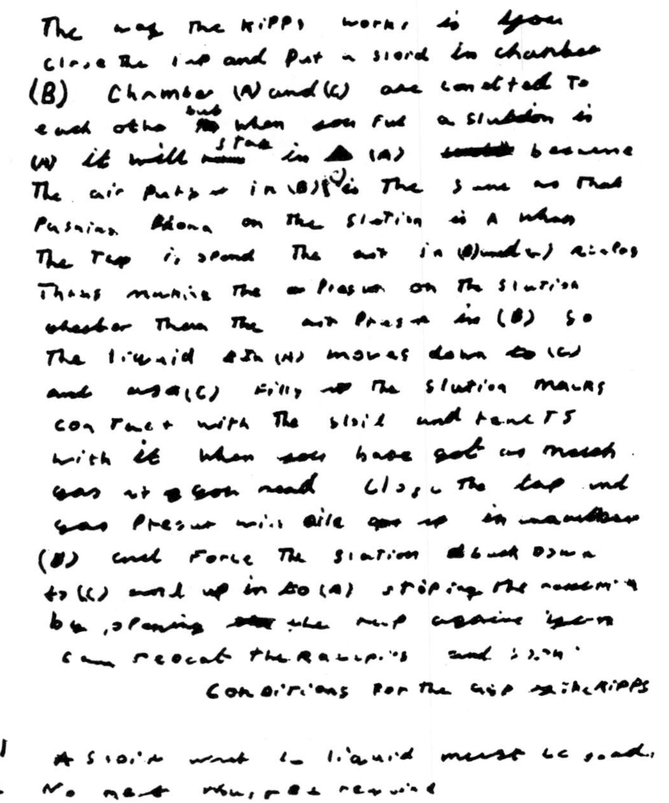

Fig. 11.3 A science lesson copied from the board by a 15-year-old boy. He had an IQ of 139 (W.I.S.C.) but was unable to understand these notes.

Because his spelling is poor he may be very bad at copying words. This is important, especially if he can read, and if he is familiar with the content of the material he is copying, as his teacher is unlikely to accept that simply 'copying' words can be difficult. But though he may recognise words, he may not be able to remember what they look like when he cannot see them. He cannot recall them. When he looks back to his own book, he cannot remember how to spell the word. He looks up again. He finds the place — although it may be the wrong place. He looks back to his book. Copying a long word, he may have to look at the text several times. His copying will be inaccurate. He is sure to take much longer than his colleagues (Bradley, unpublished data). Visuo-spatial and visual discrimination difficulties, and difficulty in concentrating, can only add to his problems.

If he is copying from the board, he has two alternatives. He can 'read' the text into a tape recorder, and then take it down later in his own time, using the spelling strategies he has been taught. Or he can be given a photocopied print taken from the book of a competent child. If neither of these alternatives is possible, he should be provided with a copy of the text by the teacher. One boy managed to cope if his neighbour softly read the text to him, so that he could copy 'by ear'. If the text to be copied is in a book, a card or marker under the line being copied is an invaluable aid, and will substantially reduce both the time taken and the number of errors (Bradley, unpublished data).

Having established a relaxed relationship, the experienced teacher will be able to make an assessment of the needs of the child based on observations such as those described here, and on a short piece of undirected writing and of reading, if the child can read and write at all. The most reluctant child quickly responds and cooperates when he realises that you are competent to help him.

If a child can only read and write poorly, or can read but not write, and it is obvious that this is related to his clumsiness but not to other influences, more formal investigation of his written language skills can provide diagnostic information.

The following tests and procedures are useful, but many other tests are available. Some are described by Thomas (1970), and most available assessment material, as well as teaching aids and reading material, are permanently exhibited at the Centre for the Teaching of Reading at Reading University.

Formal assessment

Reading

If the clumsy child cannot read, does he understand that print stands for the spoken word? Show him a small illustrated book, and see if he can guess what the words are likely to be. *The Neale Analysis of Reading Ability* (MacMillan, London) tests accuracy, time and comprehension when reading in context. Is the child reading in line with his age and intelligence? What type of errors does he make? Does he read one word at a time? Does he 'predict' or guess intelligently? *The Schonell Graded Word Reading Test* (Schonell and Schonell, 1950) tests whether he is reading in line with his age and intelligence. Can he read words out of context? Can he analyse words? Look for a discrepancy between his performance on this test and his performance on the Neale test.

Miscue analysis (Goodman, 1969).   The child reads a passage which has been selected as appropriate for his age and ability, but on which he is likely to make a reasonable number of errors. The errors that the child makes as he reads aloud are noted on the tester's own copy (and recorded on tape if possible). These are analysed as grapho-phonic, syntactic or semantic errors. Take, for example, the sentence, ' "He was swaying" said the judge.' If 'swaying' is read as 'swinging', it does not alter the sense or structure of the sentence, but indicates that more attention needs to be paid to the grapheme-phoneme correspondence within the word. However, to read 'sand' for 'said' would substitute an unsuitable part of speech, a noun where a verb is needed; 'jug' for 'judge', though both nouns, would not be meaningful. Most children would correct such syntactic or semantic errors because they would not 'sound right'. But some children hear, but are not aware of such errors. Or they may say 'that doesn't sound right', but not realise why, or that they have to look more closely. Practice in listening, using language, word games (particularly those where he has to supply a missing word) and reading stories written by the child himself about his own experiences should prove helpful.

Silent reading.   A suitable passage is selected. Questions can be answered orally, though in some tests the answers to questions can be underlined. Many children, particularly those with speech production difficulties, are happier and more competent at silent reading that at reading aloud.

The information from these assessments should enable you to decide what strategies the child is using to read, and how to help him. With a non-starter, you may have to begin by explaining what reading is. It is also surprising how some intelligent children try to decode one word at a time, and 'prediction' needs to be explained to them. Games can be played: 'You opened a letter to yourself. It said Dear . . . '. 'Once upon . . . , there were three . . . ' . Record the sound/symbol associations he does not know (Cotterell, 1969). Associations that he confuses visually/aurally/orally may be clarified through handwriting lessons and the alpha-beta letters. Does he need practice in blending sounds? Phonic Rummy (1973) is a simple card game devised for just this purpose, but is also useful for practice in word recognition and in categorising sounds, and recognising sound families. All children consider it a treat, and the first of the twelve graded packs is suitable even for 'non-starters'.

Can he analyse a word that he does not know? Non-starters learn to construct and to analyse words using the alpha-beta plastic letters, and then through writing. Analysis is best taught through writing, beginning with the child's speech. 'Spellbound' (Rak, 1972) is a useful workbook for more advanced children, which shows how to construct and analyse words. The spelling rules are systematically introduced, with related exercises to be done using a multi-sensory approach.

Does he guess a word by its shape? He must learn to analyse words. If he consistently guesses words from their outline, he will need to learn how words are constructed, by using the plastic letters, and through writing words that are meaningful to him.

If he recognises 'chunks' or groups of letters, but finds it impossible to blend sounds or analyse words, you should use the 'chunks' that he knows to introduce new words, for example, 'and', 'h/and', 'st/and'.

Does he need to have his attention drawn to consistent inaccuracies? Many clumsy children are late starters at reading, but often catch up by the age of nine or ten, when they can read in context about familiar subjects. They may miss a line, or be unable to decode a difficult word when the context gives them no clue. But slight inaccuracies seem acceptable when they do not distort the meaning. However, it can be a different story when they have to cope with new subjects and therefore new words and context, often during their secondary education. Children who rely on the twin strategies of word recognition and context but have not developed an adequate phonological/analytical strategy, 'inexplicably' begin to fail (Bryant and Bradley, 1978b). One bright teenager explained: 'I like reading novels now. But when I read a text book, I have to read every sentence three times. The first time I work out each word. The second time I put the words together. The third time I read the sentence to get the meaning'.

In these circumstances, context and prediction cannot help the child. Word construction and analysis skills must be developed. Discussing the content of a text with him before he reads it would help, but this is not always possible when someone is searching for information. But obviously we must help the poor reader by reading to him and helping him to 'keep up' with information and literature comparable with his intelligence and understanding.

Spelling

Schonell Graded Word Spelling Test (Schonell and Schonell, 1950). Is the child's spelling age near his reading age? Is there a recognisable pattern of errors e.g. using the *Schonell Diagnostic Spelling* test (Schonell, 1932) of regular and irregular words. This test often pinpoints the problem of a child who can read but is still experiencing unexplained frustration with his written work. Frequently he will score well on the regular words, but fails on the irregular words. Moreover this failure often reveals more about his knowledge, or lack of knowledge, of spelling rules and strategies than is apparent when he writes regular words. His problem is difficulty in the recall of words; because he can work the regular words out phonetically and he can read, his very real problem is often missed.

Children who perform equally badly on both lists are usually trying to recall the word visually, without recourse to phonetic strategies.

Teachers may find that they can devise similar, but more appropriate lists to test their pupils. The 'regular' list, for example, could include more simple consonant blends.

There are many excellent remedial spelling manuals available (Cotterell, 1969; Rak, 1972), but Cotterell's comprehensive work on the teaching of spelling is to be particularly commended. She points out that no regular word needs learning, as it can be worked out. If the child can write 'hip', he can write hippopotamus! It often helps to make this point with a child who only feels competent to write one-syllable words. A simplified version of this approach to regular words is as follows:

Regular words, e.g. re mem ber, up set
1. Say the word clearly (and correctly).
2. Say the word (tap it out if necessary) in syllables.
3. *Rule:* each syllable must contain at least one vowel.
4. Write the word, vocalising as he writes.

Irregular words can be learned using the multi-sensory technique where each letter is named (not sounded) as it is written. This form of Simultaneous Oral Spelling was first described in the Gillingham Stillman programme (1977).

Irregular words, e.g. light, ought
1. Have the word written correctly.
2. Say the word.

3. Write the word, spelling out each letter as it is written. (Thus, as he sees each letter, he hears its name and also receives kinaesthetic feedback through the movement of the arm and throat muscles. This not only reinforces sound/symbol association but also sequencing and recall in each modality.)
4. Check to see if the word is correct. Cover it up and repeat the process.

Ideally, the words to be learned come from the child's own vocabulary, and will be used in sentences. Words are learned as groups or families, so that the child learns to generalise. This will quickly reduce his learning load.

Words that cause particular difficulty at school (for example, science vocabulary) should be considered. Can they be worked out, or do they need to be learnt?

The second method, for irregular words, is effective for learning the most resistant word, which will be 'fixed' if it is practised correctly three times each day (which takes no more than thirty seconds) for five or six consecutive days. But this must not deteriorate into rote spelling, which is a different thing entirely. Indeed, one boy succeeded in raising his school spelling test score from three words to sixteen words correct out of twenty by changing to this method. He also reduced the time he spent learning the words that week from his usual 90 minutes each night, to ten minutes. Children who find a phonic approach difficult are usually surprised to find that they succeed using this method.

It is vitally important that words are not mis-spelled. Unless words are written correctly, the right motor patterns are not reinforced.

Writing

Ask for a story to be written, but provide an unusual subject so that a 'prepared' piece cannot be written.

Usually the clumsy child will say that he cannot write one. If he does write, his story, or even sentences, may be repetitious, and words, and even phrases, may be missing.

Difficulty with handwriting apart, the most usual reason that the clumsy child produces little or no written work is that he does not know where to start. If the structure is provided, as for example where he has only to write one-word answers, or underline an answer, he frequently finishes his work at the same time as the rest of the class. This in itself should provide a clue to the teacher. If he does write, the order of the words in the sentence are often incorrect. He seems to lose the thread.

He is trying to carry too heavy a load. He has to think out his answer. This may be his first problem — how to structure it? Then he has to organise it into the correct sequence, into sentences, perhaps paragraphs. He has to remember capital letters and full stops. He also has to work out how to spell the words. Finally, he may manage these tasks quite well, but then his mind races ahead of his clumsy hand, and he omits words, even phrases, that he 'wrote' in his head.

Even young children can learn to do a simple précis. Using a piece of scrap paper, he thinks his answer or story out in three parts. 1. Introduction. 2. Ideas (development). 3. Conclusion. He writes (1) at the top of the page, (2) beneath it and (3) at the bottom of the page. He then 'thinks' through his story, writing key words in the appropriate section. (1) and (3) may only rate one word each, to provide the ideas for an introductory and a concluding sentence. 'Ideas' are jotted down, using only key words, as they occur, and then 'ordered' (by numbering) to the desired form. The story proper is then begun, falling automatically into three paragraphs if this is required. Only one sentence has to be 'structured' at a time, and the idea of the 'whole' stays there without parts being forgotten, or left out, whilst words which are difficult to spell are worked out.

For older children who find both the physical and the structural aspects of writing difficult, and who have to learn to cope with exams, it is a good idea to practice exam techniques. They must learn to allocate time for reading the whole paper first and to selecting the questions they can best answer. A précis which can be done in a few minutes is time well spent. For the child who has a real struggle against time an elaborated précis is an effective answer.

By reminding the child that originality is important if work is to be individual the verbal non-writer may be persuaded to express his ideas in poetry. He often finds that he can express his original ideas in his own language in writing once he is released from the notion that lines in poetry must be structured to be equivalent, and words rhyme.

The tape recorder is an invaluable aid for children who find that a written record is beyond their capabilities in certain situations. At all ages it can be used to record information in class. Notes can then be made from the recording in the student's own time. Children who are too young to 'précis', or whose writing skills are inadequate, can learn to record coherent stories on tape. Homework can be 'said' rather than written.

The child who can read, but not write, can make an important contribution to class project work by finding information for the group.

Different types of problems among clumsy children

We began by pointing out that clumsy children are individuals, and as such they have different types of problem to each other. Now that we have reviewed the possible areas where problems can occur we can see how likely it is that this should be so. Some of these problems can be illustrated with examples.

The non-starter

Tom is an intelligent boy of seven and a half years. He cannot read or write. He tries to work words out phonetically as his teacher has shown him, but he does not know the sound/symbol associations and cannot analyse or categorise words visually or aurally. His school books are full of inaccurately copied work which he cannot read.

Tom is clumsy. His poor sense of rhythm is obvious in his writing. He has a sweet voice but his 'tune' is a collection of notes, without form. He cannot break words up into syllables.

His spoken language is disorganised and muddled. He mixes the order of sounds in a word, and the order of words in a phrase. He frequently 'loses' the word he wants to use.

He has a good vocabulary. His immediate recall of a story is good. But he cannot remember the words of any songs or rhymes. His attempts are incorrectly ordered.

Tom's school class is formal and structured. His family expect conformity in standards of behaviour. He is told to 'stand up; sit down; say thank you'. This structuring helps him present as a charming, well-behaved though clumsy little boy. But it is possible that he has not had as much opportunity for practising structuring his own language as he needs.

Programme: Poor Tom is attacked on all fronts simultaneously! He begins physiotherapy. He starts with a programme of movement/rhymes/songs/singing games to help him develop a sense of rhythm both in movement and in language, and to further develop his body image. *This Little Puffin* (Matterson, 1969) is an excellent source book, and there are several children's records which prove popular. Singing games require rhythm and sequence in tune, words and movement. Memory for one helps recall in the other modalities. Using bright felt-tip pens, large patterns can be made on newspaper with rhythmical movements to songs and records. All these activities must be undertaken in such a way that the child thoroughly enjoys them. Some children will prefer pop songs to nursery rhymes, square dancing to singing games.

Tom's written language programme begins with the organisation and structuring of his own language. He is encouraged, in conversation, to think carefully about what he is saying. He will write his own book, which will be 'published'. His 'book' will be typed so that he sees the words in a new setting, in typeface. One 'edition' will be the same as the original, but another will use the same words to make a different story so that he must recognise the words in a different context.

He wants his book to be about an airport crash truck. We cide that 'All Sorts of Transport' will allow more scope. It also provides us with our first word group, 'or'.

We tip the Alpha-beta plastic letters on to the table (see Fig. 11.2). In four lessons, using the plastic letters that he can feel, he masters all the sound/symbol associations that he failed to learn using letter cards at school.

Rules are introduced as they arise. The first one is to tap out the syllables in a multi-syllable word. Each syllable must contain at least one vowel.

Some children do not know what to say. Tom does not know when to stop. He has to be heped to slow down and to structure the first sentence. It begins 'The airport crash truck . . . '. With irregular words that the child does not know, name the letters that are needed one at a time and let the child find them, or show him what they are. When the 'plastic letter' word is complete, let him have a good look at it. Then, push the letters apart, and ask him to make the word again. When he can do this, push the letters back into the pile of all the plastic letters on the table, and ask him if he can make the word now. Help him until he can do it.

If the word is a regular one, Tom is encouraged to say the word, to listen, and to say what he thinks the first sound is. If he is correct, he says the whole word (or syllable) again, and then the first part of it (for example, crash, c; crash, cr) and listens to hear what letter or letters he needs next. At first this can be a painstaking business. In Tom's case he had great difficulty with the blended sounds. But as long as the words are his, so that they are in his vocabulary and are meaningful to him, and he does not undertake too much at a time, progress will be slow but sure. When the word has been made with the letters, it is jumbled up again, but this time he says the word in the same way as before, as he finds each letter.

When his first sentence has been made with the letters, it is recorded in his book. Tom has been taught how to write the letters correctly, so he will check that he can still make the first word with the plastic letters, and will discard it before he records it. If he can make it but not remember it, it stays on the table. He begins the sentence with a capital letter, and uses cursive writing. He names each word before he writes it, and vocalises it as he writes if it is a regular word, or spells it out if it is an irregular word. He illustrates his work.

If the child cannot write the letters, the teacher must instruct him in this, and he makes his first copy on a piece of paper. Systematic teaching of letter writing follows in ensuing lessons.

It is pointed out to Tom that 'transport', 'airport', and 'sort' have a sound in common. Leaving the letters for 'or' on the table, and making each of the words around them in turn, he soon 'sees' what it is. He can think of one more — 'sport'. He begins a second book for word groups, in which he records his 'or' words.

Each day he spends a few minutes using his plastic letters to make his new words. He refers to his record if he cannot remember them. He writes them in his practice book using the appropriate multi-sensory method. He tries to think of another sentence using the same words.

Tom plays Phonic Rummy. Set 1 introduces the vowel sounds which he finds difficult, but his pleasure in the game overrides this.

Tom has learnt to recognise words more quickly than to recall them. He learned to used context and prediction in his reading so that by the time he was eight years one month his reading age on the Neale Analysis of Reading Accuracy was seven years, ten months, Comprehension eight years, one month, but on the Schonell Graded Word Reading it was only six years, six months. Schonell Spelling age was seven years.

In class, he was now able to read board work into a tape recorder, and write it down when he had time. His spelling was taken mostly from phonically irregular words that he needed for class subjects.

Penny was a teenager with a reading age of seven years. She could not analyse words. She could write 'and', 'the', 'it', and her first name. She had had endless remedial tuition without success. She felt that the plastic letters were babyish, but tolerated them when they were kept in a chocolate box.

Her 'book' centred around her interests in clothes, shopping, and outings. She could not read or spell 'out', but happily recited the old counting rhyme 'O.U.T. spells 'out' and 'out' you must go'.

She knew much more than she thought she did, once she learnt how to integrate her knowledge. She learnt word groups based on letter 'chunks', 'and', 'all', 'ent', using the multi-sensory techniques. She was recently prompted to write a letter of complaint to a shop.

Adam was nine and a half. He could not read or write even his name. He did not talk much. After much motivating talk about writing his own book, he uttered only one word — 'apple'. Eventually, The Apple Book, by Adam (in the shape of an apple!) was made. The content was simple — just Adam, a tree, a car, and his dog, illustrated. But before it was finished the sentences were being written without help, and new ideas were being offered for the next book.

Children who can read but not write

Brian was only six and a half but had been referred earlier still for the same reason — he was a behaviour problem. He was also of superior intelligence, very verbal, and a mine of information. He managed to knock over a mattress that was leaning against the wall as he walked through a hall ten feet wide.

He had no friends. He was depressed and anxious. He could read the encyclopaedia. He could not write. He could not do art, games, tie his shoe laces, or sing in tune. Other children found his clumsiness and dribbling obtrusive.

He would not write, so he was persuaded to try some of the Frostig (Frostig and Horne, 1964; Frostig and Maslow, 1969) visuo-motor exercises whilst he learnt to handle a pencil, as his awkward grip had impeded his movements, and covered the direction he was following. He progressed to designing Norman shields for a class project. It was time to insist on writing. The first lessons were fraught. His hand tired easily. The letters he made were gross. But this physical problem obscured another.

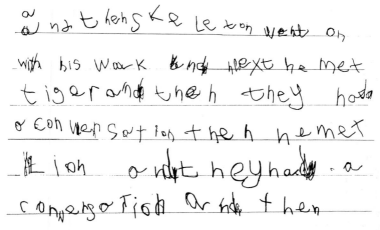

Fig. 11.4 Brian describes the skeleton's adventures in huge, sprawling writing. Note the difficulty in forming certain letters, e.g. d, e, n, h.

Though he was such an excellent reader, he could not remember the letters, or the order of letters, in his own name. He wrote bus, 'bsu'. He began, without being told, to spell out the names of the letters in all the words he wrote. Suddenly he was writing incredible stories in huge, sprawling, untidy writing.

Sean was an older version of Brian. He was nine years old, of superior intelligence, clumsy, hopeless at all games and activities; reading, but sitting through each school day without writing a word. He could write, very untidily. His spelling was in no way adequate to express his ideas. He had no knowledge of word structure or of spelling rules. He said that when they were given a topic to write about in class, he had many ideas, but he didn't know how to start. His teacher admitted that if the class had to fill in one word answers, Sean's were as quick as anyone else's.

Sean was pleased to learn that 'regular' words could be worked out. Once he realised that there were rules that would help him know how to spell, he set about learning the word groups and irregular words that he most needed.

His first précis took an hour with the teacher's help. He took it home to write the story. When he returned he brought a note from his mother which said 'Sean began his story on Friday evening. The first sentence took him an hour and a half. Then I sent him to bed. He continued all Saturday morning, and by lunch time had written half a page. Would you please tell him how long he is to spend on his work'.

The second précis took Sean eight minutes, and he almost completed his story in the lesson. His first poem summed up his problems beautifully.

Fishing
Hook in finger, line in tree
Fishing is the thing for me.

Shortly afterwards, he wrote the poem 'Autumn'. (Fig. 11.5)

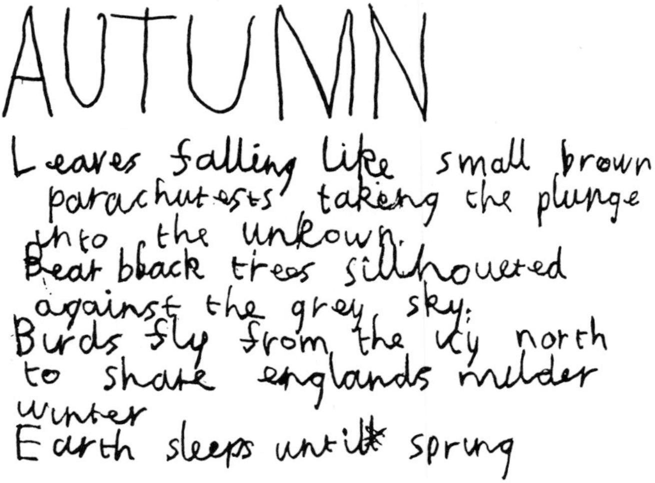
AUTUMN
Leaves falling like small brown parachutests taking the plunge into the unkown.
Beat black trees sillhoueted against the grey sky.
Burds fly from the icy north to share englands milder winter
Earth sleeps until spring

Fig. 11.5 A poem about Autumn by a nine-year-old boy who could not write before remedial help but who was of superior intelligence.

Jan was a delightful, well adjusted ten year old, who was referred for investigation because she never stopped talking to herself. Her problems were with visual perception, fine motor coordination and auditory discrimination. In fact, this clever little girl had devised her own method of compensation for her difficulties, for by talking to herself she provided a verbal cue to coordinate her visual and motor activities. In written language this frequently broke down because of her auditory perceptual problems and lack of rhythm, and the sub-skills involved in word construction; auditory discrimination; blending; syllable breakdown and rhythm.

She had incredible insight into her behaviour: 'I talk out loud because it helps me, to remember where I am (when writing) and to remember what I've put. If it's not all right I put words in.'

Most tasks involve a spatial relationship, and it was interesting listening to Jan telling herself what to do, so that she made the correct move. When asked not to talk, she failed.

Jan attended a speech and drama class. Listening helped improve discrimination and pronunciation of words. This helped syllabification and subvocalisation for spelling. Dancing helped her develop motor coordination and rhythm, and mime helped her to integrate and direct movement and vision without the verbal cues. With lessons on word structure and spelling rules, and an understanding of her problem by those helping her, she progressed well.

REFERENCES

Beck A, Talkington L 1970 Frostig training with head start children. Perceptual Motor Skills 30: 521–522

Boder E 1973 Developmental dyslexia: A diagnostic approach based on 3 typical reading-spelling patterns. Developmental Medicine and Child Neurology 15: 663–685

Bradley L, Bryant P E 1978a Difficulties in auditory organisation as a possible cause of reading backwardness. Nature 271: 746–747

Bryant, P E, Bradley L 1978b Why children sometimes write words which they do not read. In: Frith U (ed) Cognitive processes in spelling. New York, Academic Press

Bradley L, Bryant P E 1979 The independence of reading and spelling in backward and normal readers. Developmental Medicine and Child Neurology 21: 504–514

Cotterell, G 1969 Check list of basic sounds (also in appendix of: Assessment and teaching of dyslexic children (eds) Franklin and Naidoo

Cotterell G 1970 Teaching procedures. In: Franklin A, Naidoo S (eds) Assessment and teaching of dyslexic children. I.C.A.A., London

Cotterell G 1973 Diagnosis in the classroom. Centre for the Teaching of Reading, Reading University

Fernald G 1943 Remedial techniques in basic school subjects. McGraw-Hill, New York

Frith U 1976 How to read without knowing how to spell. Paper to British Association (Lancaster Conference)

Frith U 1978 Spelling difficulties with and without reading difficulties. In: Frith U (ed) Cognitive processes in spelling. New York, Academic Press

Frostig M, Horne D 1964 The Frostig program for the development of visual perception. Follett Educ Corp, Chicago

Frostig M, Maslow P 1969 Move-grow-learn. Follett Educ Corp, Chicago

Gillingham A, Stillman B W 1977 Remedial training for children with specific difficulty in reading, spelling and penmanship, 7th edn. Massachusetts, Educators Publishing Service, Cambridge

Goodman K 1969 Analysis of oral reading miscues; applied psycholinguistics. Reading Research Quarterly, V: (1): 9–30

Gorelick M 1965 The effectiveness of visual form training in a prereading program. Journal of Educational Research, 58: 315–318

Jarman C 1977 A helping hand for slow learners. Special Education, Vol 4, No 4

MacKeith R 1977 Children who are not speaking at three years of age. Developmental Medicine and Child Neurology, 19: 573

Matterson E 1969 This little puffin: nursery rhymes and songs. Penguin Books

Naidoo S 1972 Specific dyslexia. Pitman, London

Nelson H, Warrington E K 1974 Developmental spelling and its relation to other cognitive abilities. British Journal of Psychology 65: 2, 265–274

Peters M 1970 Success in spelling. Cambridge Institute of Education

Phonic Rummy 1973 (Kenworthy Educational Service, Inc., Buffalo, New York)

Rak E 1972 'Spellbound': Phonic reading and spelling. Educators Publishing Service, Cambridge, Massachusetts

Reid J F 1969 Dyslexia: a problem of communication. Educational Research, 10: 2, 126–133

Rosen C 1966 An experimental study of visual perceptual training and reading achievement in first grade. Percept Motor Skills, 22: 979

Schonell F J 1932 Essentials in teaching and testing spelling. Macmillan Education, London

Schonell F J, Schonell F E 1950 Diagnostic and attainment testing. Oliver & Boyd, Edinburgh

Spalding R 1957 The writing road to reading. William Merrow, New York

Thomas R 1970 Reading and spelling tests. In: Franklin A, Naidoo S (eds) Assessment and teaching of dyslexic children. Invalid Children's Aid Association

SUGGESTIONS FOR FURTHER READING

Atkinson E J, Gains C W 1973 An A-Z list of reading and subject books. National Association for Remedial Education.

Burgess T, Burgess C 1973 Understanding children writing. Penguin, Harmondsworth

Clark M M 1974 Teaching left-handed children. Hodder & Stoughton, London

Cambridge J, Anderson E M 1979 The handwriting of spina bifida children. An advisory booklet for teachers and students. Association for spina bifida and hydrocephalus, London

Dean J, Goodacre E, Root B 1976 Teaching young readers, part 1, (age 4–9). ed. Longley C, B.B.C. Publications

Foster J L (ed) 1977 Reluctant to read. Ward Lock Educational, London

Farnham-Diggory S 1978 Learning disabilities. Fontana/Open Books, London

Goodacre E, Harris J, Harrison C, Foster J, Walker C, ed: Longley C 1977 Reading after ten: teaching young readers part 2. B.B.C. Publications

Jarman C 1979 The development of handwriting skills. Blackwell, Oxford

Mackay D, Simo J 1976 Help your child to read and write, and more. Penguin, Harmondsworth

Rutter M, Maughan B, Mortimore P, Ouston J 1979 Fifteen thousand hours. Open Books

Psychiatry

Origins of emotional disturbance in the clumsy child
There are two major sources of anxiety for the clumsy child: his fear of
being 'handicapped', of being made to feel different from his peers,
stigmatised, labelled 'physically inept'; and frustration within him
which creates tension and rejection within the family. When motor
incoordination is found in association with other neurodevelopmental
delays, intellectual retardation or hyperkinesis, the stress and anxiety
arising within the child, may so completely dominate the clinical
picture that a child may be initially referred to a Child Guidance Clinic
for psychiatric help (Walton, 1965; Bakwin, 1968) or deemed
'maladjusted' and a recommendation made for special education
(Dare and Gordon, 1970). Often only after diligent enquiry into the
child's developmental history and an objective assessment of basic
academic attainments may the true origin of a child's feelings of guilt,
inadequacy and resentment be identified and remedied.

There are few systematic studies of the psychopathology of clumsy
children. Gubbay (1975) describes the temperamentally vulnerable
pre-school child who may withdraw when confronted by failure and
frustration; and the more assertive, extroverted child who may be
subject to violent temper tantrums, restlessness or negativistic
behaviour. In the early years at primary school, there is increasing
need to be physically and emotionally independent. P.E., a dance
class, or team games can become the sole reason for school refusal on
that day (Annell, 1949). The physically inept child quickly becomes
the class scapegoat and a focus of teasing and bullying by staff and
pupils. A child 'rejected' at school will turn increasingly to the
sanctuary of an accepting home and over-protective parents, and
succumb to a lifelong dependent existence. He may also become
depressed (Weinberg *et al.*, 1973).

Neurodevelopmental delay and cerebral immaturity associated
with emotional immaturity, poor impulse control, and poorly
developed psychological defences against anxiety, may further render
the child vulnerable to stress (British Medical Journal, 1962; Bakwin,

1968). The clumsy child with a sufficiently resilient personality can learn to compensate in some other sphere of activity. Sadly, it is often the child from the disadvantaged home who, when frustrated and demoralised, may resort to serious anti-social activities such as firesetting and vandalism, with the self-perpetuating cycle of alienation, negativism and academic failure (Wolff, 1967). In addition to the anti-social and neurotic disorders, a smaller group of hyperkinetic children has also been described by Francis-Williams (1963), Illingworth (1968) and Shaffer (1973).

Parental reactions to a clumsy child

Alternating over-protection and feelings of resentment are common reactions to the demands of coping with the handicapped child. Extremes of either attitude can give cause for concern. Excessively anxious, worrying parents may find themselves unwittingly complying with the child's every wish, thus creating an artificially non-stressful environment for the child, in which the developing personality remains emotionally immature, dependent and egocentric. The child may also be a victim of the parents' own projected anxiety and guilt feelings for their 'afflicted' child. Conscious or unconscious rejection of a child by its parents should be viewed with concern. Perfectionist parents' unrealistic expectations of their child's abilities may unknowingly arouse resentment and anger in the child, in response to their unrelenting disapproval. Overt parental rejection and in particular early maternal rejection and deprivation has been suggested as a cause of delayed physical maturation in the child (Powell, 1967). Bentovim (1973) has commented on the serious impairment to the child's capacity for forming stable relationships in later life, when parental rejection is overt.

Parental indulgence of the 'over-valued' child may ultimately exclude other healthy offspring from their affections: sibling protest, in the form of aggressive, anti-social acting out behaviour, and a depressive withdrawal (Mattsson, 1972) may be the prime presenting feature of a child referred to a psychiatric clinic.

In summary, the clumsy child is particularly vulnerable to developing a psychiatric disorder that may be more incapacitating than the physical disability (Graham and Rutter, 1968). Early recognition of the disturbance with the appropriate therapeutic intervention will be rewarded, with the child and his family maturing through their experience.

Case history: Steven D

Steven was six years old when brought to the attention of his local school psychological service, as a result of a routine screening programme for educationally 'at risk' children.

Detailed psychometric assessment suggested areas of retarded development of motor coordination. (Assessed on the Stott Test of Motor Impairment). Perceptual maturity on the Frostig Developmental Test of Visual Perception was consistently twelve months below chronological age. Assessment in the physiotherapy department confirmed poor eye-hand coordination, intense fidgetiness and restlessness with associated movement of face and feet throughout the assessment session. His IQ on the Stanford-Binet Scale was 97. His primary school had commented on the child's restlessness and distractibility in class. Attempts at written work were 'clumsy' and 'untidy' (Fig. 12.1), but reading ability was good.

Fig. 12.1 Steven's handwriting.

A remedial physiotherapy programme was instituted on a regular basis, only to be interrupted shortly afterwards by Steven's sullennness and refusal to participate in exercises either at hospital or at home. Continued anxious and negativisitic behaviour led to his referral to the child psychiatric clinic.

Steven is the younger of two children by his father's first marriage. Fetal distress during the second stage of labour necessitated his delivery by Cesarian section and later nursing in a special care baby unit for a seven day period. His subsequent neglect and rejection by his natural mother (Fig. 12.2) effectively deprived Steven of the opportunity to achieve any degree of emotional or physical independence. When Steven was five years old, his father married a widow, a caring, concerned and maternal figure whom Steven accepted after a short but stormy period of readjustment. The arrival of his step-mother and her own two children and the diagnosis of his clumsy handicap were coincidental, but only served to accentuate Steven's personal feelings of alienation and rejection. At school he became difficult and demanding and on a number of occasions was incontinent of faeces. His sleep was repeatedly disturbed by frightening dreams of monsters and trolls. At the initial psychiatric interview, Steven impressed as an anxious fidgety child, a reluctant participant in an unstructured play situation. In later play sessions he became more relaxed, talkative and demonstrated his exceptional gift for story-telling. Two themes were to be repeatedly re-enacted in the course of six one-hour play sessions: the conflicting loyalties he felt for members of his family, and in particular his natural mother whom he felt had abandoned him; and his anxious rejection of his clumsy handicap.

To relieve himself of the burdens of his clumsy handicap, Steven often created his own imaginary companion, 'Naughty John' (Fig. 12.3), an impish lad who 'lived in

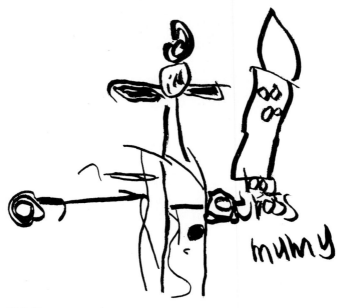

Fig. 12.2 'Cross mummy'.

Steven's tummy' and whose sole task in life was to make Steven drop things, and put objects in his way for him to fall over. In individual play sessions repeated references were made to 'fast-running trolls with strong arms and legs' that inhabited his fantasy world. Steven would often differentiate 'good trolls' from 'bad trolls', in respect of their superior agility. In a joint interview with the boy and his step-mother, later in therapy, we were to highlight a conversation Steven had overheard of his step-mother discussing the death of her first husband from a brain tumour. Ataxic symptoms had predominated in the clinic picture initially; and in Steven's mind, clumsiness became a sign of impending death and a source of extreme anxiety. Reliving this experience in the play situation appeared to have a strong cathartic effect upon Steven, with an immediate relief of his symptoms. Thereafter, Steven was to return to normal functioning emotionally. His school work progressed, his concentration improved, as did his active participation and enjoyment of his physiotherapy programme.

Psychiatric help for the handicapped family

Previous chapters have discussed in detail aspects of the practical and material help that is so necessary in the treatment of these children. By repeating what are possibly obvious principles of mental hygiene, I hope it will serve to remind us all, as professionals involved with clumsy children, not to lose sight of the child's own emotional needs when planning our treatment programmes. Diagnosing a clumsy handicap can represent a major emotional crisis for the child and his family. His parents may have sufficient personality resources to make the necessary adjustments, to accept their 'disabled child' and continue family life without disturbing the child's personal equilibrium. It is the less resourceful family or the family in adversity

Fig. 12.3 'Naughty John'.

that require most help from health and possibly mental health professionals. Pless and Pinkerton (1975), in their exhaustive review of the psychiatric sequelae of chronic childhood illness, have formulated the threefold principles of therapeutic intervention, through education, counselling and practical provision for helping handicapped families.

Education

Information, explanation and instruction are the therapist's prime educational tools. Parents need to understand what is happening to their child, how his coordination difficulties can be treated and the possible long-term effects of his handicap. This basic information should be imparted as quickly as possible after diagnosis in a factual and authoritative way, using simple and unambiguous language.

Practical provision

It is a healthy sign when parents ask how they may involve themselves more in the treatment of their child. We need to anticipate their request and be prepared to give them the specific help they require. Material provision for the handicapped child undoubtedly minimises any ambivalent or rejecting feelings parents may have towards a child they may regard as 'slow' or 'backward'. Indeed, parents use of such negative terms as 'awkward', 'hopeless or 'useless' will only serve to reinforce the childs' already dwindling self-esteem. Parents should be encouraged to emphasise the assets of their child's personality. Explanatory booklets and pamphlets can be valuable guidelines to the parent; discussion of the contents may provide an ideal opportunity for counsellors to correct misconceptions or the semantic confusions that frequently arise during the early months of treatment.

Counselling

Perhaps the key to helping the family with a handicapped child is the establishment of a trust and confidence between child, parent and the helping professional through a positive supportive relationship (Pless and Pinkerton, 1975). Freeman and Pearson (1978) have cogently detailed the principles of counselling, and stress the need for special counselling skills. The author refers the reader to their work for a more detailed account of counselling services for the physically handicapped child.

Counselling with parents. The therapist may not always find acceptance and caring attitudes in parents for their clumsy child, particularly if the child has become aggressive or oppositional in behaviour towards family or school. Psychiatrically disturbed parents, parents who are rigid disciplinarians or have unrealistic expectations of their childs' abilities, may succeed only in making their child feel worthless and hopeless, and be in danger of completely losing their childs' affections. Some rigid and defensive attitudes of parents may mellow with the establishment of a counselling relationship. However, it may be necessary to discover the origins of certain attitudes or feelings within a parent, to give them sufficient emotional insight to modify their behaviour towards their child. Enlisting the help of a psychiatric colleague should be considered. Parents often instictively resist referral to a psychiatrist, but a joint interview with the parents, the therapist and the professional counsellor can be a most productive way of securing the vital psychotherapeutic link. When referral to a mental health professional is not possible, counselling can be successfully continued by the primary therapist, with direct consultation with the professional counsellor. Psychologists in local child guidance centres may influence parents indirectly through the child's teachers. Their local knowledge of remedial guidance services and special educational facilities may prove invaluable, particularly so when prolonged parental rejection may necessitate residential schooling.

As a preliminary to the counselling process, making a formal contract with the family may inspire not only trust and confidence in the counsellor, but it ensures continuity of care, as well as providing a vehicle for the definition of one's therapeutic goals. The counselling role allows one to monitor family adjustment reactions and to identify early prejudicial parental attitudes.

Counselling the child. Although much of one's time is spent supporting the parents of the clumsy child, one must also give time to the child. Young children need to communicate their anxieties, whether it be worrying over their poor school performance, their criticism of a smothering parent, their loneliness or alienation from peers, or despair and a sense of total failure. Having a supportive relationship with the child can only increase the child's sense of self-worth. Psychiatric help for the child may be necessary when excessive anxiety, morbid thinking or persistently negative and difficult behaviour creates discomfort or suffering within the child, restricts his social activities or leads to conflict between the child and authority. Psychotherapy may take the form of supportive or play therapy in younger children (as illustrated in Steven's case history, pages 156 to 158) or interpretive or brief psychotherapy in the more mature child. Detailed description of the psychotherapeutic process is beyond the scope of this book and interested readers are directed to standard textbooks.

In conclusion, it is important to be aware of the predicament of counselling services at present. Many professionals who work with handicapped children are in a position to counsel, but the work is often poorly done; conversely, too few mental health professionals are either interested, or sufficiently cognisant of handicap in childhood (Minde *et al.*, 1971; Freeman and Pearson, 1978).

Suffice it here to remind therapists, teachers, or parents involved with clumsy children of the need for vigilance in recognising early signs of emotional distress, thereby averting the development of a psychiatric disorder that may be more incapacitating in the long term than their clumsy handicap. Behaviour checklists and questionnaires for screening children for emotional disorders are available for use in health clinics, hospital out-patient departments and schools (Rutter *et al.*, 1970; Richman and Graham, 1971).

Helping parents and children through counselling can be a most rewarding experience; it does demand a high level of professional competence and expert knowledge, a skill for the management of interpersonal relationships and a capacity for self-scrutiny. With our increasing awareness of the needs of the clumsy child and his family for long-term psychological support, there must inevitably be an expansion of services and greater opportunities for training of professional counsellors to accommodate these needs.

Medication

Clumsy children may present hyperactive or restless behaviour of sufficient intensity as to interfere with their education or treatment. The judicious use of stimulant drugs (Cantwell, 1975), minor tranquillisers or tricyclic antidepressants (Huessy and Wright, 1970; Winsberg et al., 1972; Waizer er al., 1974) have been found to be effective; major tranquillisers, however, may produce a deleterious effect on learning or cognitive functioning (Hartlage, 1965; Conners, 1972).

Prognosis

There is as yet little available data on the long-term outcome of children with specific neurological disabilities; the overall impression (Dare and Gordon, 1970; Denhoff, 1973; Gubbay, 1975) is a favourable one for their physical disability. The relatively poor prognosis suggested by prospective and retrospective studies of clumsy hyperactive children (Weiss et al., 1971), with antisocial behaviour, educational retardation, depression and psychosis prevalent in early adult life (Spivak, 1967; Menkes, 1969), should serve to remind therapists involved with clumsy children of the constant need for vigilance for early signs of emotional disorder so that if necessary the child can be referred for psychiatric help immediately. The findings of Rutter and his colleagues (1970) from the Isle of Wight study indicate the five-fold increase in psychiatric disorders in children with neuro-epileptic disorders and the two-fold increase over children with other chronic physical illness. The increased association of psychiatric disorders with central neurological disorders alerts us to the mental health of clumsy children and their families.

REFERENCES

Annell A L 1949 School problems in children of average or superior intelligence; a preliminary report. Journal of Mental Science 95: 901–909
Axline V M 1964 Dibs in search of self. Ballantyne, New York
Bakwin H 1968 Symposium on developmental disorders of motility and language. Forward, Pediatric Clinics of North America 15: 565–567
Bentovim A 1973 Disturbed and under five. Special Education 62: 31–36
British Medical Journal 1962 Clumsy children. British Medical Journal ii: 1665

Cantwell D 1975 A critical review of therapeutic modalities with hyperactive children. In: Cantwell D (ed) The hyperactive child: diagnosis, management and current research. Spectrum, New York

Conners C K 1972 Stimulant drugs and cortical responses in learning and behaviour disorders in children. In: Smith W L (ed) Drugs, development and cerebral function. Thomas, Illinois

Dare M T, Gordon N 1970 Clumsy children: A disorder of perception and motor organisation. Developmental Medicine and Child Neurology 12: 178–185

Denhoff E 1973 The natural life history of children with minimal brain dysfunction. In: de la Cruz F F, Fox B H, Roberts R H (eds) Minimal brain dysfunction N.Y. Academy of Sciences, New York, p 188–205

Francis-Williams J 1963 Problems of development in children with 'minimal brain damage'. In: Bax M, MacKeith R (eds) Minimal cerebral dysfunction. Little Club Clinics In Developmental Medicine No 10, London Spastics Society, pp 39–45

Freeman R D, Pearson P H 1978 Counselling with parents. In: Apley J (ed) 'Care of the handicapped child, Clinics in Developmental Medicine No 67, London Spastics Society, pp 35–47

Graham P, Rutter M 1968 Organic brain dysfunction and child psychiatric disorder. British Medical Journal 3: 695–700

Gubbay S S 1975 The clumsy child. Study of Developmental Apraxia and Agnosic Ataxis. Saunders, London

Hartlage L 1965 The effects of chlorpromazine on learning. Psychological Bulletin 64: 235–245

Huessy H, Wright A 1970 The use of imipramine in children's behaviour disorders. Acta psychiatrica 37: 194–199

Illingworth R S 1978 Delayed motor development. Paediatric Clinics of North America 15: 569–580

Mattsson A 1972 Long-term physical illness in childhood: Challenge to psychosocial adaptation. Paediatrics 50: 801–811

Menkes M, Rowe J, Menkes J 1967 A twenty five year follow-up study on the hyperkinetic child with minimal brain dysfunction. Paediatrics 39: 393–399

Minde K, Silver S, Killou D 1971 Some aspects of cerebral palsy and its treatment as perceived by the families of 49 children. Lával Medical 42: 1041–48

Pless I B, Pinkerton P 1975 Chronic childhood disorders — promoting patterns of adjustment. Henry Kimpton, London

Powell G F, Brasel J A, Raiti F, Blizzard R M 1967 Emotional deprivation and growth retardation simulating idiopathic hypopititarism. New England Journal of Medicine 276: 1279–1283

Richman N, Graham P 1971 A behavioural screening questionnaire for use with three year old children: preliminary findings. Journal of Child Psychology and Psychiatry 12: 5–33

Rutter M, Tizard J, Whitmore K (eds) 1970 Education, health and behaviour. Longman, London

Shaffer D 1973 Psychiatric aspects of brain injury in childhood: a review. Developmental Medicine and Child Neurology 15: 211–220

Spivack G, Haines P E, Spotts J 1967 Adolescent symptomatology and its measurement. American Journal of Mental Deficiency 72: 74–95

Waizer J, Hoffman S P, Polizos P, Engelhardt D 1974 Outpatient treatment of hyperactive school children with imipramine. American Journal of Psychiatry 131: 587–591

Walton J 1963 Clumsy children In: Bax M, Mackeith R (eds) Minimal cerebral dysfunction. Little Club Clinics in Developmental Medicine No 10: London Spastic Society, p 29–45

Weiss G, Minde K, Werry J, Douglas V, Nemeth E 1971 Studies on the hyperactive child VIII: Five year follow up. Archives of General Psychiatry 24: 409–414

Weinberg W A, Rutman J, Sullivan L, Penick E C, Dietz S G 1973 Depression in children referred to an educational diagnostic centre: diagnosis and treatment. Journal of Paediatrics 83: 1065–1072

Winsberg B, Bialer I, Kupietz S, Tobias J 1972 Effects of imipramine and dextroamphetamine on the behaviour of neuropsychiatrically impaired children. American Journal of Psychiatry 128: 1425–1431

Wolff S 1967 Behavioural characteristics of primary school children referred to a psychiatric department. British Journal of Psychiatry 113: 885–893

Conclusions

Although the majority of children with significant learning, coordination and/or perceptual motor disorders will only be mildly to moderately affected, little is known about the exact prognosis for these children and which are the factors that enable apparent recovery to occur. Overall intelligence must be important in overcoming any difficulty, but not necessarily in removing it. There is no doubt that specific learning disorders can persist into adult life, for example reading difficulties which remain in spite of adequate help during childhood. In many instances the causes are a complicated mixture of social, educational and medical factors. It may be possible to deal with some of these, for example bad housing denying the child any chance of doing satisfactory homework, inappropriate teaching from the child's point of view, and unrecognised refractive errors distorting the visual input. In some ways the more complicated the aetiology the better the prognosis may be, given the possibility that there may be a number of contributing causes that can be rectified.

The brain in early life is a very adaptable organ: for example, after acquired lesions in infancy it is remarkable how the central nervous system can compensate for injuries. However, there must be a limit to this adaptability. If for some reason connections cannot be made between one part of the brain and another and there is no way of circumventing such defects so that the necessary associations are developed to acquire a skill, the disability will persist into adult life. There are many among us who avoid some aspect of motor or language skills because we are no good at it, however well we may learn to compensate. The reasons for this are likely to be complex. In spite of the possibilities for the maturing brain to circumvent anatomical lesions there may be instances where this is impossible. If a skill is not acquired at an optimum period of learning it will become increasingly difficult as we grow older, not least because of the changing educational curriculum. However, if sensory input is not meaningful for prolonged periods it is likely to be inhibited. The ability of the brain to inhibit stimuli is considerable, as is shown by the amblyopic eye in the squinting child when the affected eye may remain virtually blind throughout life although it is usually functionally normal as a sensory end organ. This raises the possibility that sensory input of various kinds (e.g. auditory) may be inhibited if they are distorted or not of immediate use. If this continues for any length of time the inhibition may become permanent. Such mechanisms interfere with learning and may be one of the reasons why, if a special skill is not acquired by a certain age it is possible that it never will be, or that it will become very difficult to acquire later.

Other factors which affect prognosis will include motivation, appropriate treatment and teaching, the seriousness of emotional and behavioural disorders, and the personality of the child.

Difficulties of prognosis and of evaluating treatment and special education must underline the importance of well planned follow-up studies and well organised therapeutic trials, but are no excuse for doing nothing to help these children in need. Early recognition and sympathetic help are likely to prevent many of the emotional and behavioural complications of learning disorders. It seems logical for anyone who is tackling a new task and having difficulties in so doing to obtain advice and guidance from someone who has mastered it. This may make the learning of the skill considerably easier and will also tend to build up confidence and improve motivation, which is so essential. The difficulties experienced are unlikely to be the same from one child to another, so that although there can be guidelines in the approach to remediation it does seem important to adapt any theory of teaching to the child and not vice versa. Also it must be accepted that it is equally important to identify the child's assets so that these can be developed and success can be ensured in some tasks.

It is hoped that the various suggestions that have been made to assist the clumsy child will be useful, but careful management is essential. When the child and parents are first seen there must be a detailed explanation of what is thought to be wrong and how this may explain what has happened in the past. Then the reasons must be given for the analysis of the child's difficulties in greater detail, and also for the need to find tasks which are likely to be relatively easy. It is particularly important to discuss the necessity for having to involve a number of different people. Most parents will realise that no one person can give all the answers, and that those who claim to do so are to be mistrusted. The doctor, although not an educational expert, can coordinate the services for the child with learning difficulties. He may be the first professional person to be involved outside the immediate school situation and is in a good position to take an independent view of the child's predicament. Medical diagnoses may have to be made in the first instance, such as short sightedness or high-tone deafness. Emotional problems have to be dealt with, involving as they do more often than not the whole family. The doctor can ensure that the services available are mobilised on behalf of the child. He can explain to the parents the role of each expert asked to see the child, and help to interpret the results of the various examinations to them. It is essential that the parents are involved in a number of the assessments, such as that of motor performance, so that they can realise just how significant their children's difficulties are. Also if possible they must play their part in treatment, as the majority of them wish to do. Their role in the educational field may be limited and require careful guidance but it has been shown how much they can do to help at home. However, some children will accept tuition from almost anyone except their parents, and a watch must be kept for tensions that may develop.

The doctor therefore has a role to play in diagnosis and assessment and in organising the services available. Problems often persist so that the doctor has to remain involved for long periods. He must maintain his efforts to try to solve difficulties as they arise and be ready to discuss the current situation; all of which is time consuming but may be an economy in the long run. As time goes on, the doctor's role may change, in part, to that of a questioner. He must check on the progress at school of a child with learning difficulties. If remedial education is suggested and arranged, there is no certainty that it will be of benefit, as with any other form of management, and there are certainly arguments for an outside agency occasionally asking for a report on school progress. The doctor may well have to elicit the help of the social services. In fact a strong case can be made for the doctor working closely with a social worker who is experienced in the type of problems which may arise. The opportunity to visit the home to see the family circumstances at first hand, and to dicuss the difficulties in an informal atmosphere can be invaluable.

This underlies the desirability of the 'team approach'. This concept may have given rise to a lot of platitudes but, nevertheless, if people from various disciplines are involved their benefit to a particular child is likely to be lessened if they hardly know each other and rarely meet. If the doctor is to act as the coordinator he must know the ideas and opinions of the psychologists, therapists, teachers and others. If not, the parents are likely to be given contradictory advice and the end result may be increasing confusion and a deteriorating situation. There are sometimes advantages in 'case conferences' when all the members of the team can meet and discuss the problems of a particular child. Divergent views can be expressed, if these exist, and a consensus opinion reached before this is given to the parents, with the reasons for the course of action suggested. However, case conferences must not be an end in themselves and, if there is not careful selection, time and resources can easily be wasted. Quite often it is sufficient for members of the team to talk to each other informally, although this is usually only possible if they work in the same building.

Although the doctor may be the best person to act as the coordinator, there will be occasions when someone else will be more acceptable, for example if the parents have a particular rapport with another specialist. It is also essential that personal links are developed between those working in the health services and those in the educational field. Otherwise the problems faced by different experts will not be appreciated. Whatever may be said and done by all the different people involved in trying to help the clumsy child, the teacher in the classroom will almost always be a key figure.

Communication is bound to raise problems, for example ensuring that assessments carried out in a hospital-based unit ever reach the classroom where they are most needed. The more personal these communications can be the more efficient will be the results, although this is likely to be a counsel of perfection when so often there is no time for members of the assessment team to visit individual schools. Invitations can always be offered to teachers and others to be present at the assessment, and visits to schools made whenever possible.

Difficulties of communication are an argument for carrying out most assessments within the community, either at the Health Centre or in the school. It should be possible to assess and plan management for most clumsy children within schools with cooperation between class teacher, psychologist, remedial teacher, physical education teacher and school doctor. Specialist clinics could not cope with referral of all clumsy children. If 2 per cent of children in a population of 1 million are severely affected this would imply referral of 20 new children per week. Such referrals would not be in the interest of most children in any case. Specialist opinion is best reserved for children with complex problems or where a second opinion is necessary.

Although in the past children with learning disabilities or perceptual-motor difficulties were often not identified or given the help they needed; times are changing. The increased interest shown by so may people working in different disciplines must be consolidated to the benefit of these children. There is much still to be learnt and the ideas expressed in this book are only a start, and hopefully an incentive to better management of the problems presented by this common disability.

Appendix 1: Illustrative case histories
Children's work; parents' letters; school reports

Clumsy children and their parents are among the most appreciative of all patients. These case histories illustrate their problems in the words of the children, their parents and teachers.

Case T is Tom and Case S is Sean in the chapter by Lynette Bradley, which includes details of their remedial help. (W in the headmaster's letter in Case T was a similar child to T.) Case G is also of good average ability but illustrates problems of speech, relationships with peers and late academic development with sympathetic help. Case N is of very patchy ability (SS 4 to 13 on the verbal scale and 4 to 12 on the performance scale of the W.I.S.C.) However, he performs in the low average range overall (V.Q. 85, P.Q. 92, FS 87 on W.I.S.C.). On the Neale Reading test, at age 7 yrs 2 mths, his accuracy was 7.0 yrs and comprehension 8.2 yrs. He tended to rush at tasks in a disorganised fashion and to concentrate poorly and attempt to change the subject if he was in difficulty. He had a poor short term memory for sounds and scored very poorly on the Visual Memory sub-test of the W. I.S.C. On two visual sequencing tasks from the Aston Index he experienced great difficulty, scoring well below the norms for his age. When reading he used a 'look and say' approach, finishing off sentences in his own words after picking up the gist from the first part. He has little idea about spelling and has great difficulty in putting his ideas on paper but chatters constantly. Performance improves when structure is imposed on him but he resists imposed discipline strongly. Thus, socially and academically he is unsuccessful and poses great problems for parents, teachers and peers. Group play or drama therapy might help him but his needs are so individual that they are very difficult to meet. Cursive writing, individual remedial teaching and a programme of varied physical activities have led to some improvement.

Case J illustrates typical feeding and dressing problems with later perceptual-motor educational difficulties in certain subjects (maths, geography). The patchiness of his coordination is common and still unexplained. He is of placid temperament and average ability; though there have been problems at different stages his outlook is good.

Case T aged 7 yrs 6 mths

Extract from a letter from T's headmaster dated February 1977

Thank you very much for your letter about W. But, although he had a better term in the autumn, the word 'better' is, I am afraid, stricly relative. From your point of view, dealing as you do with children who are very backward for one reason or another, there has been encouraging progress. But from our point of view, of course, he is still at a stage well below that already reached by boys in his form who are two years younger. We now have another boy T whose parents have been in consultation with one of your colleagues, who is just as backward (though two years younger). Neither of these are anywhere near being able to tackle the very simple exams set to the rest of the form at the beginning of this term, when we do our half-yearly exams; and consequently have to appear as unplaced at the bottom of the list.

We can obviously persevere with T for another year or more, but W has now reached the stage when he still cannot cope with the normal curriculum of our lowest form, yet is the oldest and biggest boy in the form and is beginning to show signs of 'feeling his age'. It is quite clearly useless to promote him on social grounds, as he will simply learn nothing in the form above, where there is not the expertise from which he has certainly benefited in our bottom form.

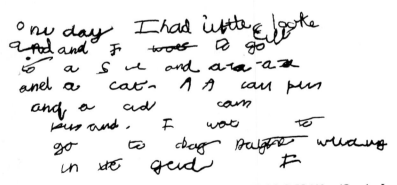

Fig. A.1 Writing to dictation. T, aged 7 yrs 4 mths with W. I.S.C. IQ 110+. 'One day I had a little look. I looked and looked with all my might. I saw little daffodils wandering on the hill like little crowds of people.'

We are fast approaching the stage, in fact, when I shall have to tell his parents (as I warned them initially I might have to) that not only can we do no more for W here but that, if he stays on beyond July he is going to be an embarrassment to us and to himself. Indeed, not to put too fine a point on it, in everybody's interest, I ought to give his parents notice to take him away at the end of July, or, to stretch a

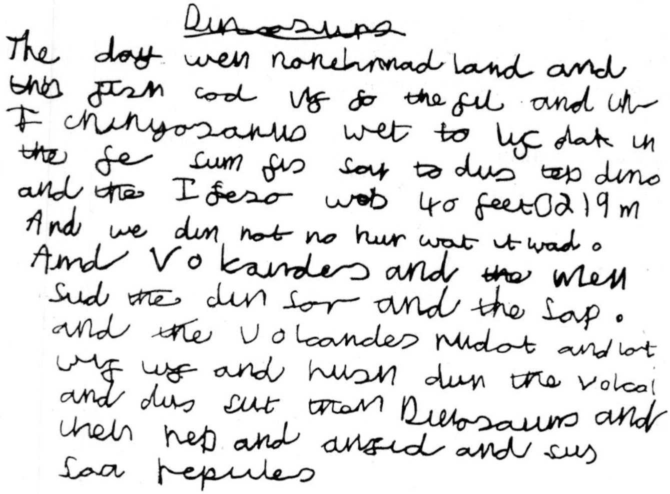

Fig. A.2 Performance aged 7 yrs 4 mths by T copying from the blackboard.

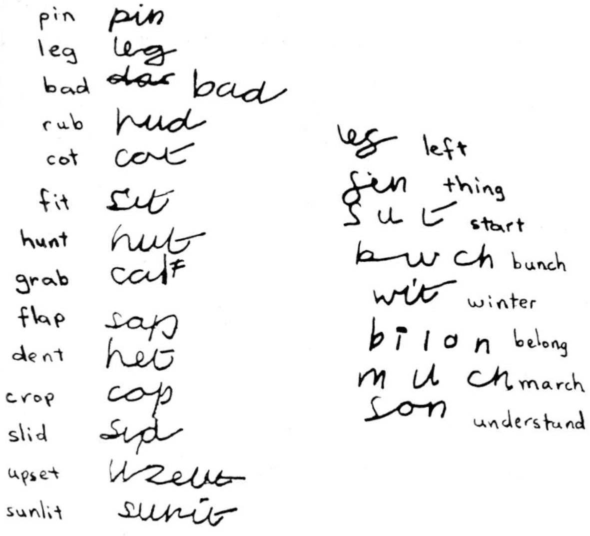

Fig. A.3 T: spelling test aged 7 yrs 4 mths.

point, my successor here (I am retiring then) ought to get him removed next December.

Obviously here is where we all very urgently need your expert advice. He needs a special school. I think his parents can afford some

HELPING CLUMSY CHILDREN

fees, but probably not boarding fees. Can you advise us as to the best course for action for W? We shall all be most grateful for your help in what is now becoming an urgent situation.

T aged 8 yrs 7 mths
School report spring term, 1978
Final place: 7th   No. in form: 16

General report	This report is a joy to write. We are all delighted with T's progress, as you must be. I admire his tremendous effort and determination. What more can I say except well done both of you!
Maths	His enthusiasm is a delight to watch and his progress in the last three weeks has been unbelievable. I am delighted with his progress.
English	He has worked so very hard for such a long time. This term he has seen the rewards of his hard basic work. With this foundation he will I feel sure go on from strength to strength. Well done.
Science	Has continued to make good progress this term, his written work and retention of facts is good. I wish I could say the same about his behaviour.
Geography	An encouraging result. T has worked well and deserves his success.
History	Only a poor test mark at the end of the term prevented T from coming top in this subject.
Scripture	He has worked hard and deserved this success more than anyone else. I admire his determination.
Games/P.E.	Has adapted to this game very well and is a promising player in the making. Needs plenty of small skill practices to improve and understand the game further.
Art	An enthusiastic artist! He always works hard.

Headmaster: I am delighted with the progress made by T during the term. He contributes greatly to all aspects of school life and is a thoroughly pleasant member of the school. Well done!

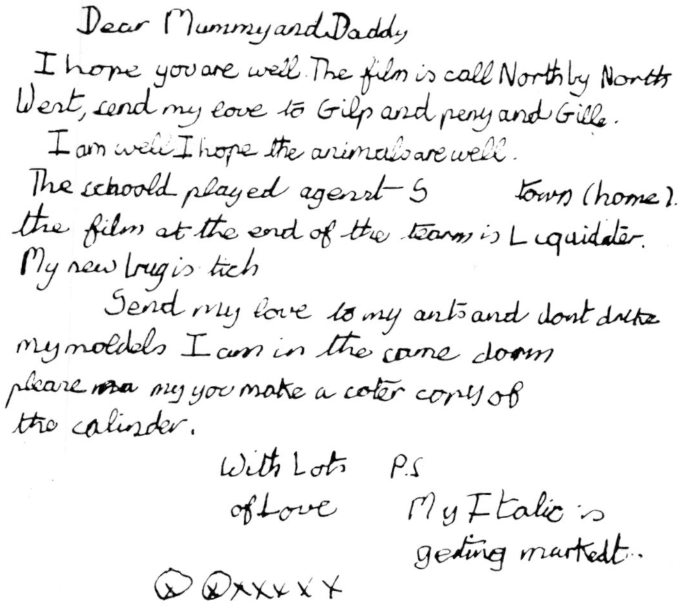

Dear Mummy and Daddy,
I hope you are well. The film is call North by North West, send my love to Gilp and peny and Gill.
I am well I hope the animals are well.
The school played agenst 5   town (home).
the film at the end of the team is L iquidater.
My new brug is tich
          Send my love to my arts and dont drtke my moldels I am in the came doom pleare rna my you make a coter cony of the calinder.

          With Lots   P.S
          of Love   My I talic is
                         geding markedt.

          ⊙ ⊙xxxxx

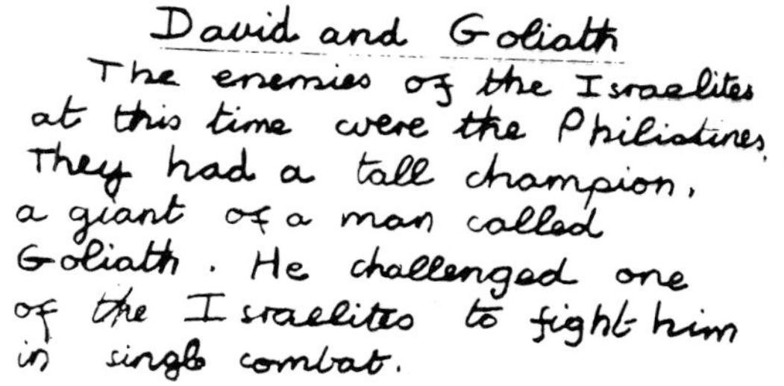

          David and Goliath
          The enemies of the Israelites at this time were the Philistines, They had a tall champion, a giant of a man called Goliath. He challenged one of the Israelites to fight him in single combat.

Fig. A.4 Now 9 yrs 2 mths, T's spontaneous writing (above) and copying (below) are much improved and he is coping at an academic private boarding school.

T aged 8 yrs 10 mths
School report, summer term, 1978
Final place: 8th   No. in form: 18

General report   I am again delighted with T's effort and progress this term. He is building steadily and surely on strong foundations. I am sure he will take this determination and go on from strength to strength. I am sorry to see him go. I have learnt from him myself.

Maths	A very disappointing exam mark because no one could question his hard work this term.
English	Again we have seen the results of his determination and dedication. His sentence construction has improved and he is developing a good style
Science	Examination: 3rd. Term: 8th. This is a very good result. He has worked well and deserves his success. Well done.
Geography	An amazing result. He has done very well.
History	An excellent term's work. Well done.
Scripture	This mark has been earned by sheer hard work.
Games/P.E.	I will be sorry to see T leave as he has made tremendous improvement since he came to the school. General coordination and basic skills are good. Always keen and enthusiastic.

Headmaster: T is a most polite and helpful member of the school and we will all miss his cheerful presence next term. I wish him every success.

T aged 9 yrs 3 mths
In December 1978, T's new school (which was a very academic, private school tolerant of eccentrics) gave the following report.

Latin	He is quite good at Latin but is held up by spelling (mainly copying) and reading problems. He will have to concentrate very hard to keep up.
English	He has produced some very clear and careful handwriting which has been pleasing. The content has been variable, sometimes quaintly expressed but he has got some quite fair work done.
History	He has done some very reasonable work on his project.
Geography	Tracing needs practice. Knowledge a little thin.
Maths	He tends to confuse methods, and is apt to jump to answers rather than write sums and work through intermediate stages.
Science	He has tried hard and made a little progress throughout the term.

French   Certain points he has grasped quite well but
                              others elude him. A great deal of work needed.

House report: T is finding some of the work difficult, and careful note
must be taken of the remarks above. He has settled in happily as a
boarder but is inclined to argue noisily if he cannot get his own way
especially at billiards! He must also learn to listen to instructions
carefully, and to act on them.

Case S aged 8 yrs 11 mths: test findings

With a discrepancy of 30 points between verbal and performance scale
scores, and individual subtest scale scores ranging from 6 to 19
(average score 10), an overall IQ figure would clearly be misleading.
Instead, it is better to quote the test ages scored for each subtest.

Clearly, with regard to pure verbal ability, S is intellectually
superior.

Information (from experience and education)	Adult
Similarities (logical/abstract thinking ability)	Adult
Arithmetic (concentration/arithmetic reasoning)	11 yrs 6 mths
Vocabulary (word knowledge from experience and education)	Adult
Comprehension (practical knowledge/ social judgement)	Adult
Digit Span (attention and rote memory)	12 yrs 6 mths
Picture Completion (visual alertness/ visual memory)	15yrs 10 mths
Picture Arrangement (interpretation of social situations)	12 yrs 10 mths
Block Design (analysis and formation of abstract design)	11 yrs 2 mths
Object Assembly (putting together concrete forms)	12 yrs 10 mths
Coding (speed of writing and learning symbols)	less than 8 yrs
Mazes (planning and following visual patterns)	10 yrs 6 mths

On the Raven's Progressive Matrices Test, his score places him in
the top one per cent of his peer group.

S's lack of manipulative skills must frustrate him since he is verbally so very gifted. It also presents problems of relating to his peers, since his conversation is too adult for them, yet he cannot compete in things like football and running.

He needs very sympathetic handling — someone to cope with his verbal expertise whilst at the same time slowly teaching him practical skills.

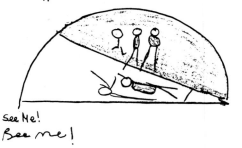

Fig. A.5 S: brilliant clumsy boy aged 8 yrs 11 mths referred because of difficulty relating to peers and academic underachievement. While he could have been seen purely as a gifted emotionally disturbed boy, an alternative remedial teaching and O.T. approach has been successful, combined with the boy's insight and determination. Note

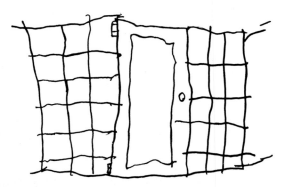

Fig. A.6 S: Asked to 'draw a man', S replied 'I can't draw, the man's on the other side', and drew a door.

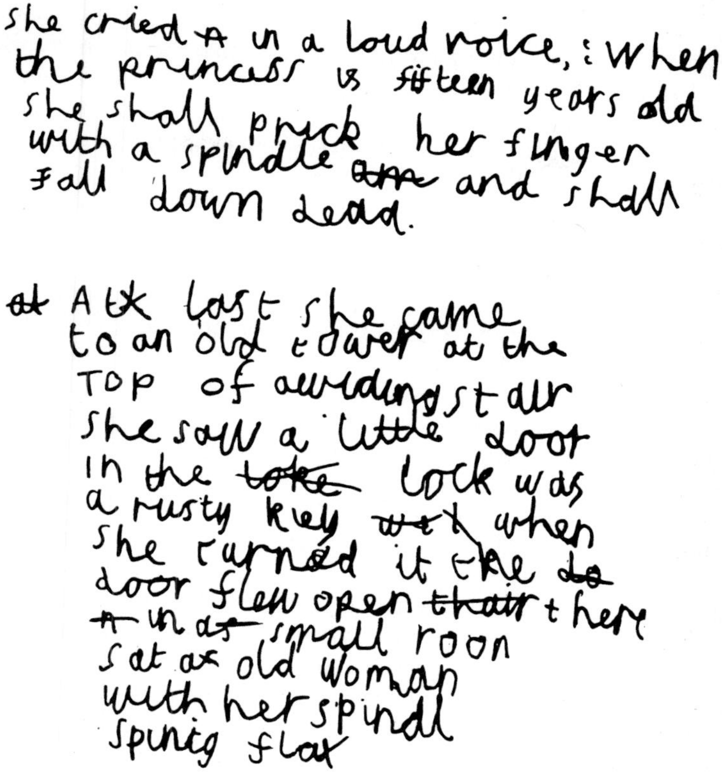

she cried A in a loud voice, : when
the princess is fifteen years old
she shall pryck her finger
with a spindle and and shall
Fall down dead.

at A tk last she came
to an old tower at the
Top of awinding stair
she saw a little doot
in the lock was
a rusty key when
she turned it the
door flew open there
A in a small roon
sat ax old woman
with her spindl
spinig flax

Fig. A.7 S: three months later showing difference between copied passage and writing to dictation.

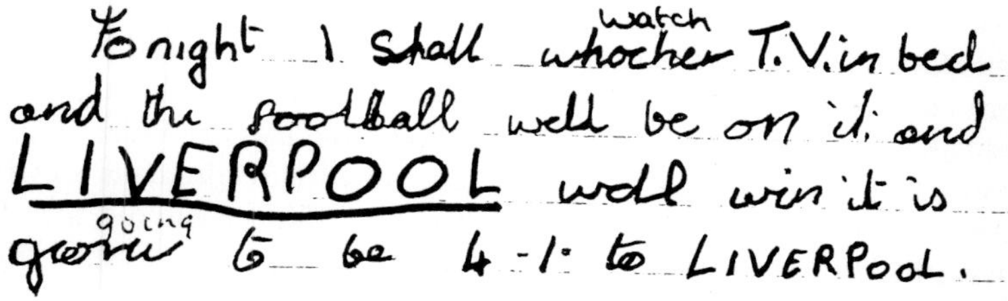

Tonight I shall watch whocher T.V. in bed
and the football well be on it and
LIVERPOOL wold win it is
goving to be 4-1 to LIVERPool.

Fig. A.8 S: now 9 yrs 7 mths after systematic remedial teaching and physiotherapy his spontaneous writing and spelling are much improved. This extract suggests that physical prowess might be more important to *him* than might be realised.

Case G

G's mother reports: he was a difficult and cantankerous baby who cried frequently and always at night. He eventually began sleeping through the night when he was 18 months old. Although G never crawled, by the time he was 12 months old he could pull himself up by grabbing hold of a piece of furniture and walk several yards. Unfortunately he was unable to organise his limbs sufficiently either to stand still or sit down and consequently overbalanced and fell, always banging his forehead.

From birth to 5 years G was a particularly demanding child, unable to amuse himself for any length of time, easily frustrated and subject to frequent temper tantrums. Apart from odd words, he did not really begin to talk until he was two and a half years old, and then it was very difficult to understand what he was saying. He did not play easily with other children but did not show any particular antipathy to his baby brother, three years younger than himself.

G did not learn to read or cope with number work in the infant school. His spatial relationships were poor for his age group and he had great difficulty in copying correctly and forming letters and numbers easily. He also had speech problems which took the form of stammering or rushed speech that did not make complete sense to the listener. G was unable to catch a ball or succeed in any physical activity which required careful physical coordination. His sense of rhythm was poor and he was unable to reproduce variations of pitch when he was singing.

We moved to Kent when G was eight and due to enter primary school. He attended a small village school and we grew increasingly concerned at his lack of progress. The headmaster said that we should reconcile oursleves to the fact that we had a child who was of very low intelligence. I insisted that G should be seen by the educational psychologist and this was done in 1968 (I think).

After the testing the only information I received was that although G obviously had some learning problems, his IQ was 'grammar school standard'. At the end of that school year I was able to send G to the primary school where I had been a supply teacher and which I knew had an excellent remedial teacher. G was in this class two years before going to secondary school. During that time his reading age slowly crept up to 8.9 yrs but he gained greatly in confidence and did so well in maths (after mastering reversals of numbers) that he was able to join the top set for maths at his new school. He was not put into the remedial group for English as I was taking it, but was placed with an experienced teacher in the set above. During this year G appeared to concentrate to some extent on developing his memory in order to

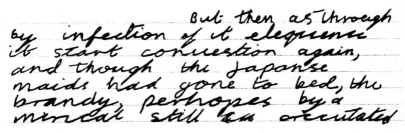

But then as through by infection of it elequence it start convuestion again, and though the Japanse maids had gone to bed, the brandy, perhapes by a mircal still am orculated

Fig. A.9 G: this boy aged 17 yrs 8 mths still has some difficulty with writing and spelling, has intermittent verbal dyspraxia and is very poor at ball games. However, by sustained effort with extra help his educational attainments have far exceeded expectations. He has become a karate expert also. The passage written here was dictated.

make up for his poor reading and writing skills. Thus, in tests which required one word answers to spoken questions he could come within the top five of a mixed ability group. It was towards the end of this year that a colleague gave G a Stanford Binet test which indicated an IQ of 119.

At the end of G's first year at secondary school we had to move back because of my husband's job. G had a very unfortunate term at the secondary school where he was 'dumped' in the remedial class and bullied unmercifully. By the Christmas he appeared to be developing school phobia, having constant headaches and stomach pains. I felt obliged to take him away from the school and succeeded in obtaining a place for him at . . . It was during this year at the age of 12 he achieved some success with reading (reading age of about 10 yrs) and was able to cope with the reading material connected with his school work.

During his time at this school G's academic standards began to improve although spelling and written English were very poor. He also began to enjoy rugby where brute force was more necessary than an exact skill. During his last two years there he became very highly motivated and surprised his teachers and myself by obtaining the following examination results in his fith year:

C.S.E.	Grade	O Level	Grade
Art and design	2	Art	D
Chemistry	1	Chemistry	C
Geology	1	Geology	C
Maths	1	Maths	E
Physics	1	Physics	C
Geography	1		
English	4		

G obtained a place at . . . College of Further Education the following year as there is no sixth form at . . . He took four O level subjects but spent a great deal of his time trying to bring his English up to standard. He obtained the following results:

Subject	Grade
Maths	C
Art	D
Computer studies	C
English language	C

G is taking Computer Science, Maths and Physics at A level in 1979. He has great difficulty in coping with the note-taking in Physics and producing neat and legible work under pressure.

Case N, now 9 yrs old

Early development

N's mother reports that he was: slow at walking, talking and sitting up unaided. Never crawled. (I have no great experience of children, but used his contemporaries as a yardstick.) He was 11 months old before he could sit without falling to one side.

Always very slow at feeding. N was never able to finish a bottle and during the week following his birth Baby N was the bane of the nurse's life. I would still be trying to feed him when all the other babies had finished their bottles and had been returned to their cots.

Feeding always has been, and still is, a problem. When a toddler he would never attempt to feed himself. He never appears to be hungry or particularly thirsty, although he has improved considerably in the past few months. As a toddler and a young child he could never be tempted by sweets, chocolates, etc. At the present time he disappears whenever I start to make a meal and will completely miss a meal if I allow him to. I have to coax him to eat. When he has been to parties, even though the other children will be eating jelly, etc., N will just sit there and not eat. Several mothers have told me this.

He has never put things into his mouth. He would not accept a dummy and never sucked at toys or ever attempted to put them to his mouth. I have noticed many children 'explore' things with their mouth, but I have never once seen N do this.

As a baby and toddler, I was never able to get N into any kind of routine, day or night. He has had periods of waking in the night, from birth to the present time, and even now has a very fitful kind of sleep. I

can never keep him covered in bed and he travels all over the bed
during the night.

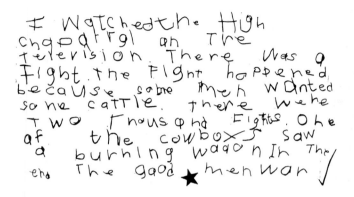

Fig. A.10 N: a boy aged 7½ of average intelligence. These samples contrast his
spontaneous writing to dictation ('big red bus' and 'an elephant has a trunk at the front
and a tail at the back') with his work for his tutor. The former was typical of his school
work. The latter, though the ideas are his, represents copied work, hence the seemingly
perfect spelling. However, it does illustrate difficulty in distinguishing upper and lower
case letters. He also shows confusion between some vowels (o/a) and uncertainty in
writing some letters (r, n, h, a, g, m, f). More detailed and systematic remedial teaching
has led to a substantial improvement and his school reports are now encouraging.

At the time I first went to Dr . . . , N was particularly bad and
Melleril syrup was prescribed for him, but even this did not seem to
improve matters.

When N began to walk, he was always falling and constantly
stumbling. Outings were a nightmare, as they always ended in tears,
cuts and bruises; sometimes he hurt himself quite badly when he fell.
When he got tired, he was much worse. This still applies today
although he is at times very sure-footed and adventurous.

When he was three to four years old, compared with other local
children N was very timid — he could not use the rides, etc. on the
recreation ground with anything like the skill of children of his age
and younger.

N has always had difficulty drinking from a cup, and even now he
will very often jerk and spill. I have to only half-fill cups.

N wanted to ride a bicycle (two-wheeler) like the other children. It
took many many weeks of intensive learning sessions before he could

get the hang of it and even now he cannot turn in tight circles, or do any of the 'circus' tricks that my next door neighbour's little boy can do at the age of five.

He would never attempt to dress himself, do up buttons, put on gloves, etc.

Schooling

N went to a playgroup for two mornings a week for two hours each morning at the age of three. He then went to a pre-school nursery for three mornings a week from 9 to 12 o'clock. He had difficulties at both these places as I was told he would not join in with the other children, would not do as he was told, would not play at one thing for even a short space of time. As he kept having bad chests and would go for a week and then be off for two, I ascribed a lot of his difficulties to this. With the benefit of hindsight, I see these difficulties in a different light, but at the time it seemed that N was just an extremely naughty child.

He then went to primary school. His infant teacher told me eventually that she could not do anything with him and that she had washed her hands of him. She said she left him all day to play in water as that at least kept him quiet. She said he had 'social difficulties' and hinted that I was to blame.

One of the things I had noticed when N attended this school was that every day the other children came out carrying little things they had made such as hats and never once did N make or paint anything. I pointed this out to her and she said it was because N *would* not do anything. I questioned if this was *would* not, or *could* not, but she said it was his negative attitude to everything. She also said he was lazy and would not attempt to do anything for himself, i.e. dress himself or fasten his shoes. She told me do do nothing at all for him, and I was to leave him to sink or swim. Needless to say, this approach achieved nothing.

Incidentally, while all this was happening, I had consulted the Health Visitor on several occasions, made frequent trips to the Clinics and been to my G.P.

We then decided N should go to a private school with small classes and he started there in April, 1976.

From the moment he commenced, Miss K (Head of junior school) picked up his abnormal behaviour and advised me to consult my G.P. I did this and he told me to come back in six months. Miss K persevered, but with no success and the school eventually gave me a letter to take to my G.P. Even then my G.P. did not take much notice (I gained the impression that I was considered to be the neurotic mother of an only child) and it was only after my G.P. had had a conversation with the Head that we were referred to Dr . . . (psychiatrist).

Present situation with regard to schooling

Miss K is concerned regarding N's future. She feels she cannot keep him with the kindergarten much longer, and yet if he is put with the boys of his own age, he will be totally out of his depth. She wants to be told how to deal with him as apparently he has retreated into his shell. He lolls about and will do nothing unless forced to do so on a one-to-one basis. He remains silent and does not talk to the staff. This is totally unlike N at home.

The other boys tease him and ridicule him because he cannot do the work, and because he cannot play cricket and football. This in turn makes him peevish and upset as apparently he desperately wants to join in. Miss K says she has tried, in a simple way, to explain his problem to the other boys but because they cannot see anything wrong with N they are unable to grasp the situation.

N goes to a private tutor (Mrs P) for 1½ hours every Thursday afternoon. He loves to go and does not regard the work he does with her as *work*. It appears to me that he gets through as much work with Mrs P in the short time he is with her as he does all week at school.

Extra activities

N goes boxing twice weekly. I explained his difficulties to the coach when N first started, and the coach has been very tolerant and patient with him. N cannot do exercises, etc. as well as the other children and cannot keep up any degree of concentration. This means that one minute he will be lined up with the other children and the next wandering away.

He goes horse riding twice weekly. More or less the same things happen here. As with the boxing and everything else he does, he never wants to go and is tremendously nervous. It would be so easy to say 'Oh, well, you don't need to go'. However, once he actually gets on the horse, he loves it and tries hard to ride properly. With all these activities he loves the associated hustle and bustle, and wants to know about everything, i.e. how to feed the horses, how are they ill, what all the men at the boxing do, what jobs have they got, and so on — question after question.

He goes to a little music class to learn to play the recorder and he goes to drama. Both the teachers (who were warned beforehand!) say the same thing about N — that he lacks concentration and confidence and yet is talented. The recorder teacher cannot get him to do the simple fingering of which he should at seven be capable, but she does other things to compensate for this.

General remarks

N irritates most people. He is restless, appears not to listen, and unless told beforehand of his problems, people jump to the conclusion that he is lazy, spoiled, and just plain naughty.

N craves the company of other children — when I take him to the beach or the recreation ground, he will run to join other gangs of children. He loves to play with other children in the road, but he gets on better with children younger than himself. Older children and children the same age reject him. They start off well enough, but when it becomes apparent he cannot play football or games as well as they can, they push him out.

N appears at times not to listen, or to hear what we say to him. He constantly says 'pardon' and will ask us to repeat what we have said. This prompted me to take him to the clinic for a hearing test but they assured me that N had perfect hearing.

N has great difficulty remembering things which happened only a short while ago. He tends to talk to me about things which happened last week or before. He can never tell me what happened at school that day for instance, but eventually I get little stories in great detail. This has caused confusion at school as he has never been able to remember simple messages, or tell me what is going on. Miss K now tells me everything directly, but the other children in N's group are perfectly able to relay happenings daily.

N at home

N is a chatterbox. He talks constantly — following me round the house asking questions, making up stories, experimenting with words. He cannot bear to see either myself or my husband sit quietly even for a few moments — there must be a constant interaction. He is a tease, and will aggravate us just for the hell of it. He does this with other children, and they do not like it either!

He is affectionate, easily upset and touched by distress, illness, misfortune. He has a very sympathetic nature and responds to old people and crippled or ill people. I have had children at my house and when they have watched television together, N has been distressed by scenes where people have been in danger, and yet the other children have been apparently unmoved. A recent case was a war film where a pilot was shot down and had to be left. N was horrified by this and came to me in the kitchen, very agitated because the other airmen had left this pilot in the sea, apparently to die. 'How can they do that?' he wanted to know. If he was in their gang, they should help him. The other two little boys watching were totally unconcerned; all they could think about were the planes on fire and how smashing it was.

N has a zany imagination. He will pick on a word and by word association invent a story which can be described only as 'way out'. He does this all the time. He will invent stories to please people. He has no intention of lying, but that is in a way what it appears to be. Some people respond to this, and then his imagination runs riot and the only way I can describe what goes on is — an 'Alice in Wonderland' conversation.

N likes to please. I have one neighbour who knows that eating and drinking has been a problem. She therefore always gives him something to eat and drink when we visit and he always makes an obvious effort to please her by having a token mouthful of everything offered. Nothing more; he then politely explains that he is not hungry.

N has an iron will. Nothing will deflect him from what he wants to do. He cannot be browbeaten, bribed or beaten into submission. We constantly have confrontation situations. He also refuses to accept that every good thing must come to an end — so if we take him on an outing to the lake, or the beach, or to the amusements at Blackpool, we have to manhandle him home. His tantrums have lessened, but he can be very difficult to handle as he will kick us, or hit us.

Yesterday we took him to the fair and because he did not want to leave (after a very good time) no amount of firmness would induce him to leave. Of course, it ended in yet another fight.

N's kindergarten report
No. of pupils in form: 8   Age: 6.1   Average age of form: 5.9

Art	He occasionally tries, but his work is very immature for his age.
Handwork	Fair. He lacks patience.
Mathematics	He still rarely puts pencil to paper except under pressure.
French reading	Quite good.
English	He has just started to write three letter words on his own.
Science Nature	Very good.
Scripture	Satisfactory.
Games	Good.
Swimming	He has done very well.

Report of headmaster.   It is very hard to assess his ability because he does not do much to help himself, and it was hard in the first place simply to get him to do as he was told.

N's school report at age 8½
Form VIA   Place in form: 13   No. of pupils in form: 14   Age: 8.6   Average age of form: 7.4

	Position	
Latin reading		Good, but he tries to read too quickly and so makes mistakes.
Mathematics	14	Occasionally he works quite well, but he quickly confuses himself and so his general results are poor.
French		He has tried.
English	13	He is starting to make much more effort with improving results, although he is still well below average.
Science/Nature	14	His oral work is very good indeed, but he is unable to reproduce this in his written work.
History	13	He has started to answer oral questions well but he is still unable to write legibly or to spell.
Geography	13	He does not concentrate in class but absorbs a lot of information. A good examination result.
Scripture	8	Quite good.
Games/P.E.		He does not concentrate on the game in hand. He tries very hard but he is unable to perform the same range of movements as the other children.
Art		He tries hard and is quite imaginative.

Report of headmaster. I have been pleased to see his general behaviour very much better this term. Orally, he has come on very well, but we have the greatest difficulty in getting him to transfer any of it on to paper.

Case J Extract from a letter from J's mother
I have listed below the many small instances which, added together over the years, led me to believe that J had some difficulty in coordinating his fingers and hands with distance and space. It was very difficult for me as a mother to try to explain J's difficulties to his

teachers because I was repeatedly told that it was J's inattention in class and his lack of concentration which led to his difficulties with written work. I cannot express my gratitude enough to your staff who have been so understanding and helpful. Even now after only a few weeks of treatment he is a much more confident child and has a willingness to beat his problem.

As a tiny baby he was, in my opinion, *too* placid and calm. He never cried at all until he was three months old. I did not have an induced labour but he was due on 11.11.64, and I went into labour normally on 17.11.64 and he was born just before midnight on the 18th. He weighed only 6 lbs at birth and was in considerable distress towards the end of my labour and was given oxygen at birth. From about three months old he developed normally; stood up at 10 months and walked

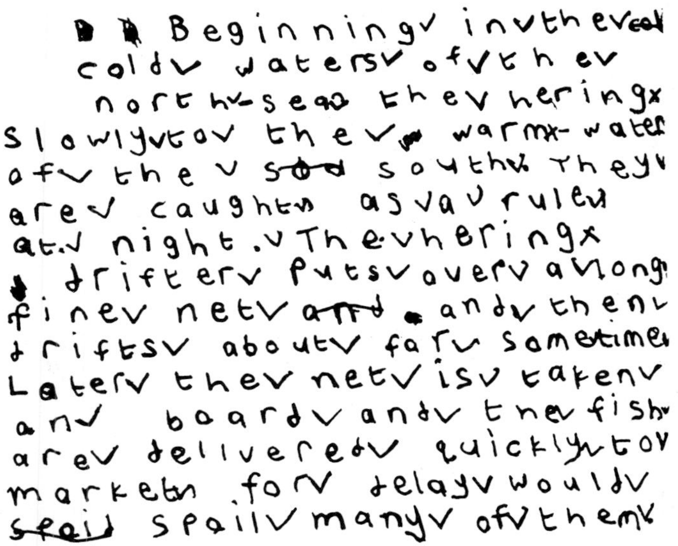

Fig. A.11 J: a boy aged 10½ (superior intelligence). Normally did not leave gaps between words when copying but is shown here trying to teach himself by inserting a 'v'. The teacher's comment at the end of this exercise was 'Incredible!')

at 13 months, but he was still very placid and not at all adventurous. He showed no inclination at all to feed himself, even with 'finger' foods, e.g. bread, toast, bacon, sausage, etc. He was extremely clumsy when he did feed himself, far more than one would expect. Even now (13 yrs) he has trouble scraping his plate and tends to leave bits of food on his plate.

As a toddler he was easily bored in the house and seemed to have no

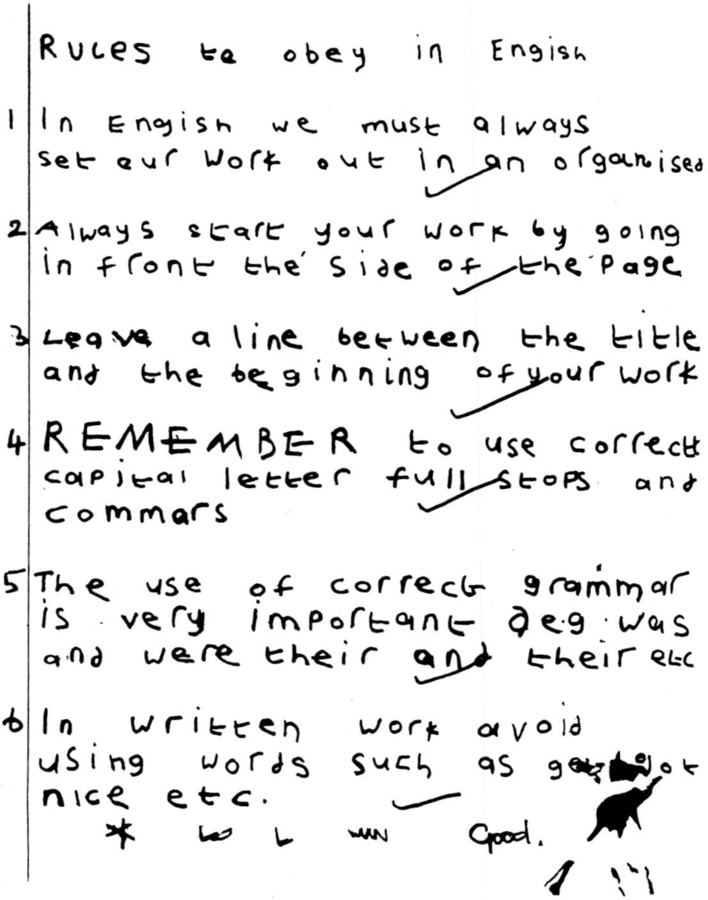

Rules to obey in Engish

1 In Engish we must always
   set our Work out in an orgaunised

2 Always start your work by going
   in front the side of the Page

3 Leave a line between the title
   and the beginning of your Work

4 REMEMBER to use correct
   capital letter full stops and
   commars

5 The use of correct grammar
   is very important aeg was
   and were their and their etc

6 In written work avoid
   using words such as get not
   nice etc.
          * ᴸ ʟ ⌇ Good.

Fig. A.12 J: a bright 11-year-old's account of the rules of English (sic). Though marked correct these copied rules contain errors. However, the boy could not read much of this, for him, inappropriate exercise.

interest in construction toys such as plasticine, jigsaws, lego, scissors, etc. With hindsight, this can be explained by the fact that he couldn't use any of these toys. He still cannot do jigsaws. His main pleasure in the house was being read to and conversing, although his speech was not clear to other people until he was about six years old. He had great trouble dressing himself because he never seemed to know which was the front or back of his sweaters/tee-shirts, even though they had buttons or patterns etc. to denote which was front or back. His shoes and sandals were always a problem, especially the buckles on sandals. Wellingtons were *always* on the wrong feet. We got over the problem of the shoelaces by making a large 'shoe' out of a cardboard box and using long wide crepe bandages as laces. Eventually we were able to narrow it down to his own shoes and laces. The problem of the wellingtons was solved by putting a coloured mark inside one only. Buckles were never mastered until he was about nine years old and he still has trouble with the belt of his scout uniform and the open-ended zip on his anoraks.

Just before he was due to start school I spent time with him trying to teach him his letters, and it soon became obvious to me that he could not copy the simplest shape. I eventually taught him his letters by talking him through the shapes and he learned this method very quickly. At the infants school his inability to copy was spotted immediately but because he could not write anyway it was never followed up. It was some time before he decided which hand to use and he eventually wrote with his left hand; but for other purposes, e.g. using his knife and fork, he uses his right hand. He was slow to read but once he started (after about three months) he overtook the class and has been excellent in both reading and spelling. He has always read a lot for pleasure. His written work has always been untidy and very slapdash, and he is now having trouble trying to learn 'real writing' and I am having to teach him myself by our old method because, once again, he cannot copy the shapes of the letters. He is also unable to write on the lines, and he is very slow at writing and will only write a small amount at a time, as he complains, most genuinely I feel, that his fingers, arm and shoulder ache. Mathematics still remains a mystery to him and he has had remedial maths since he was seven. He cannot seem to understand shapes and areas. When he started secondary school, geometry, technical drawing, woodwork and map reading made him desperately unhappy. During this time, I saw him change from a happy, placid child to a weepy, frustrated one. In his geography homework on one occasion he had to reduce a map to half scale. He knew exactly *how* to do it but was unable to put it on paper. When he was put into a remedial class, where he was working with boys of lower intelligence, he was completely demoralised and at home he stopped eating and sleeping properly and became very 'edgy'. It was this change in his behaviour which made me determined not to be put off once again when I voiced my worries. I was not content to be told that this time it was his age that was causing the trouble. I might also add that he was sent, by the school, to have his eyes tested even though I knew his vision was excellent and I was extremely upset when the eye specialist at the clinic told me in no uncertain terms that I was a fussing mother. I mention this because I am trying to explain how difficult it is for an untrained person like myself to try to pinpoint the problem. I feel that there are many occasions when a caring parent knows when things are not right.

I hope that by listing the problems that J has had, some child elsewhere will be able to be helped at an earlier date than J because it is obvious that the earlier a child can receive help the easier it will be for that child to overcome the difficulty. The following points may seem trivial but I had come to realise as J grew older that it wasn't a question of his being careless but that he just could not help it. Even now he is still clumsy about the house, especially at the table. He sprinkles salt everywhere not just on his meal, he spills sugar every time he sugars his tea, and if he refills the sugar basin he always spills a lot. He cannot pour milk or cereals without making a mess, nor carry a cup and saucer without spilling it. He still cannot comb the back of his hair and has only just learned how to turn the back of his coat/shirt collar down. It has been very frustrating for me over the years and I can imagine very easily how a mother will do jobs for her child rather than have these irritating mishaps day in, day out. The fact that J has remained a placid, happy-go-lucky child is very much to his credit but it has also helped to mask his problem because he does have a lazy streak which has tended to make him give up or lose interest when things have got difficult. I also know that he is a strong-minded child and he will give 100 per cent of his attention to anything that really interests him. Because of this, I feel that his inattention in some subjects at school is caused by the fact that he just cannot do them. This is proved by his good work in oral lessons of geography, history, French, English, classical and religious studies. It is his written work and/or drawings that let him down. He has recently been moved up into a top work group and he is quite able to cope with the work if he could have longer time to write. This is his one big worry now.

I should perhaps add that he could ride his first two-wheeler bike, without stabilisers, within half an hour of receiving the bike. He has always been able to control a bike very well. He plays rugby and soccer by the hour, plays good tennis and squash, he can ice skate and has been an excellent swimmer from being a toddler. His only problem seems to be his finger movements and relating space and this has tended to make him lack confidence in himself. I feel sure though that with the help he is now receiving he will overcome this in time.

Once again may I say thank you very much for your help. My husband and I and J will always be in your debt. I do hope that these points in my letter will be of assistance to you in your work.

Appendix 2: Arithmetic problems

This book has not discussed arithmetic problems in detail though there is no doubt that many clumsy children have problems with numerals. Less is known about the subject and relatively little has been written about it. Interested readers are referred to the texts below for more detailed discussion.

The difficulties encountered are of several types, apparently, though to some extent the categories described are speculative rather than proven. Children may have difficulty copying shapes or figures, particularly copying from a blackboard. At an older age, written problems present difficulties to children who cannot read well or have language comprehension difficulties (e.g. 'How much change from 50p should a man be given if he buys 6 packets of crisps at 7p each?'). If there are difficulties in spatial organisation, the child may not put figures in the right line or the right column. There may be logical deficits in understanding concepts such as thousands, hundreds, tens and units or difficulties in writing these concepts in the correct notation (e.g. 4003 for 403). Concepts of addition, subtraction, multiplication and division may be difficult to teach and require constant use of apparatus.

There may be defects in the preliminary analysis of a problem and consequent inability to formulate a solution. A child may perseverate with an incorrect strategy for solving any problem. There may be difficulty remembering automatic schemes such as multiplication tables (or even counting) with consequent calculation difficulties.

Specific 'dyscalculia' has been described in adults with acquired focal brain lesions. In children 'developmental dyscalculia' seldom occurs in the absence of reading difficulty except insofar as arithmetic may sometimes be less well taught than literacy skills. Focal lesions are not generally demonstrable. Up to a point, children (or adults) who cannot count can get by to an extent which is difficult to achieve without literacy. It is is possible to offer the shop assistant more money than is necessary, for example, and expect to receive the correct change when the individual could not offer the correct money.

Fingers can be used for simple sums, adding or subtracting one at a time. However limited numeracy can present practical problems and embarrassment so it is to be hoped that better understanding will be achieved in future.

SUGGESTIONS FOR FURTHER READING

Cohn R 1971 Arithmetic and learning disabilities. In: Mykelbust H R (ed) Progress in learning disabilities. Grune & Stratton, New York

Department of Education and Science (1979) Mathematics 5–11. A handbook of suggestions. HMSO, London

Farnham-Diggory S 1978 Learning disabilities. Fontana Open Books, London

Ginsbury H 1977 Children's arithmetic: the learning process. Van Nostrand, New York

Luria A R 1966 Human brain and psychological processes. Harper & Row, New York

Tammage A, Starr P 1977 A parents' guide to school mathematics. Cambridge University Press, Cambridge

Young J 1979 It figures. BBC Publications, London

Index